A CENTURY OF CHILDREN'S BOOKS

A CENTURY
OF CHILDREN'S BOOKS

BY
FLORENCE V. BARRY
B. LITT.

LONDON
METHUEN & CO. LTD.
1922

Now Reissued by
Singing Tree Press
1249 Washington Blvd., Detroit, Michigan 1968

Library of Congress Catalog Card Number 68–23467

PREFACE

THIS book was begun at Oxford before the War, when I had the great privilege of being a student in Sir Walter Raleigh's class. Through his generous encouragement, it was continued at intervals and under many difficulties ; and if he had not found some things to like in it, I should hardly venture to put it forth in its present shape.

It is true that the interest of great men in little books (a token of romance since the eighteenth century) is no gauge of public favour ; but the history of children's books is in some sort a record of childhood. Lovers of children may be willing to look through the shelves of old nurseries, if only for the portraits.

The farther one goes upon such small business, the more intricate it seems ; and although I began with some knowledge of the treasures that Mrs. Field had unearthed in her study of *The Child and His Book*, I had no idea there were so many of these books, or that I should find it so difficult to choose. In this I was helped by the older reprints, by the collections of Mr. E. V. Lucas, and later by Mr. Harvey Darton's chapter in the *Cambridge History of English Literature*.

The book itself is a poor acknowledgment of my gratitude to Oxford : to Sir Charles Firth and Mr. Nichol Smith for their advice and criticism ; to the late Mr. R. J. E. Tiddy and Mr. Percy Simpson for help in the early stages ; to Miss Helen Darbishire, Miss Janet Spens, and not least to my fellow students at Somerville who, in the midst of serious things, found time to be amused.

F. V. B.

CONTENTS

A CENTURY
OF CHILDREN'S BOOKS

INTRODUCTION

TO open a child's book nowadays is to discover some part of that unknown world which touches experience at so many points. The city beyond the clouds, the underground country, all the enchantments of woods and islands are open to the little traveller. From *The Water Babies* to *Peter Pan* there has been little else in nursery tales but the stuff of dreams.

It is hard to believe that the child who read the story of Rosamond and the Purple Jar, less than a hundred years ago, had no curiosity about dream countries, no sense of poetry in nature ; yet the first sign of a romantic movement in children's books was the printing of unknown or forgotten fairy tales under the title of *The Court of Oberon*, in 1823. The actual awakening came later, with the nature stories of the Howitts and the imaginative nonsense of Edward Lear.

A century of little books had passed before a child could read fairy tales without shame, and the taste for true " histories " prevailed long after Miss Edgeworth had written her last sequel.

For although there were eighteenth century chap-books that kept alive old tales of chivalry, these had no proper place on the nursery shelves. Books written for children were always designed to instruct as well as to amuse, and it was only because the human interests of the eighteenth century included children that it became a century of children's books.

Those that survived the use of their first owners,—a little company in old sheepskin or flowered paper covers,—are either treasured by collectors or hidden away in some old library ; but some of the best are still to be had in reprints and collections of " Old-fashioned " or " Forgotten " children's books.

The new generation, pressing forward to discover more of the dream country, cares little for tales that reflect the quiet schooling of its ancestors ; yet the most moral and instructive of these books mark the child's escape from a sterner school.   It was on his way to the Child's Garden that he passed through this town of Georgian dolls' houses, where, indeed, he found some rare and curious things.

In the earlier centuries a child made shift with such tales as his elders chose to tell him.   There were few books that he could call his own, and those were devised to advance him in knowledge or courtesy.   Yet the monks of the eleventh and twelfth centuries had a way of turning the natural instincts of children to account.   They taught Latin by means of imaginary conversations, and put the raw material of wonder tales into their instructive " Elucidarium ", a sort of primitive " Child's Guide " which told of fabulous beasts and gave miraculous accounts of heaven and earth.

The successors of these old schoolmasters devised a book for parents which they might share with their children.   This was the *Gesta Romanorum,* a collection of stories put together in Latin about the fourteenth century to serve as texts for " Moralities ".   It became the popular story-book of the Middle Ages, and a woodcut in the early editions shows a whole family gathered round the fire on a winter night telling stories to pass the time.

This was no book for children, even in the days before

nurseries ; yet it contained variants of the Arabian Tales, a story that Chaucer afterwards used for his " History of Constance ", and two strands of the *Merchant of Venice* plot.

Travellers' tales, also shared between men and children, filled a gap between the truthful records of King Alfred and Caxton's new-discovered wealth of romance. Marco Polo and other voyagers brought back stories and fables from the East ; Sir John Mandeville wrote of " the Meruayles of Ynde and of other diuerse Coûtries ". These cross the border between truth and fancy much as children do ; but children knew them only from hearsay.

Caxton alone, had he been so minded, could have filled a child's library ; for besides his *Recuyell of the Historyes of Troye,* he printed Sir Thomas Malory's *Noble Histories of King Arthur* with many romances of his own translating and legends and lives of Saints. He was actually the first printer and editor of the very books which Locke, in the eighteenth century, prescribed for children : Æsop's *Fables* and *The History of Reynard the Fox* ; but Caxton intended none of these for children. The *Fables* showed men their follies ; and *Reynard* was then a satire that ridiculed unjust rulers under the figures of beasts. For children, he chose the kind of books that their parents would buy : the instructive *Parvus et Magnus Chato,* with its woodcut print of a monastery school ; *Stans Puer ad Mensam,* a museum of quaint formalities, and *The Book of Courtesy,* addressed to " Lytyl John " in " tendre enfancye".

Thus early did grown-up persons monopolise the pleasures of fiction, while they prepared handbooks of learning and courtesy for youth. Chaucer, it will be remembered, wrote a scientific treatise instead of a story for his little boy ; and *The Babees Book,* designed for the royal wards and pages of the fifteenth century, had not a word of romance or fable ; nothing but precepts of fair behaviour, and lessons that should teach those " Bele Babeës " how to give their reasons smoothly, " in words that are gentle but compendious ".

There were many such books, nor were they all confined to children of gentle birth. *The Book of Courtesy* was for the sons " of gentleman, yeoman or knave ", and Symon's *Lesson of Wisdom* (1500) " for all manner children ".

As for Caxton's successors, they were content with his ideas about children's books ; it was simply a choice between manners and learning. Wynkyn de Worde, though he printed the splendid romance of *Bevis of Southampton*, gave his child-readers a " Wyse Chylde of Thre Year Old " that could answer the fearful question : " Sage enfaunt, how is the skye made ? " ; and William Copland produced *The Secret of Secrets of Aristotle*, " very good to teach children to read English ", while he lavished the adventures of Guy of Warwick upon their parents.

It is true that the child of the sixteenth century had much to compensate him for a lack of books. If he dwelt in the country, he saw *Robin Hood* and *St. George* played out upon the village green, or if in a town, he might meet with strange merchantmen in any street. He lived in an age of practical romance, and could match you the exploits of Guy or Bevis any day from the adventures of his neighbours. Moreover the Elizabethan child, if he could not read the old stories, at least had a chance of hearing them set to a new measure. Puttenham in his *Art of English Poesie* (1589) writes of the " Blind Harpers and such like taverne Minstrels " who sang " stories of old time " to ballad tunes : " the tale of Sir Topas, the reportes of Bevis of Southampton, Guy of Warwick, Adam Bell and Clymme of the Clough, and such other old romances or historical rimes ".

But a boy had to evade his schoolmaster before he could

listen to such things ; and the schoolmaster saw to it that he had no English story-books. The new learning, which poured out its treasures for scholars, meant little more to the average boy than longer hours of study and more stripes ; and reformers in education, although they looked upon him as a creature of promise, and were concerned to make his lot more bearable, came no nearer than their predecessors to the secrets of his mind.

Companies of schoolboy-players,—the children of the Chapel, or of Paul's—might make the most of such plays as they could understand ; and the Queen's wards had times of " honest recreation " when they might tell each other stories ; but their hours with tutors and music-masters would astonish the youth of these days.

Perhaps the happiest child of the great age of romance was the truant who could follow some pedlar along the road. For the pedlar's songs were more enthralling than his " unbraided wares " ; and he had ballads, such as " The Two Children in the Wood " and " Chevy Chace ", that a child could paste upon his nursery walls.

There was at least one writer who recognised the pedlar's claims, and made him the hero of an instructive book. This was Thomas Newberry, who in 1563 wrote " A booke in English metre, of the great Marchaunt man called Dives Pragmaticus, very pretye for chyldren to rede : wherby they may the better, and more readyer, rede and wryte Wares and Implements, in this World contayned ".

This merchant knows all crafts and deals in every kind of wares ; but he does it in the manner of Autolycus, calling all men to come and buy. His " Inkyll, crewell and gay valances fine " perhaps made copy for *A Winter's Tale* ; his " ouches, brooches and fine aglets for Kynges " might lie in the pack with

> " Bugle bracelet, necklace amber,
> Perfume for a lady's chamber " ;

and though he had neither songs nor ballads, he spoke in
verse and could find poetry in the " chyselle " and " blade "
which Stevenson, more than three centuries later, praised
in his *Child's Garden* :

> " A chisel, both handle and blade,
>   Which *a man who was really a carpenter made*."

It was a hard day for the men of the road when the
Roundhead prevailed over King Charles. Had the Puri-
tans been gifted with the worldly wisdom of old religious
orders, the pedlar's songs, interpreted as allegories, would
have passed, with a word or two altered here and there ;
as it was, many of these poor merchants were reduced to
carrying tracts that reflected the gloomy spirit of the times.
But the seventeenth century garlands still preserved some
of the older ballads, and the true Autolycus was never
without copies of *Tom Thumb*, *The Wise Men of Gotham*,
and other chap-books for the unregenerate. He suffered
the penalties of rogues and vagabonds, and the child shared
his disgrace.

George Fox, in his *Warning to all Teachers*, condemns,
among other sins of children, " the telling of Tales, Stories,
Jests, Rhimes and Fables ". The doctrine of Original Sin
left no hope of grace by means of books. Courtesy, as
concerning the mere outward forms and carriage of a
child, was held of no account, and instruction itself was
abandoned in favour of " Emblems ", " Warnings ", and
morbid " Examples for Youth " : such books, for example,
as James Janeway's *Token for Children*, which contained
" an exact account of the conversion, holy and exemplary
lives and joyful deaths of several young children " : a
literature of denial and negation.

And yet the greatest child's book of the age was written
by a Puritan. John Bunyan was the first to reconcile the
claims of religion and romance, and he never could have
written *The Pilgrim's Progress* if he had not been a good

customer of the pedlar in his youth. But in writing it, Bunyan had no more thought of children than Caxton when he printed the stories of King Arthur. Both were thinking of grown-up children. And when, some eight years later, Bunyan tried his hand at a *Book for Boys and Girls*, he made it a mere collection of " Emblems " in doggerel verse. The alternative title, *Country Rhimes for Children*, seems to refer to certain farmyard creatures which he introduced to point analogies even more absurd than those of the old monkish Bestiaries ; but the monks had sirens and other wonderful things in their natural history. There is nothing to atone for the dulness of these rhymes ; any child would be better entertained in the Interpreter's House.

After the Restoration, the pedlar had a better market for his books, but he also came upon new enemies ; for it was then that members of the Royal Society were beginning to question those " strange and wonderful Relations " which simple folk, seeing them in print, received as true.

When Shakespeare's shepherdess asked the pedlar " Is it true, think you ? " he answered " Five justices' hands at it, and witnesses more than my pack will hold " ; but these men of letters and science accepted no evidence save that of their own reason, and this was fatal to the common matter of chap-books. It is the more surprising that one of their number should have been an unacknowledged maker of children's books.

John Locke was the first to apply the methods of the Royal Society to education. He cared neither for creeds nor grammars, followed Montaigne in denouncing the pedantry of the old schoolmasters, and held with Rabelais that " the greatest clerks are not the wisest men."

It is true that his concern for literal truth made him a very imperfect reader of children's minds. He never understood the part that imagination plays in a child's life, and his plan of education allows no scope for it ; yet he understood children so well on the practical side that every eighteenth century writer of little books quoted his maxims, despised romance and produced " fables " that made a certain appeal to childish interests while they proved the advantages of common sense.

Locke's book, *Some Thoughts concerning Education*, which he published in 1693, was put together from the letters he had written during his exile in Holland, to Edward Clarke ; but it suggests notes rather than letters. Locke so condenses the human element that it reads like a book of educational prescriptions.   The key is to be found in the letters of his friends, and in the records of his pupil, the third Lord Shaftesbury, author of the *Characteristics*. Locke was the first earl's friend and medical adviser, and for a time had taught his son ; the third earl came to him as " Mr. Anthony " at the age of three, and was his " more peculiar charge " till he was twelve years old.   After the grandfather's death, they sent him to Westminster, entirely against Locke's wish, for he hated schools ; but when " Mr. Anthony " came to write about his childhood, he had not a good word for " pedants and schoolmasters " ; only for Mr. Locke to whom, next his " immediate parents ", he owed " the highest gratitude and duty ".

Men do not write thus of tutors who were not their friends ; and doubtless others could have said the same of Locke : the younger brothers of Lord Shaftesbury, the Dutch Quaker's little boy, Arent Furly, a kind of foster-child of his in Holland, or little Frank Masham, his last pupil, who was between four and five when Locke came to live with his family.   They all owed him good health and a happy childhood, and it does not appear that they hankered after the forbidden joys of romance.

Locke's belief in physical training was a welcome contrast to the average tutor's insistence upon books.   He put aside the rod, invented games for his pupils and, as soon as possible, treated them as " rational creatures ".

By reversing the order of Books of Courtesy, he relieved them of rules and maxims. Virtue stood first in his judgment, then wisdom, then breeding, and learning last. At heart he was not less concerned for manners than the old masters of courtesy ; but he thought they could only be acquired by habit and good company. It is the more curious to find him, in another part of the book, assuming that the right kind of tutor could teach Virtue and Wisdom as another might teach Latin. Locke himself came as near as a man could to his ideal of a tutor more wise than learned, a man of the world that knew how to bear himself in any company ; and it mattered little to his pupils that such a tutor could not be found for every child.

Intelligent parents found in his published *Thoughts* some confirmation of their own experience, and his very inconsistencies made his ideas seem the more reasonable to them. For it cannot be denied that Locke, although he believed in teaching children not what, but how to think, yet fell into the error of impressing facts upon their memory, and facts that could only be learned from books. His Irish friend Molyneux, on whose advice the *Thoughts* were put together, brought up his little boy according to Locke's plan, and proved that the system could produce a rival to Wynkyn de Worde's Wyse Chylde : one that at five years old could read perfectly and trace out upon the globes " all the noted parts, countries and cities of the world ". At six, his knowledge was incredible, he was " obedient and observant to the nicest particular ", and his father believed that no child " had ever his passions more perfectly at command".

There is nothing in Locke's theory to account for the encyclopædic knowledge of this child ; but in practice he had replaced Latin and Greek with Geometry, Chronology,

the use of the Globes, and even some part of " the incom-
parable Mr. Newton's " Philosophy, so far as it was justified
by " Matter of Fact ".

This helps to explain the little pedantries of later
children's books, although many of these do not go beyond
Locke's directions for teaching a child to read.

" There may be Dice and Play-things with the letters
on them," he says, " to teach Children the Alphabet by
Playing ; and twenty other Ways may be found, suitable
to their particular Tempers, to make this Kind of Learning
a Sport to them.   Thus Children may be cozen'd into a
Knowledge of the Letters . . ."

If this smacks of artifice, there is no question of his
wisdom about essentials : " If you have any Contests with
him, let it be in Matters of Moment, of Truth and Good
Nature ; but lay no Task on him about A.B.C."

About books he is very plain : when " by these gentle
Ways " a child begins to read, " some easy pleasant Book,
suited to his Capacity should be put into his Hands, wherein the Entertainment that he finds might draw him on,
and reward his Pains in Reading, and yet not such as should
fill his Head with perfectly useless Trumpery, or lay the
Principles of Vice and Folly.   To this purpose I think
Æsop's Fables the best, which being Stories apt to delight
and entertain a Child, may yet afford useful Reflections
to a grown Man ; and if his Memory retain them all his
Life after, he will not repent to find them there, amongst
his manly Thoughts and serious Business ".

Then, after recommending an *Æsop* with pictures in it,
he adds : " *Reynard the Fox* is another Book I think may
be made Use of to the same Purpose ".   Talking beasts
that can be made the mouthpiece of a moralist are Locke's
nearest approach to the supernatural.   In another place,
he admonishes parents to preserve a child's mind " from
all Impressions and Notions of *Spirits* and *Goblins*, or any

fearful Apprehensions in the Dark ". Thus the child is to be protected from ghost-stories or fairy-tales and " cozen'd " into reading what will be useful to him when he is a man.

Locke knew no other books in English " fit to engage the liking of children and tempt them to read " ; and indeed there were few to know. *The Seven Wise Masters of Rome* is an example of what was thought fit for children. This was a very old sequence of Eastern parables first printed by Wynkyn de Worde. Francis Kirkman, who translated it from the French in 1674, declared that it was " held in such estimation in Ireland that it was always put into the hands of young children immediately after the horn book ". English copies were common ; but the tales had less interest for children than those of the *Gesta*. " Pedants and Schoolmasters " must have conspired to keep it in print.

Thus at the close of the seventeenth century the greater number of children, if they read anything, amused themselves with chap-books or broadsheets,—all of which, doubtless, came under Locke's ban as " perfectly useless Trumpery " ; and for those that read no books, in spite of Locke, there were still tales " of Sprites and Goblins ".

CHAPTER I

CHAP-BOOKS AND BALLADS

Children and the Supernatural—Steele's Account of a boy's reading—Characteristics of chap-book " histories "—Folk-lore and legendary settings—*The History of Friar Bacon*—*Fortunatus*—Other chap-book survivals—The Georgian Autolycus—Travellers' tales—A great chap-book—Books for men and children—Chap-books and ballads—Treatment of romances—The fairy world—Legend and history—Border and Robin Hood ballads.

STEELE'S account of his two god-children[1] (perhaps the choicest of his *Tatler* papers) discovers the weak point of Locke's philosophy. Nothing could so shake a blind faith in Æsop as the frank words of Steele's little boy who, at eight years old, although he was " a very great Historian in Æsop's Fables ", declared " that he did not delight in that Learning, because he did not believe they were true ".

His sister Betty defied Mr. Locke upon another side, for she dealt " chiefly in Fairies and Sprights "; and would " terrifie the Maids with her Accounts " till they were afraid to go up to bed.

Now, neither of these children had the least difficulty about the supernatural. The boy could have believed in beasts that talked ; but he detected the man inside the lion's skin : the man that pointed a moral. These *Fables*, once understood as ridiculing the follies of mankind, were no longer " true "; but there were other stories of the boy's own choosing which, though full of magic, were true to the spirit of their kind.

Steele says he had " very much turned his studies for about a Twelvemonth past into the Lives and Adventures

[1] *The Tatler*, No. 95.

of *Don Bellianis of Greece, Guy of Warwick*, the *Seven Champions*, and other Historians of that Age ".

Not only does the sympathetic godfather enter into these literary adventures, as Mr. Locke, with all his wisdom, never could have done, but he knows the virtue of an unpointed moral: the boy, he says, "had made Remarks, which might be of Service to him during the Course of his whole Life. He would tell you the Mismanagements of *John Hickathrift*, find Fault with the passionate Temper in *Bevis of Southampton* and loved *St. George* for being the Champion of *England*; and by this Means had his Thoughts insensibly moulded into the Notions of Discretion, Virtue and Honour ".

In the reign of Anne, these stirring " Histories " were a part of every pedlar's stock-in-trade. They were sold at fairs or hawked from door to door ; and a boy that could never stumble through the maze of a seventeenth century folio might read as many romances as he had halfpence. Some had been among the earliest printed books. They were mostly from French originals, though Sir Bevis and Sir Guy had been " *Chevaliers d'Angleterre* " from the beginning. The chap-book *Seven Champions* and *Life and Death of St. George* were both based on Richard Johnson's *History of the Seven Champions*, a medley of other romances in which Caxton's " Saynt George of Capadose " had become St. George of Coventry. But the romance spirit was cosmopolitan, born of the Crusades, and foreign champions like Don Bellianis of Greece were hardly less popular.[1]

Late writers varied the old adventures ; but the chapbook printer, who did his own editing, cut down the heavy matter of the folios to a bare chain of incidents. His words were few and ill-chosen, he had neither style nor grammar ; but the core of interest was sound : the stories

[1] See Appendix A. I.   Note on these and other romances.

touched the imagination of his readers like ballads and fairy tales.

Gallant Knights came straight from the fields of France to the magnificence of Eastern cities ; youths, setting out from the English towns, adventured among dwarfs and Saracens, giants and dragons, and won their knighthood by the way.

If the hero never failed to subdue his enemies and win a lady of surpassing beauty, there was still a doubt (enough to keep the reader curious) whether a rival would snatch her from him and put him upon a more dangerous adventure to win her back ; or whether, if they fared on together, they would meet an enchanter or a giant first.

Repetition seldom tires a child. The feats of Acquitaine could be repeated at Damascus ; and the wood-cuts in the chap-books proved that Montelion and Parismus could fight in the armour of Don Bellianis or St. George. Nor was it a chance association of the pedlar's pack which threw these champions into the company of a village strongman, John Hickathrift, more commonly called Tom ; for although Hickathrift fought with a cart-wheel and axle-tree for shield and sword, he could beat the best of them at giant-killing.[1]

The romances, indeed, are full of the common stuff of folk-lore. If the hero blow a trumpet at a castle-gate, a giant may be expected ; if he blow it at the mouth of an enchanted cave, a prophetic voice replies, or if he enter the cave by chance, he may find the prophecy inscribed on a pillar of sapphire—the prelude, in *Don Bellianis*, to the coming of the Enchantress through a pair of ivory gates.

A hundred folk-tales tell of the Princess rescued from a dragon ; transformation is an affair of every day : Don Bellianis slays a magician " in the shape of a griffin " ;

---

[1] *The History of Thomas Hickathrift*, 1750 (?). See below. Chapter II and Appendix A. II.

St. Denis, in the *Seven Champions,* is transformed into a
hart, the Princess of Thessaly into a mulberry-tree ; and
St. David sleeps seven years in an enchanted garden—
the Magic Sleep of the fairy tales.   Nor is the champion
of romance without his wonderful sword or cloak.

The Sword " Morglay " (no more than a stout weapon
in the old version of *Sir Bevis*) is called " wonderful " in the
chap-books.   Don Bellianis draws a magic sword from a
pillar, as Arthur pulled his out of the stone ;   St. George
has invincible armour ;   and the later *History of Fortunatus*
is the tale of a Wonderful Purse and a Wishing Cap.

But whoever looks upon a child as a pure romantic, has
learned but half his lesson ;   for in many tales that have
stood the test of time, there is little interest outside sheer
matter of fact ;   and even the romances owed something
to legendary settings which touched a borderland of
truth.   To know that Bevis lived in the reign of Edgar,
that Guy, returning from his pilgrimage, found King
Athelstane at Winchester, beset by the Danes, would
confirm a child's belief ; but the little reader of chap-
books knew more than this ;   he could give the exact
measurements of Tom Hickathrift's grave in Tilney
Churchyard, knew where to find Guy's armour and his
porridge-pot at Warwick, and never doubted that Bevis
built Arundel Castle for love of his horse.

It might be done indeed, for such a horse : no mere
product of a wizard's cunning, but a steed fit to carry a
champion :   alive as the persons of the romances never
were.   He figures in every adventure, carries the thread of
the story from point to point, and yet stands out, a very
symbol of romance.

The chap-book writer makes no picture of the knighting
of Bevis, and never mentions his shield with the three blue
eagles on a field of gold ;   but he remembers well enough
how the Saracen King's daughter, Josian the fair, presented

Bevis with the sword "Morglay" and the "wonderful steed called Arundel".

From that point the story goes to a sound of hoofs ; and though the King betrayed Bevis into the hands of his enemy and gave the horse Arundel to Bevis's rival, King Jour, and though Bevis lay in a dungeon for seven years, Josian herself was not more faithful to him than Arundel ; for when at last he escaped, and came, disguised as a poor pedlar, to the castle of Jour, Josian knew him not ; but Arundel, hearing his master speak, "neighed and broke seven chains for joy".

As to the men and women of romance, they borrowed life from their adventures, but apart from these, were mere types of strength or beauty. The original portraits, though vague, were not without poetry : the impression of "The Squyere Guy" has a hint of Chaucer :

> "Feyre he was and bryght of face,
> He schone as bryght as ane glace."

The chap-book writer contents himself with the remark that King Ermine was "prepossessed with Guy's looks". He bestows more care on the heroine, Felyce, but covers the faint outline with his trowel. Felyce, once

> "the Erlys Doghtur, a swete thynge",

becomes "this heavenly Phillis, whose beauty was so excellent that Helen the pride of all Greece might seem as a Black a Moor to her".

Many striking situations and dramatic incidents of the older stories are lost in the chap-books, for want of picture-making phrases and live speech. A name here and there, such as Brademond, King of Damascus, would lift a boy like a magic carpet, and set him down among Saracen pavilions ; bare facts might call up pictures ; there was the ransom of King Jour,—"Twenty tun of gold and three hundred white steeds " ; but the unlettered writer shirked

2

most of the details which, in telling the story aloud, he would express by gestures. The fine fight with the dragon, in *Guy of Warwick*, makes but a paragraph in the chap-book ; the monster's head is off before the fight is well begun. Not even a " picture of the dragon, thirty feet in length, worked in a cloth of arras and hung up in Warwick Castle for an everlasting monument " could make amends for this.

Yet a child, making his own pictures out of the poor phrases of these writers, might have in his mind's eye something not unlike the images of the old translator : the boy Bevis on a hillside with his sheep, looking down at the Castle " that should be his " ; the four Knights selling him to the Saracen merchantmen ; or the giant Ascapart wading out to the ship, with Bevis and Josian and the horse Arundel tucked under his arm.

These stand in clear outline, and, in the roughest shape, have suggestions of pathos or incongruity ; but they pass at once into action, which is what a child wants : the boy comes down from the hill, forces his way into the castle and attacks the usurper with his shepherd's crook ; the Saracens carry him overseas, and set him in the way of adventure ; Ascapart proves himself " a mariner good at need ", hoists sail and brings his master and mistress safely into harbour.

Laughter is rare in the romances, but this story of Ascapart has a humour of its own. Bevis, having beaten the giant, spares his life on condition that he becomes his servant ; and in the course of their adventures the van-quished rescues the victor, the servant picks up his master and carries him about like a toy. Such a feat measures the great creature more effectually than the exact method of the chap-book writer : " thirty Foot high and a Foot between his eyebrows ".

Another " famous History " which came with these

into the chap-books, was that of *Valentine and Orson*, first printed by Wynkyn de Worde, and reprinted at the close of the nineteenth century as an " old fairy tale ". It has some novel features besides the usual stage properties of romance. Of the twin brothers separated in childhood, one is brought up at Court and trained in knightly exercises ; the other carried off by a bear and nourished with her cubs. This is a foretaste of *The Jungle Book* :

" In a cave, the bear had four young ones, among whom she laid the child to be devoured, yet all the while the young bears did it no harm ; but with their rough paws stroked it softly. The old bear, perceiving they did not devour it, showed a bearish kind of favour towards it, inasmuch that she kept it and gave it suck among her young ones for the space of one year ".

The second chapter records how the bear's nursling, Orson, grew up into a Wild Man, and how the young knight Valentine, his brother, meeting him in a wood, won a victory of skill against strength ; after which, still unconscious of their relationship, he tamed the Wild Man and taught him the arts of chivalry.

The more magical elements of the story have a flavour of the East, and doubtless belong to the older strata of Eastern romance. The adventure of the Dwarf Pacolet suggests the tale of the " Magic Horse " in the *Thousand and One Nights* ; for by his art this dwarf, who was an Enchanter, " had contrived a horse of wood, and in the forehead a fixed pin, by turning of which he could convey himself to the farthest part of the world ".

Many such marvels, related during the Middle Ages by merchants or Crusaders returning from the East, had been caught up in the weavings of romance ; but it is a sort of magic that has little to do with the myth-making power of childhood. Pacolet's flying horse is made of wood ; the touch of its hoof never brought water from a mountainside. It represents the magic of ingenuity which comes half-way between pure romance and the practical marvels of a scientific age.

Indeed, it is but a step from the flying horse of Eastern tales to Roger Bacon's horseless chariots and flying "instruments ". The " Learned Friar ", a clerk of Oxford in the thirteenth century, foretold many things to be performed by Art and Nature ", wherein should be " nothing magical ". Yet he studied such strange matters that he was persecuted for practising magic, and the chap-books set him down a conjurer. The Enchanted Head of Brass which in *Valentine and Orson* reveals the parentage of the brothers, reappears in the *Famous History of Friar Bacon*, as the Brazen Head, wrought in so many sleepless nights by the Friar and his brother-in-magic, Friar Bungay.

Greene, in his play of *Fryer Bacon and Fryer Boungay* (1591), follows this well known tract,[1] which came down with few changes to the eighteenth century. Here the old magic machinery goes with the light movement of a popular tale. The Brazen Head should have disclosed a secret whereby Friar Bacon " would have walled England about with brass " ; but the stupidity of his servant Miles prevented it. For when the two magicians, worn out with toil, lay down to sleep, they set him to watch the Head, commanding him to call them the moment it should speak ; and he, the while, kept up his spirits " with tabor and pipe and song ".

When at last the Head spake these words :   " Time Is," and no more, Miles, understanding nothing by that, fell to mockery : " If thou canst speak no wiser, they shall sleep till doomsday for me. Time is !   I know Time is, that you shall hear, Goodman Brazen Face ! "

So saying, he fitted the words to the tune of " Dainty,

[1] See Appendix A. I.   Note on *Dr. Faustus*.

come thou to me ", and sang for half-an-hour. There-
upon the Head spake again, saying two words and no
more : " Time Was " ; whereat the Simpleton railed
afresh, and another half-hour went by.

Then the Brazen Head spake again, these words :
" Time is Past ", and then fell down ; and presently
followed a terrible noise, with strange flashes of fire,
so that Miles was half-dead with fear.

" Out on thee, villain," cried Friar Bacon, " thou hast
undone us both ; hadst thou but called us when it did
speak, all England had been walled about with brass, to its
glory and our eternal fame."

Locke's followers were never tired of setting the " plain
Magique of tru Reason's Light " against Friar Bacon's
conjurings. There were later moralists who recognized
the Wizard as a pioneer of science ; but these would have
none of his magic, and rejected all tales of undeserved
good fortune.

Wordsworth alone had the courage to turn a child loose
in the enchanted woods. He praised *The History of
Fortunatus*, which is more like " Aladdin " than any tale
of chivalry. By sheer luck the Spendthrift finds a Galley
of Venice lying at anchor and gets his choice of gifts. These
vanished like fairy gold in the hands of his sons, and
children remembered little else but his Wishing Cap and
his Purse that never was empty. Yet Fortunatus was
a name to conjure by, and the pure spirit of adventure
was in his first setting out, as the woodcut shows, " with
a Hawk in his Hand ".

It seems odd that the eighteenth century child should
have ballads about King Arthur and his Knights, but no
account of them in prose. Malory's " Noble Histories ",
like the once famous cycles of Amadis and the Palmerins,
escaped the chap-book writers; but they had one or two
relics of the old *Historyes of Troye*, in which Priam's

palace had become an enchanted castle, and Hector a knight errant.

The pedlar had no chronology. Patient Grissel, fresh from a new translation of Boccaccio, was a lady of the eighteenth century, and what pleased the country fireside of 1700 still pleased it in 1760. The tales that Mr. Burchell gave the children in *The Vicar of Wakefield* might have come out of a chapman's bundle in almost any part of the century : " the story of the Buck of Beverland, with the History of Patient Grissel, the Adventures of Catskin and then Fair Rosamond's Bower."

Among other " useless Trumpery " were riddles, non-sense-books and farcical tales of rogues or simpletons.[1] These are full of the topsy-turvy nonsense that children love, and the coarse jests from which they were seldom guarded. The older stories, even when they deal with everyday life, give it a romantic flavour. The Cobbler feasts with the King ; the Valiant London Prentice leaves his shop on London Bridge, and sets out to joust with eastern princes. A Tudor pedlar, Tom Long, in the course of his absurd adventures, visits the Cave of the Seven Sleepers, whose story makes a welcome interlude :

" Coming to the town, they found everything altered, the inhabitants being other sort of people than they were the night before. So, going to buy food, the people refused to take their money, saying they knew not the coin ; but enquiring further, found that since their being there, three generations had been dead and the fourth was in being ".

Tom Long was the puppet of a nonsense-book ; but other chap-books, following Deloney, told the " true histories " of industrious fortune-makers who were not out of place in a commercial age ; and the life of an eigh-teenth century pedlar was plain enough to pass for truth. An account (in a late Stirling tract)[2] of the " Flying

[1] See Appendix A. I. Note on Nonsense Books.
[2] For details of this and of other tracts, see Appendix A. I.

Stationer ", Peter Duthie, shows that he took up his trade
in 1729, when he was eight years old, and was upon the
road for eighty years—a Georgian Autolycus, kncwn for
his quaint wit " in every city, town, village and hamlet
in great Britain ". At some time, perhaps, he sold " lives "
of his brethren Dougal Graham and John Cheap the
Chapman, whose story was " moralised " by Hannah
More.

The traveller is always a romantic figure. No amount
of fact can take the pleasure of expectation and surprise
out of a journey, and the setting of most chap-books was
a journey by land or sea. The " Flying Stationer " asked
no more for the Wonderful Voyages of Sir John Mandeville
than for the rough yarn of a ship-wrecked sailor.

This last, if it pointed a moral, might serve a double
purpose, for the old allegories were dying out, except in
burlesques. Abstractions always had a way of coming
alive when they set foot on English ground, and *The
History of Laurence Lazy*, of " Lubberland Castle in the
County of Sloth " was no mere allegory of Idleness, but the
tale of a scapegrace who, to the joy of all children, got the
better of the Schoolmaster, the Squire's Cook and the
Farmer. His " Arraignment and Trial " in the Town Hall
of " Never Work " was a triumphant apology for idlers ;
yet a scene like this may have suggested the symbolic
trial of Christian and Faithful in the Town of Vanity.

That splendid chap-book, *The Pilgrim's Progress*,[1] is
built up of such things. Bunyan's reading, outside the
Bible (although he counted it among his sins) had
acquainted him with romances, tales of magic and enchantment, " histories " of live persons ; and all these, or
nearly all, were concerned with adventures upon the road.[2]

---

[1] First edition, 1678.
[2] See Introduction to *The Pilgrim's Progress* (Methuen) by
Prof. C. H. Firth.

Bible stories and Christian legends were common in Bunyan's youth. There was a versified "history" of Joseph and his Brethren, and the beautiful legend of the Glastonbury Thorn was as well known as that of *The Seven Sleepers* or *The Wandering Jew*.

But *The Pilgrim's Progress* dealt in terms of unmistakable experience with the journey that every man must go ; the figures of its allegory were live persons, such as a man might meet upon any road, and its setting changed as the way ran through towns and villages, past fields and sloughs and thickets, over hills where the surest-footed might fall "from running to going and from going to clambering upon his hands and knees, because of the steepness of the place ", or beside rivers that ran through meadows and orchards, with lilies underfoot, and above, " green trees with all manner of fruit ".

These things give place at certain points, as they do in life, to the scorched plains of torment, the overwhelming Shadow of Death, or, where the river and the way for a time part, to the Dungeon of Despair.   There are glimpses by the way of strange and beautiful lands, of vineyards and mountains upon which " the sun shineth night and day " ;   but here also is the road running through the midst of the country to a city more splendid than the cities of romance, for " it was builded of pearls and precious stones, also the streets thereof were paved with gold ".

The child would start on this journey with some knowledge of his bearings, for, like Bunyan, he had set out on an earlier pilgrimage with Guy of Warwick.[1] At the Palace Beautiful, he would remember how Montelion had been armed by nymphs, and at Doubting Castle, how Bevis had escaped from his prison in Damascus.

[1] Richard Graves, in the *Spiritual Quixote* (1772), likens the adventures of Christian to those of Jack the Giant Killer and John Hickathrift.

No knight ever strove with giant or dragon as Christian struggled with Apollyon ; none of the Seven Champions had encountered the dangers of this road. Yet these were adventures that might happen to a man in the midst of his ordinary business ; that much a child might understand beneath the surface of romance which for him is the chief matter of the book.

This was the first of three great books which pleased both men and children in the eighteenth century. The others are *Robinson Crusoe*[1] and *The Travels and Adventures of Captain Lemuel Gulliver.*[2] Each, in its own kind, is a *Voyage Imaginaire* and the unwrought matter of all three was to be found in chap-books. The tale of the shipwrecked man had never been told with such apparent truth as in *Robinson Crusoe.* Readers of the chap-book history of Drake, who were familiar with accounts of " Monsters and Monstrous People ", would read this sober journal as the purest matter of fact ; nor was there anything beyond belief in Gulliver's adventures, to anyone who knew the pedlar's book of *Sir John Mandeville.* For here, among greater marvels, was a notable account of giants and pigmies.

The island setting of *Robinson Crusoe*, the figure of Friday, the footprint in the sand, belong to the world of romance ; so do the giants and dwarfs of *Gulliver.* Yet in both books, the things that happen are human and practical ; the setting gives scope for the chief interests of the century : men and morals and matters of fact. Defoe pointed his moral, and as an afterthought explained the Voyage of Robinson Crusoe as an allegory of his life ; Swift used the contrary device of satire. But no child was ever concerned with an under-sense, where he could

---

[1] Published 1719. Abridged 12 mo. in the same year. See Note on *Philip Quarll*, Appendix A. I.

[2] First edition, 1726.

follow every turn of the adventure. A philosopher would not have discovered Crusoe's allegory, and a child is more likely to suspect satire in *Reynard the Fox* than in *Gulliver*.

The adventures of Lilliput and Brobdignag are the convincing "histor_" of a nation of Tom Thumbs and a nation of Blunderbores; only a little Gradgrind would question their truth. A child reading *The Pilgrim's Progress* is himself the Pilgrim; in the adventure of the island he is the shipwrecked man; and in the Travels, first the big man upon whose body the little men climb with ladders, then the little man, paddling his toy boat to amuse the giants.

These books, like the romances, were for little men as well as big ones; but their authors renewed the old devices by a masterly simple style. They made pictures such as were never found in chap-book prose, and rarely in tales that had passed into ballad form.

The eighteenth century pedlar had fewer ballads than his predecessors; yet those he had, like the songs of Autolycus, were " for man or woman, of all sizes ".

Ballad tunes, from Shakespeare to Wordsworth, were " Food for the hungry ears of little ones," and there is something in the simple conventions of ballads that suggests the story-telling of a child. Those printed ballads, " darling songs of the common People ", which Addison found upon the walls of eighteenth-century houses, attracted him by their classic simplicity, but the two he liked the best : " Chevy Chase " and " The Two Children in the Wood ", had been the joy of Elizabethan nurseries.[1]

Most of the chap-book stories were sung as ballads. " The Seven Champions ", " St. George ", " Patient Grissel " and " The London Prentice " were all in the

[1] *Spectator*, Nos. 70, 74 and 85. See Appendix A. 1.

Collection of Old Ballads printed in 1723, with " The Noble Acts of King Arthur " from Malory; [1] and others were reprinted in Percy's *Reliques* (1765) from a folio manuscript of the seventeenth century.

The ballad maker, dealing with romances, preferred short episodes. A tedious story would never go to his quick measures ; but by laying his chief stress on speech and movement, or adding a refrain, he made a thing quite unlike the short versions of the chap-books, and gave a certain dramatic unity to the separate parts.

Thus the incident of " Guy and Colebrande ", in Percy's folio, had been chosen from *Guy of Warwick*, and the ballad of St. George, in the Collection of 1723, deals only with the dragon story. Some ballads, it is true, cover a sequence of adventures. " The Lord of Lorn,", like *Bevis of South-ampton*, gives the whole story of a child robbed of his inheritance : a shepherd boy that should have been a lord ; and the scene changes from Britain to France and back again ; but so much is told in dialogue that the story dances to its end :

> " Do thou me off thy sattin doublett
>   Thy shirtband wrought with glistering gold,
> And doe mee off thy golden chaine
>   About thy necke so many a fold.
>
> " Do thou me off thy velvett hat,
>   With fether in that is so ffine ;
> All unto thy silken shirt
>   That's wrought with many a golden seam.
>
> .   .   .   .   .   .
>
> " ' What must be my name, worthy Steward ?
>   I pray thee now, tell it me : '
> ' Thy name shalbe Pore Disaware,
>   To tend sheepe on a lonelye lee.' "

Of the fairy world revealed in " Thomas Rymer ", the ghostly suggestion of " The Wife of Usher's Well," there

[1] See further Appendix A. 1.

is no trace till the close of the century.   The true ballads of
Elfland are more song than story, and rise by suggestion
above the simplicity of fairy tales :

> " O they rade on and farther on,
>   And they waded rivers abune the knee
> And they saw neither sun nor moon,
>   But they heard the roaring of the sea."

The breath of enchantment is rare in English ballads.
There is nothing in print before Scott's *Minstrelsy* like the
magic of these lines ; but Percy reprinted a sixteenth
century ballad, " The Mad-Merry Prankes of Robbin
Goodfellow " which Puck himself might have sung :

> " From Oberon in Fairyland
>   The King of ghosts and shadows there,
> Mad Robbin I at his command
>   Am sent to view the night-sports here.
>   What revell rout
>   Is kept about
>   In every corner where I goe
>   I will oresee
>   And merry be
> And make good sport with ho, ho, ho."

This is the triumphant laughter of a child.   The " shrewd
and knavish sprite " has neither the delicacy of smaller
fairies nor the courtly dignity of his master. He is the
spirit of childish mischief : greeting night-wanderers " with
counterfeiting voice ", shape-changing, " whirrying " over
hedges and pools, or playing tricks on lads and lasses at
village feasts. " Hobgoblin " or " sweet Puck ", half-child,
half-fairy, he roams the English country,

> " Through woods, through lakes.
>   Through bogs, through brakes,
> Ore bush and brier ",

and boasts of greater powers.
   There is no doubting either voice or words :

> " More swift than lightning can I flye
>   And round about this ayrie welkin soone,
>   And in a minutes space descry
>   Each thing that's done belowe the moone ".

There are two more fairy songs in the *Reliques* : one given " with some corrections " from a seventeenth century garland, the other, Bishop Corbet's " Farewell " to the fairies. The first contradicts the second, for obeying the invocation

> " Come, follow, follow me
>   You fairy elves that be ",

a team of little atomies appear, proving that they were never out of England since Shakespeare wrote, but " unheard and unespy'd ", were gliding through Puritan keyholes and spreading their feasts while the Bishop was composing his lament,

> " Farewell, rewards and fairies ! "

Yet these, like Robin Goodfellow, are spirits of Earth ; they eat more than fairy bread. A mortal surely suggested the details of their feast, but they dance a fairy measure :

> " The grasshopper, gnat and fly,
>   Serve for our minstrelsy ;
>   Grace said, we dance awhile,
>   And so the time beguile ;
>   And if the moon doth hide her head,
>   The gloe-worm lights us home to bed.
>
> " On tops of dewie grasse
>   So nimbly do we passe ;
>   The young and tender stalk
>   Ne'er bends when we do walk :
>   Yet in the morning may be seen
>   Where we the night before have been."

Rhymed nursery tales seldom show the true ballad quality. The only children's stories in the Collection of

1723 are " The Children in the Wood ", and " Sir Richard Whittington " : the one a true ballad, newly licensed and approved by Addison ; the other (also mentioned in the *Spectator*) taking precedence of such rhymes as " Catskin " and " Tom Thumb " for a popular grafting of the romance of Fortune upon a stock of historical fact.

Southern ballad-printers favoured the merry or tragic themes of legend and history,[1] and if few of their songs had the trumpet-note of " Chevy Chase ", they lacked neither freshness nor vigour. Some, like " the Blind Beggar's Daughter of Bednall-Green ", gave a fresh turn to Elizabethan traditions, and made up for indifferent workmanship by a plentiful force of rhythm. Late nursery poets could not better this trick of the ballad-maker's :

> " It was a blind beggar that long lost his sight,
> He had a fair daughter of beauty most bright ;
> And many a gallant brave suitor had she,
> For none was so comely as pretty Bessee."

Another of these old broadsides, " Johnny Armstrong's Last Good Night " appeared among Dryden's Miscellanies in 1702, in the Collections of 1723 and 1724, and again in Evans's *Old Ballads* (1777).

" The music of the finest singer is dissonance," wrote Goldsmith, " to what I felt when our old dairymaid sung me into tears with Johnny Armstrong's last Good Night or the Cruelty of Barbara Allen."

These are the true stuff of ballads ; but a child cares most about action, and, asked to choose between them, would be pretty sure to call for the Border Song.

The story of John Armstrong, which came down to prose in the chap-books, has points in common with " Robin Hood ", but John and his " Merry Men " have no touch of Robin's careless humour. They fight like the heroes of Chevy Chase, and ask no quarter :

[1] See Appendix A. I.

> " Said John, Fight on, my merry men all,
>   I am a little hurt, but I am not slain.
> I will lay me down for to bleed a while
>   Then I'le rise and fight with you again."

The pirate song of " Sir Andrew Barton " [1] is a sailor's variant of this. Lord Howard defies Sir Andrew upon the high seas much as Erle Percy, in despite of the Douglas, takes his pleasure in the Scottish woods. There was never a better fight on shore, and when at last the pirate falls to an English bowman, he repeats the border cry :

> " ' Fight on, my men ! ' says Sir Andrew Barton,
>   ' I am hurt, but I am not slain ;
> I'le lay mee downe and bleed awhile,
>   And then I'le rise and fight again '."

Sir Andrew stands out from his fellows, though the portrait is not to be compared with Robin Hood's ; and the king himself speaks his epitaph :

> " ' I wo'ld give a hundred pound,' " says King Henrye
> ' The man were alive as he is dead ! ' "

Another of these narrative ballads, " Adam Bell ", [2] has a forest background that suggests Robin Hood :

> " Merry it was in grene forest
>   Among the leves grene
> Where that men walke both East and West
>   Wyth bowes and arrowes kene."

The full title, " Adam Bell, Clim of the Clough and William of Cloudesley ", has a sufficing rhythm, and the story is good ; not unlike a Norse Saga, where they set fire to the outlaw's house, and like *William Tell*, where Cloudesley splits an apple on his son's head at six score paces.

But the true Robin Hood ballads take a child into his own

---

[1] See note on sea songs and ballads—Appendix A. I.
[2] First printed by W. Copland.

country, and he finds it peopled with his friends. From
the first stanzas of " The Curtall Friar ", he is Robin's man :

> " In summer time, when leaves grow green
>   And flowers are fresh and gay
>   Robin Hood and his merry men
>   *Were disposed to play.*"

In this play-humour, the outlaws themselves are children,
as every child is by nature an outlaw.   They know better
than to take life for a serious business.   To them, as to a
child, it is one long and absorbing game of make-believe.

Robin, like Fulk Fitz-Warine or Hereward, could play
at any trade—a potter, a beggar, a shepherd, a fisherman.
His band were mostly men who had forsaken some dull craft
for this great game of hiding and hunting and robbery.
In the midst of active enjoyment, they set themselves to
redress the unequal balance of fortune ; but they never
doubted their own solid advantages over sheriffs and abbots,
—the people who dwelt in towns and cloisters, and had
forgotten how to play.

Early collectors of the eighteenth century found no
ballads that echoed the sound of the greenwood :

> " notes small
> Of Byrdis mery syngynge ",

or that made pictures of the deer shadowed in green
leaves ; but there were imitations of the older songs, and
the setting was always implied.

After 1765, there must have been children who knew the
prelude to " Guy of Gisborne ", from Percy's *Reliques* :

> " When shaws been sheene and shradds full fayre,
>   And leaves both large and longe,
>   It is merrye walking in the fayre forrest,
>   To heare the small birdes songe.
>
> " The woodweele sang and wold not cease,
>   Sitting upon the spraye
>   So lowde, he wakened Robin Hood
>   In the greenwood where he lay."

A child cares little about landscape for its own sake, but much for the things which it suggests. Here, the setting is essential to the game these outlaws are playing ; they are as much a part of it as the deer they chase. The beauty of the forest and the song of birds lead on to the adventure ; but they are as nothing compared to the romantic fact that this is a place where any man may meet with Robin Hood.

In the same way, a child appreciates character as it affects the course of events. Robin Hood's men are neither an army nor a clan ; they join his company of their own free choice, after proof of sportsmanship ; and the chief of them—Little John, Scarlett and Much the miller's son, are distinct personalities. The result is a spirit of individual adventure which gives the stories unusual interest and variety.

The earliest songs of Robin Hood had grown into a ballad-epic, " A Lytell Geste of Robyn Hood ",[1] in which Robin's character was proved in talk and incidents, and further shown by the story-teller's comments on his courage and gentleness, his respect for women, his love of the forest ; but gentle attributes failed to impress the writers of eighteenth century broadsheets. They recall the more obvious traits by a few epithets :

> " I will you tell of a bold outlaw,"

or

> " A story of gallant brave Robin Hood
> Unto you I will declare."

Taking the rest for granted, they deal directly with Robin's combats and escapes, his farcical adventures with bishops and beggars, his daring rescues ; and in these, the quality that comes uppermost is the roguish humour which above all distinguishes him from the conventional knight of chivalry.

[1] First printed by Wynkyn de Worde.

3

A single attempt to connect him with the romances—
the late ballad of " Robin Hood and the Prince of Aragon "
—marks the difference of kind ; for though Robin kills
the prince, and John and Scadlock bag a giant apiece, they
move like live men among shadows.

The children of the eighteenth century did not meet the
outlaws of the " golden world ". They knew the Curtal
Friar and Alan a Dale, and what happened when Robin
Hood

" Weary of the Wood-side
And chasing of the fallow deer,"

tried his fortunes at sea. They had two ballads at least
that varied old themes of the *Geste*, " Robin Hood and
the Bishop " and " The King's Disguise ". And Little
John was their friend,—not of course, the old Little John
who praised the season in the words of a poet ; but " A
jolly brisk blade right fit for the trade", more like the
scapegrace in a popular " History ".

Robin Hood's Garland, printed in 1749, gave a mere
collection of stories for the sequence of the *Geste*, and many
chap-books copied it in prose ; but a rough cadence is better
than none, and Robin Hood was first praised in a ballad.

The chap-books, indeed, were no more than the dead
leaves of romance ; it took the vivid play of a child's
fancy to revive them ; but whatever the ballad-maker
touched,—fairy tale or legend or history,—he made a new
thing of it : a story to sing or tell, but short enough to
be sung or told many times over.

CHAPTER II

FAIRY TALES AND EASTERN STORIES

Unwritten fairy tales—" Child Rowland "—Traditional matter and printed books—*The History of Thomas Hickathrift*—Giants and Dwarfs—Logic and Realism in *Tom Thumb*—Lack of Magic in English Folk-tales—Whittington and his Cat—Perrault's *Contes* —The partnership between Youth and Age—English versions— " Court " adaptations and " moral " fairy tales—Eastern stories— The " little yellow canvas-covered book "—Nursery criticism— Aladdin and Sinbad—The " Oriental Moralist "—Traditional tales moralised : *Tom Thumb* and *Robin Goodfellow*—*The Two Children in the Wood—The Enchanted Castle.*

FAIRIES were not altogether unknown in the Age of Reason, though the Royal Society kept no record of their delicate transactions. The little Betty of Steele's paper, who terrified the maids with her accounts of " Fairies and Sprights ", must have learned them, as children do, from the " Grasshoppers' Library " ; for the pedlar had no such tales in print.

They were sometimes told as a mixture of ballad and fairy tale—a story with snatches of ballad rhyme. Children guarded them jealously, passing them on word for word, with none of the slips that a printer would have made.

Such a tale was " Child Rowland ", first set down by Jamieson in 1814,[1] as an old country tailor told it to him when he was seven or eight years old. But that old tailor had heard it in his own childhood, and so, doubtless had his great-grandfathers in theirs ; for this tale of the three

[1] *Illustrations of Northern Antiquities*, by Weber, Jamieson and Scott.

brothers seeking their lost sister, of her being stolen by the King of Elfland and kept under a spell, is the same that Shakespeare quoted in *King Lear* :

> " Child Rowland to the dark tower came,
> His word was still ' Fie, foh and fum,
> I smell the blood of a British man '."

A child would remember the giant-formula, though he forgot every word of that " easy pleasant Book, suited to his Capacity " which Mr. Locke prescribed for him ; he would remember the whole exquisite story : how the youngest brother found his sister, and what passed between them (most of it in rhyme) and how he fought with the Elf-King and broke the spell.

If Child Rowland had been the only story of its kind, Mr. Locke had yet to reckon with the fancies that a child might weave for himself out of common experience : the moving tree that casts the shadow of a pursuing giant, the wind that wears an invisible cloak, the enchanter sun who can pave any road with gold. These baffled all his efforts to drive fairies out of the nursery.

But printed tales, before Perrault, were few enough : in prose, the giant killers, " Hickathrift " and " Jack " ; in rhyme, " Catskin " and " Tom Thumb " and " Whittington ". Like printed ballads, they favoured themes of action and reality. Catskin, the English Cinderella, did without a fairy godmother ; Tom Thumb, although he tilted with the knights of the Round Table, never saw Fairyland till he died, and Whittington's cat was a mere mouser, a poor relation of Puss in Boots.

The truth is that a child never asks himself whether a tale belongs to the dream world or to the world of reality, because either will serve his turn, and either may be true. Any setting convinces him if the adventure hold ; and a tale that lost its imaginative colouring in the chap-books might regain it in a winter night.

Between 1690 and 1790, there is little change in " The Pleasant History of Thomas Hickathrift ",[1] and not a trace in print of the " astonishing image " that Coleridge remembered : the " whole rookery that flew out of the giant's beard, scared by the tremendous voice with which this monster answered the challenge of the heroic Tom Hickathrift ".[2] The nearest thing to it (in a chap-book of 1780) is the likening of the giant's head, when it was off, to " the root of a mighty Oak." But this image of the monstrous beard, a piece of pure myth, if it were not the addition of some imaginative teller, came down from a time when childlike men invented it to explain the giant shapes of trees. A child, recognizing the analogy, feels the same shock of surprise and pleasure as his forest-dwelling ancestors, and finds in this play of likeness and contrast, the source and sustaining interest of all giant tales. For there never was a giant without dwarfs to measure him, nor a dwarf that had not his giant ; nor indeed is Jack's fight with Blunderbore a more engrossing spectacle than Tom Thumb dancing a Galliard on the Queen's left hand.[3]

Yet there is little of the fairy about Tom Thumb. He is a real child, mischievous, even thievish,—taking advantage of his size to creep into other boys' cherry-bags and steal. His one poor trick of magic is to hang pots upon a sunbeam, his one adventure into romance, a mock-heroic episode at King Arthur's court.

When Dr. Johnson " withdrew his attention " from the great man who bored him and " thought about Tom Thumb ", the escape was not from dull facts into a world of

[1] Printed from the earliest extant copies, and edited by G. L. Gomme. (*Chap-books and Folk-lore Tracts*, First Series, 1885).

[2] See Coleridge's *Biographia Literaria*, Vol. II., Ch. XVIII. (1870 ed.).

[3] A Douce chap-book of *Tom Thumb* (verse) is " corrected after an old copy, printed for F. Coles ". This has a note on an earlier edition (1621).

dreams, but from the pedantry of words into a simple realism.

Given a little creature in a land of giants, Tom's experiences are strictly logical. He stands on the edge of a bowl in which his mother is mixing batter, and falls in. When his mother goes milking, she ties him to a thistle, and he is swallowed by a cow. A raven that spies him walking in a furrow carries him off " even like a grain of corn ".

As for his life at Court, there is example for it, " Tom being a dwarf " ; nor was he the first mischief-maker to find his way there, nor the first poor man's son that overcame his betters. But his method of attack was new ; no champion in the annals of romance had beaten Sir Launcelot, Sir Tristram and Sir Guy with no other weapon than a laugh.

At Court, Tom bears himself as to the manner born ; wears the King's signet for a girdle, creeps nimbly into the royal button-hole, and finds a place, sooner than most courtiers, " near his Highness heart ". At home, he is still the gentle scapegrace beloved of village folk. If he craves a boon of the King, it is to relieve the wants of his parents : and the boon,

> " as much of silver coin
> As well his arms could hold ",

amounts to the great sum of *threepence*,

> " A heavy burden which did make
> His weary limbs to crack."

There is a kind of natural magic in all this that a child can grasp without the help of a magician. Tom Thumb although he is wingless, can wear a fairy dress : an oak-leaf hat, a spider-woven shirt, hose and doublet of thistle-down and

> " shoes made of a mouse's skin
> And tann'd most curiously ".

Small creatures that creep among grass-blades seem to have furnished the rhymer with analogies. Tom's house is but half a mile from the court, yet he takes two days and nights to make the journey; he sleeps in a walnut-shell, and his parents feast him three days upon a hazel-nut,

> " that was sufficient for a month
> For this great man to eat ".

" A few moist April drops " are enough to delay his return, till his " careful father " takes a " birding trunk " and with a single blast, blows him back to court.

Last comes the notable account of his death, which tells how the doctors examined him through " a fine perspective glass " and found—

> " His face no bigger than *an ant's*,
> Which hardly could be seen ".

The rhyme is a dwarf epic, perhaps begun by some child that had found an ant-hill, or a thistle taller than himself; carried on, with a phrase here and a picture there from older tales, by the " careful father ", who set it to the unequal beat of little feet at his side.

But no child could endure the unhappy end. A second part and a third (both sorry imitations of the first) brought the " little knight " back to fresh adventures; and even the printers of instructive books understood the value of his name on a title-page.

Catskin,[1] long forgotten through the more glorious transformations of her French sister, could hold Dr. Primrose's children with the old theme of disguise and changing fortune. Five parts in verse gave her whole history: how she was banished, like Cordelia, by an angry father; how she

[1] (a) " The Wandering Young Gentlewoman, or Catskin (complete) ". W. Armstrong, Liverpool, n.d. (early 19th c.) (b); " Catskin's Garland, or the Wandering Young Gentlewoman ", in five parts (verse). Printed and sold by T. Cheney, Banbury, n.d.

disguised herself in a hood of Catskin, and took service in a great house ; how (following here the very print of the Glass Slipper) she went to the ball and danced with a Knight ; and how, one day when she forgot her Catskin hood, the Knight, discovering her " in rich attire ", fell in love with her and married her.

English folk-tales, compared with others more magical, are like the toys that a child will make for himself out of a stick, beside the fine inventions of a conjurer ; they appeal chiefly to practical interests, and leave much to the imagination. Jack killed Cormoran and Blunderbore and the giant with two heads before anybody thought of giving him a cap of knowledge, or shoes of swiftness, or even a magic sword. These things were the addition of a Second Part.

Indeed, a tale never was so plain that it gathered no colour in the telling. There was an old story of Whittington without a Cat,[1] and how the cat got into the story was more than the whole Society of Antiquaries could tell, though it met together in 1771 expressly to discuss the problem. In our own time, most antiquaries are agreed that the Cat found its way from Genoa or Persia or Portugal,—no matter whence,—and that it is a piece of folk-lore grafted upon authentic biography. Try as they will, they can get little nearer to the heart of the matter than Mr. Pepys, when he watched the puppet-show of Whittington at Southwark Fair, " which was pretty to see ", and remarked " how that idle thing do work upon people that see it, and even myself too ".

The very truth underlying the modest fable of the Cat and the song of Bow Bells, had more power than the Wishing Hat of Fortunatus, and would have carried more fanciful embellishments ; but it is never safe to lose sight of the

[1] For a full account of ballads and prose chap-books, see the introduction to " The History of Sir Richard Whittington ", edited by H. B. Wheatley (Chap-books and Folk-lore Tracts, 1885). See Appendix A for references in the *Tatler*, *Spectator*, etc.

double paradox of childish imagination—that reality is romance, romance, reality. If " *Cendrillon* " had never been done into English, Catskin or Cap o' Rushes might have worn the Glass Slipper and ridden in a Pumpkin Coach. As it fell out, the little kitchen-maid surpassed them both,—the girl whose ragged dress was transformed at a touch into " *drap d'or et d'argent, tout charmarez de pierreries.*"

Cinderella's biographer was no less a person than Charles Perrault, a member of the French Academy, and a friend of La Fontaine. He also wrote the famous " histories " of little Red Riding Hood and the Sleeping Beauty, of Hop o' my Thumb (a distant kinsman of Tom Thumb), Puss in Boots, and others who have lived so long in English nurseries that their French names are forgotten.

In his youth, Perrault had rebelled against the formal education of his day, and when he was little short of seventy, he turned from his serious works and produced a children's book by which he is still remembered.

Fairy tales, indeed, were already popular in France, but they had become a part of that fantastic world into which the Court of Louis XIV had been transformed : a world of courtly shepherds and shepherdesses, who told " *Contes des fées* " (" *mitonner* ", Madame de Sévigné says they called it) to prove that they had gone back to the Golden Age.

Perrault knew better than to copy them. He wrote for a public at once more appreciative and more critical : the nursery society of which, in the introduction to his rhymed tales (1695) he wrote : " *On les voit dans la tristesse et dans l'abbattement tant que le héros ou l'héroine du conte sont dans le malheur, et s'écrie de joie quand le temps de leur bonheur arrive* ".

His knowledge of children alone might have carried him through, but his choice of a collaborator was an act of genius. When in 1697, the *Contes* were collected and pub-

lished,[1] it was not to M. Perrault of the Academy that the
" *privelège du roy* " was granted, but to his ten-years-old
son, Perrault Darmancour. The device of anonymity was
common among the early writers of children's books, and
some critics have suggested that it was beneath the dignity
of an Academician to acknowledge the authorship of fairy-
tales ; but Mlle. L'Heritier, Perrault's niece, who contributed one tale to the book, declared, before it was published,
that little Darmancour could write fairy-tales " with much
charm " ; and Mr. Andrew Lang, following M. Lacroix,
believed that the boy had a real share in the book. He
detected the actual note of a child's voice in the dialogue :

" *Toc, toc, qui est là ? C'est votre fille, le petit chaperon
rouge—qui vous apporte une galette et un petit pot de
beurre que ma mère vous envoye . . . tira la chevillette, la
bobinette chera* ". But this, after all, is the language of
fairy-tales. Here it is again, when the little princess finds
the old woman spinning : " *Que faites-vous là, ma bonne
femme—je file, ma belle enfant. . . . Ha ! que cela est
joli . . . comment faites-vous ? Donnez-moy que je voye
si j'en ferois bien autant* ".

It is the language of fairy-tales ; and that, of course, is
child's talk. But the father's part is clear in the artistic
handling of the tales, in the addition of " *Moralités* " after
the manner of Æsop, and in asides of laughter or comment
intended for grown-up ears,—a sly dig at the lawyers
in " *Le Maître Chat* ", or at women, through the Ogre's
wife in " *Le Petit Poucet* ".

---

[1] *Histoires ou Contes du Tems passé, avec des Moralités. A
Paris, chez Claude Barbin. Avec Privilège de sa Majesté, 1697.*
Title on frontispiece : *Contes de ma mère Loye.* Another
edition : *Histoires ou Contes du Temps passé, avec des Moralités.
Par le fils de Monsieur Perrault de l'Academie François. Suivant
la copie à Paris. A Amsterdam, chez Jacques Desbordes, 1708.*
For a full account of Charles Perrault and the *Contes*, see Mr.
Andrew Lang's introduction to his edition, 1888.

Some such partnership between youth and age there
must be in all real children's books ; whether it be arranged
between them is another matter. The wise writer will
always take hints from the child, will remember the way
he turns his phrases, the tones of his voice, the things that
interest him ; but if he remember his own childhood, it may
serve as well.

These stories are all memories of childhood. As their
more intimate title, " *Contes de ma Mère Loye* ", suggests,
they were handed down for centuries, gathering new
features by the way, till this boy of Perrault's had them
from his nurse. But no child could have written them as
Perrault wrote. " Cinderella "—the " story of stories " :
the boy could repeat it word for word ; but if he had tried
to set it down, he would have lost the thread at the point
of transformation. Those dramatic strokes of the clock
would have been forgotten in the music of the ball. This
balance, this art of simplicity is the work of a man,—an
academician, the writer who, in a French " Battle of the
Books ", took up the cause of the Moderns against the
Classics, and yet lived in the kindly reasonable humour
that belongs to the Augustan Age.

Perrault's *Contes* are essentially romantic ; the Sleeping
Beauty gives place only to Persephone,—she and her sleeping
household, shut in by the great hedge of thorns ; but every
tale has quaint human touches which puts it precisely at
the right angle to life : the little girl, her basket of goodies,
and the sick grandmother, all things of experience ; and
then, with a quick turn of the " World Upside Down "—
the Grandmother that was really a Wolf in bed. A nurse
might have told it well enough ; but the artist knew the
true colours, the just economy of lines, and the point where
one could turn from the pictures and listen for talk.

Perrault must have followed every footstep in the tales
with the eager sympathy of the boy at his side. Together

they hid with Little Thumb under his father's stool, and heard the poor parents' desperate shift to be rid of their children.   They were with the tiny hero when he filled his pockets full of small white pebbles, and made the trail by which he and his six brothers found their way home; and they joined in the hopeless search of the second adventure, when Little Thumb dropped crumbs instead of pebbles, and the birds ate them.   That brings the story to the very heart of interest : when the hungry boys, lost in the forest at nightfall, fancied they heard on every side of them the howling of wolves coming to eat them up.   For then Little Thumb, the youngest and smallest and cleverest of them all " climbed up to the top of a tree, to see if he could discover anything ; and having turned his head about on every side, he saw at last a glimmering light, like that of a candle, but a long way from the forest."   This is matter of romance, though there is nothing in it beyond Nature. But—that " glimmering light " threw its beams from *an Ogre's window*, and there was yet to come the Adventure of the Seven League Boots : those boots that would fit a foot of any size, from the Ogre's to Little Thumb's ; in which either Perrault *père* or Perrault *fils* could go seven leagues at a step.

No copy remains of the first translation of Perrault's tales by Samber (1729),[1] nor of John Newbery's edition ; but a seventh edition appeared in 1777, under the title of " Mother Goose's Tales ", and an eighth in 1780.   At the close of the century, Harris printed another, " Englished by G. M. Gent ", of which copies are still found. The book fits a very small hand, and though every trace

[1] The original English translation is advertised in the *Flying Post, or Weekly Medley* for June 7, 1729, " printed for J. Pope at Sir Isaac Newton's Head, the corner of Suffolk Street, Charing Cross—just published (very entertaining and instructive for children, with cuts to every tale).   Done into English from the French by Mr. Samber."

of gold be rubbed off the covers, the Dutch paper pattern can still be seen through diamond patches of colour. The frontispiece shows an old woman with her distaff, seated by the fire, telling stories to a group of children; and there are quaint woodcuts in the text.

The welcome given in court circles to fairy-tales marked the beginning, or rather, a special phase of romantic interest; but this had little to do with children. Such tales, originally simple, caught the elaborate grace of their new setting, and borrowing variations from the newly-translated eastern stories, ran into an endless series in the *Cabinet des Fées*. In English they were represented chiefly by the *Contes* of Madame la Comtesse D'Aulnoy, which were translated before Perrault's.[1] These were common as nursery chap-books in the second half of the century.

Nothing could be more unlike the simplicity of Perrault. Madame D'Aulnoy's stories are rich in embroideries of the folk-tale themes. She makes something very like a novel of her " *L'Oiseau Bleu* " ; but the adventures of the bird-lover are well known in such ballads as " the Earl of Mar's Daughter ", and no artifice can hide the traces of an old " *cante-fable* ". The wicked step-mother of all fairy-tales transforms the prince into a bird ; but the spy set to watch the princess at last falls asleep, and then the princess opens her little window and sings :

> " *Oiseau bleu, couleur de temps,*
> *Vole à moi, promptement* ".

" These," explains Madame la Comtesse, " are her own words, which it has been thought best to keep unchanged ". Elsewhere she is less concerned for her originals. Her

[1] (a) *Tales of the Fairys.* Translated from the French. For T. Cockerill, 1699. 12s. (b) The collected Works of Madame D'Aulnoy, published by John Nicolson, at the King's Arms, and at the Cross Keys and Bible in Cornhill, 1707.

"*Finette Cendron*" (the English "Finetta") is an odd mixture of Perrault's "Cinderella" and "Little Thumb", in which both stories are spoilt.

Gold and silver are the meanest ornaments in these fairy novels; they have much of the glitter of a transformation scene. When the colours fade, there is only a confused memory of the setting; but fairies and talking animals remain. Children are not likely to forget "The White Cat", "The Hind in the Wood", or that lurker in dark corners of the nursery, "The Yellow Dwarf".

As the century advanced, grown-up persons from time to time ventured into the unknown regions of romance; and it is odd to find that the more thrilling their discoveries in poetry and fiction, the more determined they were to hide them from children, or to cloak them with moral applications.

The rhymed "*Moralités*" which Perrault added to his tales were a tactful concession to public opinion. No moralist ever succeeded in reforming Puss in Boots, though one, early in the nineteenth century, claimed him as the ancestor of a *Moral Cat*. It is clear, however, that Perrault, left to himself, would have trusted his readers to find their own morals; for in the dedication to his *Contes* he says: "they all contain a very obvious moral, and one that shows itself more or less according to the insight of the reader."

The task of reconciling parents and children upon the vexed question of the supernatural was achieved by Madame le Prince de Beaumont, with her educational or moral fairy-tales.

Allegorical persons often appeared in the court adaptations with names and images drawn from classical authority. Mlle. L'Héritier had already foisted into the old folk-tale of "Diamonds and Toads" a fairy called "*Eloquentia Nativa*"; but Madame de Beaumont's tales were simpler and more convincing. From the parental point of view she had undoubted advantages over her predecessors in the fairy-tale, for, in the words of an editor of the *Cabinet des Fées*, she " devoted herself entirely to the education of children ".

Born in 1711, six years after the death of Madame D'Aulnoy, she spent a great part of her life in London. Her *Magasin des Enfans*, published in 1757,[1] properly belongs to the type of moral miscellany introduced by Sarah Fielding's Governess[2]; but the schoolroom setting could not spoil fairy-tales which, however obvious their moral purposes, had refreshing touches of humour. In her intercourse with English children, Madame de Beaumont had somehow acquired a belief in the educational value of nonsense.

Charles Lamb's rhyme of " Prince Dorus " is simply an adaptation of Madame de Beaumont's "*Prince Désir*"; her story of " The Three Wishes " found in so many chapbooks, is a well-known " droll ", and there are playful touches in her most serious tales.

Yet a child might venture a protest on discovering that the little white rabbit in " *Prince Chéri* ", that leaps into the King's arms as he rides hunting, is an educational fairy in disguise ; and it is impossible not to sympathise with the prince who, in spite of a ring that pricks whenever he is naughty, becomes a scapegrace, and has to undergo a Circeian transformation ere he is reformed.

Like all successful *gouvernantes*, Madame de Beaumont can be severe. Her fairy in " *Fatal et Fortune* " deserves a place in Spartan folklore ; this is how she answers the mother who pleads for a son doomed to misfortune :

" *Vous ne savez pas ce que vous demandez. S'il n'est pas malheureux, il sera méchant !* "

---

[1] Translated into English *c.* 1770. 3rd edition 1776.

[2] See below, Chap. VI.

One at least of Madame de Beaumont's tales is worthy of Perrault. " Beauty and the Beast " would decide her title to nursery fame, if she had written nothing else. In 1740, Madame de Villeneuve had spun out the same theme at extraordinary length ; but the story as children know it first appeared in the *Magasin des Enfans*, and it bears all the marks of a genuine folk-tale.

It was late in the century before the Arabian tales,[1] translated from the French of M. Galland in 1708, appeared in English children's books. In France, they received a welcome surpassing that of the fairy-tales, and produced a fantastic literature of supposed translations, in which Eastern imagery and the incidents of Western folk-lore were curiously mixed. Yet the new pattern was not altogether incongruous. Dwarfs and magicians were the stock figures of romance ; the Quest of the Talking Bird, Singing Tree and Yellow Water was but a variant of the Fortune-Seeker's adventures ; the Magic Mirror a commonplace of fairy-tales ; and there were old ballads, like " The Heir of Linne ", with Arabian, Persian and Turkish variants.

Eastern stories, nevertheless, had more in common with Court fairy-tales than with those of natural growth. They were woven, like oriental carpets, for Kings' palaces, and the " Folk " elements were simply repeated as a part of the design. Children as yet knew nothing of these visions of splendour and terror, which turned the French Court from its pose of simplicity, and coloured the whole fabric of the *Cabinet des Fées*.

But the British tendency to moralise was never stronger than in the eighteenth century, and eastern fables and aphorisms were rich in illustrations of philosophy. Thus,

[1] *The Arabian Nights' Entertainments*. Translated into French from the Arabian MSS. by M. Galland of the Royal Academy, and now done into English. For A. Bell, 1708, 12mo. (8 vols.). See Appendix A. II.

for the greater part of the century, the English oriental tale was moralised, and if children came into any part of their legacy, it was either by courtesy of the moralist, or through illicit traffic with the pedlar.

Neither Steele nor Johnson mentions these tales among children's books ; but the " precious treasure " of Wordsworth's childhood, a " little yellow canvas-covered book ",[1] although it was but " a slender abstract of the Arabian tales," was within the reach of other children. Wordsworth tells how he and another boy hoarded their savings for many months to buy the " four large volumes " of " kindred matter ". Failing in resolution, they never got beyond the smaller book ; yet this, if it had only the tales of the Merchant and the Ginni, the Fisherman, the Sleeper Awakened and the Magic Horse, would build them a city of dreams. Whereas it almost certainly contained the Voyages of Sinbad,[2] and the two apocryphal tales, never doubted by children, " Aladdin " and " The Forty Thieves ".

Such a book was a maker of magicians. The child that possessed it found himself richer than Ali Baba, for he knew the magic formula that would open all the treasure-caves of the East. He was the shipmate of Sinbad, that sailor of enchanted seas ; the fellow of Aladdin, possessing the ring and lamp that gave him mastery over slaves " terrible in aspect, vast in stature as the giants ", who could carry him a thousand leagues while he slept, or build in a single night a palace " more splendid than imagination can conceive ".

The tastes of Wordsworth and his schoolfellows were probably more catholic than those of the little De Quinceys, who discussed in the nursery the relative merits of the *Arabian Nights*, and dared to question the judgment of

---

[1] See Wordsworth's " Prelude ", Book V.

[2] *The History of Sinbad* was published as a nursery chap-book by E. Newbery (between 1779 and 1801) at 6d.

4

Mrs. Barbauld, " the queen of all the bluestockings ", because she preferred " Aladdin " and " Sinbad " to all the rest.[1] Most children would agree with her, for even the cave where they measured gold like grain lacks the splendour of the garden in which the trees " were all covered with precious stones instead of fruit, and each tree was of a different kind, and had different jewels of all colours, green and white and yellow and red."

The palace, though all its storeys were of jasper and alabaster and porphyry and mosaics, was not half so dazzling as this garden of jewels.

As to " Sinbad ", it may be, as De Quincey judged, " a mere succession of adventures " ; to a child, it is a second Odyssey. The giant that throws masses of rock at Sinbad's raft is a brother of the Cyclops ; Proteus is one with the Old Man of the Sea. But the adventures of Odysseus are plain and straight compared with the extravagant splendours of this merchant-adventurer. He walks by a river of dreams (which is yet a real river) till he finds the tall vessel that pleases him ; but once afloat with black slaves and pages and bales of merchandise, he cares less for the occupation of traffic than for " the pleasure of seeing the countries and islands of the world ".

This is the very desire of the child ; nor did dream-islands ever yield romance in greater profusion. One, indeed, is no island, but a great fish, on whose back the sand has been heaped up till trees have grown upon it ; no sooner is the sailors' fire alight than the solid ground sinks under their feet. In another, Sinbad descries from the top of a tree a " white object of enormous size ", the egg of a Roc, that gigantic bird whose wings obscure the sun.

Sir John Mandeville might have set down the adventures of the rhinoceros and the elephant, the valley of diamonds

[1] See De Quincey's *Autobiographic Sketches*, Vol. I, Ch. III. " Infant Literature," pp. 121–125.

or the river of jacinths and pearls ; but his account could never compare with this for reality.

These voyages among the islands, from El-Basrah to Sarandib, though they are set down in the language of myth, are as easy to trace upon a map as the wanderings of Odysseus between Troy and Ithaca. Nor is the Eastern story-teller without a Homeric interest in things seen and discovered, both great and small : a thousand horsemen clad in gold and silk, or a letter sent by the King of Sarandib to Harun Er-Rashid, written " on the skin of the Khawi, which is finer than parchment ", in writing of ultramarine.

The quality of realism is indeed one of the distinguishing features of Eastern romance. Sinbad's account of the building of his raft from the planks and ropes of the wrecked ship almost reads like an entry in Crusoe's journal, and there is the characteristic opening which simulates a narrative of fact : " In the time of the Khalifeh, the Prince of the Faithful Harun Er-Rashid, in the city of Baghdad ". All the sounds and colours of the East are in the setting of these tales, all the details of life and traffic ; and yet it is never out of keeping with the supernatural. Wizards and fairies simply move among the natural inhabitants of bazaars or palaces,—a thing in no way surprising to a child ; and forms of enchantment surpassing the illusions of a dream rise up in existing cities.

In a realistic age, such a setting would atone for the elements of unreality ; yet the authors of the *Tatler* and *Spectator* (those gentle schoolmasters of grown-up children) held it of less account than the aptness of the stories to " reflection " and philosophy. For this they could forgive " that Oriental extravagance which is mixed with it " ; but the more philosophical the tale, the less it needed a real background and moving figures. Vague allusions took the place of description, and incidents were turned to illustrate particular virtues or to point the arguments of Mr. Locke. Thus treated, the stories were said to be "writ after the Eastern manner, but *somewhat more correct*."

Johnson followed the same method, but with more profound philosophy, in the *Rambler* ; and it was in this "moralised" form that Eastern tales came, straight from the pages of the *Spectator* and the *Rambler*, into the first books which John Newbery devised "for the Amusement and Instruction" of children.

Thus the story of Alnascar, the Persian Glassman,[1] is printed in the last section ("Letters, Poems, Tales and Fables") of *A Museum for Young Gentlemen and Ladies : or, a Private Tutor for little Masters and Misses* (1763) ; and the *Twelfth Day Gift* (1767) has Johnson's tale of Obidah and the Hermit,[2] here called "The Progress of Life".

Nor was there any attempt to choose the lighter and more entertaining stories for children. Such a tale, for example, as Will Honeycomb's of Pug's adventures (*Spectator*, 343), which Addison borrowed from the *Chinese Tales*, never found its way into the early children's miscellanies, though Mrs. Barbauld, at the close of the century, produced a somewhat similar series of adventures in *Evenings at Home*.

In France, as in England, there were Eastern tales which came half way between the romance of pure adventure and the "Moral Tale". Marmontel chose an Eastern setting for two of his stories ; but English writers for children not unnaturally preferred Johnson's "oriental" examples of conduct and duty, and were willing to sacrifice interest to moral significance.

Johnson himself would have advised them better. "Babies do not want to hear about babies," he told Mrs.

[1] See *Spectator*, 535.
[2] *Rambler*, 65.

Thrale ; " they like to be told of giants and castles, and of somewhat which can stretch and stimulate their little minds." [1]

He expressly warned her against the nursery editions which contained, as a substitute for genuine romance, his own moralised " Eastern tales ". But the Great Cham's remarks upon children's books were not published with his works, and parents went on buying the books which he declared that children never read.

Mrs. Sheridan's *Nourjahad* (1767) appeared as a nursery chap-book in 1808, and Miss Edgeworth, in her tale of "Murad the Unlucky" (one of the *Popular Tales*), gives similar contrasted examples of wisdom and folly.

Minor moralists were unnumbered. Mr. Cooper, the author of *Blossoms of Morality*, having by his own account " accidentally met with a French edition of the Arabian Nights during a trip on the Continent ", and being " induced to wade through it, having no other book at hand ", was so far moved by the entertainment as to select and adapt some of the tales " for Youth ", under the title of *The Oriental Moralist*. [2]

A remark at the close of " Prince Agib and the Adamantine Mountain " gives a fair example of his treatment : " It may not be amiss to remind my youthful readers that an unwarrantable curiosity, and a degree of obstinacy too natural to young people, were the causes of the third Calender losing his eye ".

The author of *The Governess* ; or, *Evening Amusements at a Boarding School*, though she allows Persian stories, admits that whenever she found " a sentiment that would

[1] *Anecdotes of Johnson* (1786) by Mrs. Thrale (aft. Piozzi).

[2] *The Oriental Moralist, or the Beauties of the Arabian Nights' Entertainments :* " Translated from the original, accompanied with suitable reflections, adapted to each story ". London, E. Newbery, c. 1796.

answer her purpose ", she did not hesitate to " make it
breathe from the lips of the Eastern Sage ".

The Grateful Turk, one of Thomas Day's moral tales,
appeared in the same year as Mrs. Pilkington's *Asiatic
Princess*, and Miss Porter followed with *The Two Princes of
Persia*, " adapted to youth ". Alluring titles, such as
" The Ruby Heart " and " The Enchanted Mirror " were
another means of recommending improving histories.

Yet the oriental tale suffered less than native romance
and folk-lore, by this sort of adaptation. Perhaps the
Jinn, being " the slaves of him who held the lamp ", or
" of him on whose hand was the ring ", were more helpless
than other spirits in the power of the Moralist.

English fairies were not so submissive ; indeed they
played strange tricks with the little didactic works that
bore their names.

Already (in 1746) Tom Thumb had turned pedagogue
and published his " Travels ",[1] a barefaced introduction
to Topography. *Tom Thumb's Folio* (1768) was followed
in 1780 by *Tom Thumb's Exhibition*, " being an account
of many valuable and surprising curiosities which he had
collected in the course of his travels, for the instruction
and amusement of the British Youths ".

This is somewhat more entertaining than the " Travels ",
having an odd humour of its own ; but the Tom Thumb
of the Exhibition has changed his fairy dress for a schoolmaster's gown, and lies in wait for pupils " in a large
commodious room at Mr. Lovegood's, number 3 in Wise-
man's Buildings, at the upper end of Education Road ".

Here he examines, under the lens of an " Intellectual
Perspective Glass", the unreasonable things which please a

[1] *The Travels of Tom Thumb over England and Wales*, " containing Descriptions of whatever is most remarkable in the several
Counties, interspersed with many pleasant Adventures that happened to him personally during the Course of his Journey. Written
by Himself." London, 1746. Price 1s. 6d. bound.

child. For example, unripe apples or gooseberries thus scrutinized, " instantly appear to be changed into a swarm of worms and other devouring reptiles ".

From this it is tempting to infer that the same merciless glass had discovered, instead of the traditional wren or robin, that " little feathered songster called the *Advice Bird* " which a child might see at the Exhibition. Such a lens, focussed upon Whittington's Cat, would doubtless prove it a figment, or applied to a magic sword, might instantly change it to a piece of rusty iron.

Old ballads suffered the same transforming process. Robin Goodfellow,[1] dragged from his haunts to show " a virtuous little mortal " the way to Fairyland, took on the likeness of a Philosopher, the better to fool his victims.

Fairyland, he asserts, is " neither a continent nor an island, and yet it is both or either. It exists in the air, at a distance of about five feet and a half or six feet at most from the surface of the Earth ".

The solution of this pleasing riddle is found in a diagram of the human frame, whereon the Fairyland of Philosophy is shown to exist nowhere but in a man's head, hard by those notable tracts, the " Land of Courage " and the " Land of Dumplins ".

A knavish sprite, this, who can find matter for jests in a fairy revolution ; for by his account, " the reigning Monarch Fancy, and Whim, his royal Consort " have usurped the throne of Oberon ; and Imagination is their eldest son.

In such an age, the boldest outlaw would have much ado to rescue Robin Hood ; and since Robin could point but a one-sided moral, the writer of little books forgot his virtues and published his " Life " as a " Warning-piece ". He, forsooth, " did not know how to work ", had " neg-

[1] *Robin Goodfellow*, " A Fairy Tale written by a Fairy, for the amusement of all the pretty little Faies and Fairies in Great Britain and Ireland ". Printed for F. Newbery, 1770.

lected to learn a trade ", and being justly outlawed, skulked with his " gang " in Sherwood Forest, living " *what they called* a merry life ".

The Two Children in the Wood afforded ampler scope for moral contrasts. Addison's praise had included even the pretty fiction of the robins, on the authority of Horace and his doves ; but the makers of toy-books were not satisfied with this. They expunged the robins and prepared two prose versions of the ballad, one expanding the story into a novel of domestic life, and the other marring it with a happy ending.[1]

The novel, an amusing medley, deals in an underplot with the adventures of the wicked Uncle at sea, laying bare a past about which the ballad was silent ; the rest is concerned with the home life of the two children, and contains a chapter of stories told for their benefit. At the end (by way of reparation, perhaps) the ballad itself is printed. The novelist carries enough moral ballast to float it all, and anticipates its effect in rhyme :

> " The tender Tale must surely please,
> If told with sympathetic ease ;
> Read, then, the Children in the Wood,
> And you'll be virtuous and good."

But of all these " restorations ", none was a greater outrage than the attempt of a nursery moralist to rebuild the Enchanted Castle of Romance.

" The History of the Enchanted Castle ; or, The Prettiest Book for Children " appeared in Francis Newbery's list in 1777, and was reprinted for Harris early in the nineteenth century. On the title page it is further described as " the Enchanted Castle, situated in one of the Fortunate Isles and governed by the *Giant Instruction*. Written for the Entertainment of little Masters and Misses by Don Stephano Bunyano, Under-Secretary to the aforesaid Giant ".

[1] See Appendix, A. II.

The wheel has come full circle : folk-tales, ballads, romances, not one of the forms of popular literature has escaped. Here at last is the giant himself surrendering his stronghold to the moralist, delivering up captives and stolen treasure, engaging Secretaries, and parcelling out the Enchanted Castle into a Picture Gallery, Museum and Library.

The parallel between the Giant Instruction and Giant Despair is sufficiently obvious ; but the giant's under-secretary, with official sagacity, turns it to account. He boldly proclaims himself " a distant relation of the famous John Bunyan, the pious and admired author of the *Pilgrim's Progress* ", and proceeds to explain the symbolic pictures and curiosities in the Castle, after the manner of Mr. Interpreter.

Yet there is one rare thing among the oddities of this little book ; a statement of aim which involves direct criticism of existing children's books. This betrays the Giant's intention to make children " as capable of thinking and understanding what is what (according to their years) as their Papas and Mammas, or as the greatest Philosophers and Divines in the whole Country ".

To this end it is forbidden to present even " very little Masters and Misses " with " idle nonsensical stories " and " silly unmeaning rhymes ".

It is little wonder that Wordsworth, remembering

> " A race of real children ; not too wise,
> Too learned, or too good . . . ",

denounced moralist and pedagogue, and cried in vain for the old nursery tales :

> " Oh ! give us once again the wishing-cap
> Of Fortunatus, and the invisible coat
> Of Jack the Giant-killer, Robin Hood
> And Sabra in the forest with St. George ! "

CHAPTER III

THE LILLIPUTIAN LIBRARY

FOR every parent that read Locke's *Thoughts*, a hundred took his ideas at second hand from *The Spectator*. Many, indeed, seem to have confused his notion of childhood with the description of the baby Addison, who threw away his rattle before he was two months old, and would not make use of his coral until they had taken away the bells from it.

It was no new thing to regard a child as a small man or woman. Since Shakespeare's time, children had followed the fashions of their elders. But the tastes of grown-up Elizabethans were not so different from those of children. Never, until the eighteenth century, had a child been taught to think and act like a man of middle age. The little Georgian walked gravely where his for- bears danced, and was expected to read dwarf essays, extracts from Addison and Pope, and little novels after Richardson.

Swift's engrossing pictures of Lilliput had no sooner captured the nursery than grown-up persons began to fancy themselves in the part of Gulliver stooping to instruct a little nation ; and the logical outcome of this was a " Lilliputian Library ".

The ingenious artist of an older generation, who could put " all th' Iliads in a Nut " must have passed on his secret to the makers of toy-books ; and of these the first and greatest was John Newbery, a descendant of the very Newbery who, in the sixteenth century, had published the rhyme of the " great Marchaunt Man ".

There is no better portrait of John Newbery than the one drawn by Goldsmith in *The Vicar of Wakefield.* That " good-natured man " with his " red pimpled face " who befriended Dr. Primrose when he lay sick at a roadside inn, was " no other than the philanthropic bookseller of St. Paul's Churchyard, who has written so many little books for children ".

Goldsmith was writing for Newbery between 1762 and 1767, and on more than one occasion he, like his Vicar, " borrowed a few pieces " from the kindly publisher. He could not have chosen a more graceful way of thanking him, nor one more likely to give him pleasure, than by thus imitating Mr. Newbery's own method of internal advertisement, associating him with those " little books for children ", and adding that " he called himself their friend, but he was the friend of all mankind ".

The rest of the passage recalls Dr. Johnson's caricature of Newbery as " Jack Whirler, " in *The Idler :*

" Overwhelmed as he is with business, his chief desire is to have still more. Every new proposal takes possession of his thoughts ; he soon balances probabilities, engages in the project, brings it almost to completion and then forsakes it for another."

But Goldsmith again lays stress on his pet project :

" He was no sooner alighted but he was in haste to be gone ; for he was ever on business of the utmost impor-

tance, and was at that time actually compiling materials
for the history of one Mr. Thomas Trip."

An account of John Newbery's career would itself furnish
matter for a children's book. He was a very Whittington
of booksellers—a farmer's son who made his way in the
world " by his talents and industry and a great love of
books ". Every day of his life was an adventure, and he
never lost his Pepysian interest in men and things. Goldsmith's story of the inn (or its counterpart) might almost
have come out of the pocket-book in which Mr. Newbery
kept a record of his journey through England in 1740, with
notes of his various " projects " and purchases.[1]

It was at Reading, where he had begun his trade of
printer and publisher, that he produced his first children's
book : *Spiritual Songs for Children*, by one of the many
imitators of Dr. Watts ;[2] but the genuine " Newberys "
appeared after he settled in London, first at the Bible and
Crown, without Temple Bar, and afterwards at the famous
little shop in St. Paul's Churchyard.

He began with miscellanies—quaint imitations of the
periodicals, announced by whimsical " advertisements ",
and professing the aims and methods of John Locke : *A
Little Pretty Pocket Book* (1744),[3] and *The Lilliputian
Magazine*, advertised in the *General Evening Post*, March 4,
1751.

Two quotations in the *Pocket Book* suggest a connection
between two prevailing interests of the day, Education and
Landscape-gardening. The first is from Dryden :

> " Children, like tender Osiers, take the Bow
>   And as they first are fashioned always grow " ;

[1] Mr. Charles Welsh in *A Bookseller of the Last Century*, gives a
full account of John Newbery and his work. There is a complete
list of the Newbery Books in the Appendix.

[2] By J. Wright. Second edition, 1738.

[3] The " Advertisement " is quoted in Appendix A. III.

the second from Pope :

> " Just as the Twig is bent the Tree's inclined,
> 'Tis Education forms the vulgar Mind ".

But the prefatory letter addressed " To all Parents, Guardians, Governesses, etc. ", illustrates the difference between the " fashioning " of trees and children. It is all pure Locke :

" Would you have a virtuous Son, instil into him the Principles of Morality early. . . . Would you have a wise Son, teach him to reason early. Let him read and make him understand what he reads. No Sentence should be passed over without a strict Examination of the Truth of it. . . . Subdue your children's Passions, curb their Temper and make them subservient to the Rules of Reason ; and this is not to be done by Chiding, Whipping or severe Treatment, but by Reasoning and mild Discipline."

So much for the Parents who bought the *Pretty Pocket Book*. The rest is a judicious mixture of Amusement and Instruction for its readers. There are alphabets big and little, " select Proverbs for the use of children ", *Moralités* in plenty ; but by the precise authority of Mr. Locke, there are also pictures of sorts, songs and games and rhymed fables. There is even a germ of the " Moral Tale " in accounts of good children, set down somewhat in the manner of seventeenth century " Characters ".

Between this and *The Lilliputian Magazine* came an instructive " Snuff-box " series : The *Circle of the Sciences*,[1] described in the Advertisement as " a compendious library, whereby each Branch of Polite Learning is rendered extremely easy and instructive ". But the Newbery Pedant is never quite serious. When, later, he sets himself to adapt the Newtonian System " to the Capacities of young Gentlemen and Ladies ", he does it in a *Philosophy*

---

[1] Advertised in the *Penny London Post*, January 18, 1745.

of Tops and Balls,[1] and seems immensely diverted by this notion of making the Giant Instruction stoop to play.

In 1745 John Newbery left the Bible and Crown, and set up at the Bible and Sun, near the Chapter House in St. Paul's Churchyard. By this time he had become "a merchant in medicines as well as books" and had acquired a partnership in the sale of the famous fever powders of his friend Dr. James, which he advertised with other remedies in his nursery books, often working them into the story.

Like all really busy people, he could always find time for a new enterprise; but the "little books" were no mere relaxation from serious work. His son says that at this time he was "in the full employment of his talents in writing and publishing books of amusement and instruction for children", and adds that "the call for them was immense, an edition of many thousands being sometimes exhausted during the Christmas holidays".[2]

This, in fact, was a favourite "project" of Mr. Newbery's, never forsaken for another, but continued up to the time of his death.

One can imagine him, delighted as Mr. Pepys with his puppet show,—inspecting the woodcuts, examining different patterns of Dutch flowered paper for the binding, deciding the exact size (4 inches by 2¾) for the biography of Mr. Trip; or watching the young apprentices (these paper covers were painted by children) each filling a row of diamond spaces with his appointed colour.

His next venture was *The Lilliputian Magazine*[3] announced as "an attempt to amend the World, to render the Society of Man more amiable, and to re-establish the Simplicity, Virtue and Wisdom of the Golden Age".

Details of the proposed method are set forth in the

[1] Adv., April 9th, 1761. See Appendix A. III.

[2] From Francis Newbery's Autobiography.

[3] Advertised in the *General Evening Post*, March 4, 1751, Price 3d. Additions in Appendix A. III.

following "Dialogue" between a gentleman and the Author :

> *Gentleman :* I have seen, Sir, an Advertisement in the Papers of the Lilliputian Magazine to be published at Three Pence a Month : pray, what is the Design of it ?
>
> *Author :* Why, Sir, it is intended for the Use of Children, as you may perceive by the Advertisement, and my Design is, by Way of *History* and *Fable*, to sow in their Minds the Seeds of Polite Literature and to teach them the great Grammer (*sic*) of the Universe : I mean the Knowledge of Men and Things.

The framework of the book suggests a combination (in miniature) of the Royal Society and the Spectator Club ; for the various Pieces are submitted to a Society of young Gentlemen and Ladies (including a young Prince and several of the young Nobility) presided over by little Master Meanwell (who by reading a great many Books and observing everything his Tutor said to him, acquired a great deal of Wisdom).

The "Histories" and "Fables" that follow are not mixed from Mr. Locke's prescription. They are amusing parodies of Mr. Newbery's (or his contributor's) reading from the *Spectator* and *Gulliver* and Richardson's novels. Not even Gulliver escapes the moralising tendency, and Lilliput (here translated to the "Island of Angelica") is a new Utopia, where no man is allowed more money than he needs. The inhabitants are so little removed from common experience that they appear to be "no more than a gigantic Sort of Lilliputian, about the size of the Fairies in Mr. Garrick's Queen Mab ".[1]

Locke would have scorned the fanciful descriptions of this *Voyage Imaginaire* ; nor would " A History of the Rise and Progress of Learning in Lilliput " (which precedes it)

[1] An " Entertainment " later performed with Garrick's " Fairy Tale from Shakespeare " (1777). See p. 82, Note 2.

have pleased him better ; he never could have understood the sly humour of its author.

Indeed, but for the date, there might be some truth in the suggestion that Goldsmith edited *The Lilliputian Magazine*. For among its contributions was that notable " History of Mr. Thomas Trip " in which his philanthropic bookseller was engaged ; and in the " History ", a rhyme of " Three Children Sliding on the Ice " [1] that Goldsmith might well have invented to temper the virtues of Mr. Trip ; for indeed, this hero, though he scarcely overtops Tom Thumb, is the Wyse Chylde in little : " whenever you see him, you will always find a book in his hand ".

But Goldsmith was not yet in London when *The Lilliputian Magazine* appeared ; the rhyme of " Three Children " is now said to be John Gay's ; and it was Goldsmith himself who named John Newbery as Tommy Trip's biographer.

The other contributions are mere attempts to fit children of middle age with little novels of morality and sentiment,— surely not the least flattering imitations of Richardson. [2]

First comes the " History of Florella, sent by an unknown Hand (and may, for aught we know, have been published before) ", and after an interval for further reference and collation, " The History of Miss Sally Silence, communicated by Lady Betty Lively ". But neither the story nor the sentiment rings true. As yet, the Lilliputian novel has no life : and all that there is to be said of Miss Sally is condensed in her epitaph :

> " Here lie the Remains of the Duchess of Downright :
> Who, when a Maid, was no other
> than Sarah Jones
> A poor Farmer's Daughter.
> From her Attachment to Goodness she
> became great.
> Her Virtue raised her from a mean State

[1] See note in Appendix A. III.
[2] See Appendix A. III.—Novels abridged or adapted for children.

To a high Degree of Honour
and
Her Innocence procured her Peace in her last Moments.
She smiled even in Agony
And embraced Death as a friendly Pilot
Who was to steer her
To a more exalted State of Bliss."

Here the author, as if doubting his effect, adds a direct appeal :

" Little Reader,
Whoever thou art, observe these her Rules
And become thyself
A Copy of this bright Example."

It was somewhere between 1760 and 1765, when a latent spirit of romance was beginning to move the grown-up world, that the children's bookseller turned his attention to Nursery Rhymes.

Some of these were already in print. *Tommy Thumb's Pretty Song Book* [1] had appeared in 1744 : two tiny volumes in Dutch flowered boards, of which the second only has survived. This was a great advance on the song-books commonly given to children as soon as they could read ; but there is something more than the usual nonsense and rhythm in the Newbery rhymes. The very title : *Mother Goose's Melody*,[2] brings them into touch with the first book of fairy-tales ; and indeed those two voices (the child's and the man's) can be heard here as in Perrault—a merry new partnership of song and laughter—, the one piping high in lively see-saw, the other declaiming a mock-learned " Preface ", fitting each rhyme with an ironic " Note " or " Maxim ", burlesquing the commentators and setting the wit of nursery sages against the wisdom of the pedants.

The editor of *Mother Goose's Melody*, although the Preface declares him " *a very great Writer* of very little Books ", has none of that contempt for " Nonsense " which philo-

[1] See Appendix A. III.
[2] Title-page, etc. in Appendix A. III.

5

sophers are apt to show. He traces " the Custom of making Nonsense Verses in our Schools " to " the Old British Nurses, the first Preceptors of Youth ", and speaks of them with evident respect. Yet he shows no bias towards the more imaginative absurdities. It is the use of a rhyme for ironic comment, or its lyric quality that directs his choice.

The song about Betty Winckle's Pig that lived in clover (" but now he's dead and that's all over ") is annotated thus : " A Dirge is a Song for the Dead ; but whether this was made for Betty Winckle or her Pig is uncertain—no Notice being taken of it by Cambden or any of the famous Antiquarians ".

This is " Amphion's Song of Eurydice " :

> " I won't be my Father's Jack
> I won't be my Mother's Jill
> I will be the Fiddler's Wife
> And have Musick when I will.
>> T'other little Tune
>> T'other little Tune
>> Prithee, Love, play me,
>> T'other little Tune."

And this the comment (in small type, for Parents) : " Those Arts are the most valuable which are of the greatest Use ".

Such gentle irony would be lost upon the serious student of Lilliputian Ethics. Grown-up wiseacres and little philosophers must have puzzled their heads in vain over some of these " Maxims " and exclaimed at the effrontery of a Writer, however " great ", who, after suggesting that an unmeaning rhyme " might serve as a Chapter of Consequence in the New Book of Logick ", could add (in a note upon " Margery Daw ") : " It is a mean and scandalous Practice among Authors to put Notes to Things that deserve no Notice. (Grotius) ".

There is no direct evidence of Goldsmith's hand in this ; but he was well acquainted with nonsense-songs, and Miss

Hawkins, writing of her childhood in a letter, connects him with a nursery-rhyme : " I little thought", she says, " what I should have to boast when Goldsmith taught me to play Jack and Gill by two bits of paper on his fingers."

If this " very great Writer of very little Books " was not Goldsmith, it is an extraordinary coincidence that the rhyme in the Preface should be the same that he sang to his friends on the first night of *The Good Natur'd Man*, and " never consented to sing but on special Occasions "—which runs thus :

> " There was an old Woman tossed in a Blanket,
> Seventeen times as high as the moon,
> But where she was going no mortal could tell,
> For under her arm she carried a Broom,
> Old Woman, old Woman, old Woman, said I,
> Whither, ah whither, ah whither so high ?
> To sweep the Cobwebs from the Sky,
> And I'll be with you by and by."

There is only one Lilliputian book that has been attributed to Goldsmith with the consent of his biographer, and that is Mr. Newbery's masterpiece, the quaint and original *History of Goody Two-Shoes.*[1]

Here is the characteristic notice that appeared in *The London Chronicle* (December 19-January 1, 1765) :

" The Philosophers, Politicians, Necromancers, and the Learned in every Faculty are desired to observe that on the 1st of January, being New Year's Day (Oh, that we may all lead new lives !), Mr. Newbery intends to publish the following important Volumes, bound and gilt, and hereby invites all his little Friends who are good to call for them at the Bible and Sun, in St. Paul's Churchyard : but those who are naughty are to have none ".

Here follows a list of the " important Volumes " : " The Renowned History of Giles Gingerbread : a little Boy who lived upon Learning ; " Easter, Whitsuntide and Valentine

[1] First edition, April, 1765. Others in Appendix A. III.

" Gifts " ; " The Fairing " ; and after these an announce-
ment of greater interest, that " there is in the Press and
speedily will be published, either by Subscription or otherwise, as the Public shall please to determine, The History
of Little Goody Two-shoes, otherwise called Margery Two-
Shoes ".

The " Gifts " are so many variants of the Lilliputian
Miscellany,[1] and as to *Giles Gingerbread*, there is nothing
about him to attract a child, unless his name should conjure up a flavour of those gingerbread books sold at Fairs,
which could be eaten when the reading grew tedious. The
story (made to fit a penny chap-book) tells, without digres-
sion, how young Gingerbread learnt to read, that he might
have a fine coach and emulate the success of one Sir Toby
Wilson, who also was a poor man's son.

But *Goody Two-shoes*, though it offers a similar prize for
self-help, teaches no such politic morality. Indeed, it shows
what can be done with the babies' novel, by a writer who
understands children and has a winning gift of humour ;
but for all that, it presents in epitome the whole Lilliputian
Library.

The title-page at once proclaims its likeness to those
records of triumphant virtue, the nursery " Richard-
sons " ; the " Introduction " is a miniature essay on land-
reform. Mr. Welsh, who reprinted *Goody Two-Shoes* in
1882, found an exact picture of the Deserted Village in the
Parish of Mouldwell, where little Margery's father suffers
the " wicked Persecutions " of Sir Timothy Gripe and " an
overgrown Farmer called Graspall ".

A passage at the close of the " Introduction " certainly
lends some colour to the idea that it was a half-playful study
of Goldsmith's, for his serious argument :

" But what, says the Reader, can occasion all this ? Do

[1] For details of the *Valentine's* and *Twelfth Day Gifts*, see Appendix A. III.

you intend this for children, Mr. Newbery? Why, do you suppose this is written by Mr. Newbery, Sir? This may come from another Hand. This is not the Book, Sir, mentioned in the Title, but the Introduction to that Book; and it is intended, Sir, not for those Sort of Children, but for Children of six Feet high, of which . . . . there are many Millions in the Kingdom ".

The change, after all, is merely from Lilliput to Brobdignag,—a voyage that represents no more difficulty to the editor than to Gulliver himself.

It is in Lilliputian pedagogy that the writer of *Goody Two-Shoes* has so completely outdistanced his fellows.

For although none of them could produce a more wholehearted supporter of Locke's theories than " little Two-Shoes ", she wastes no time in abstract reasoning, but puts them at once into practice.

No sooner did she learn to read (and that was startlingly soon) than she began to teach her companions, and finding them by no means so quick nor so diligent as herself, she cut out of several pieces of wood ten " Setts " of large letters and ten of small (all printed very clear in the text); " and every Morning she used to go round to teach the Children with these Rattletraps in a Basket—*as you see in the Print* ".

The letter-games of Goody Two-Shoes were doubtless among the " twenty other Ways" hinted at by Mr. Locke when he described his own, in which " Children may be cozen'd into a Knowledge of the Letters ". There are minute directions for playing them in the chapter that tells " How little Two-Shoes became a *trotting Tutoress* ".

Nor is virtue (the philosopher's chief concern) neglected for this matter of mere learning. There are lessons and reflections enough for the old " Schools of Virtue "; but little Margery's true piety makes amends for her preaching and saves her from the prudential excess of the " little Boy who lived upon Learning ". When she admonished the sick gentleman for his late hours by the example of the rooks, she forced him to laugh and admit that she was " a sensible Hussey ". The Reader (more often admonished) does the same.

In this blending of morality and humour, the author is only following the practice of eighteenth century novelists. His morality (in the main, very sound and reasonable) hangs by the humour of separate incidents ; yet these, together, form a sequence of moral and " cautionary " tales. There is, for example, the warning against useless display in the account of Lady Ducklington's funeral,— " the Money they squandered away would have been better laid out in little Books for Children, or in Meat, Drink and Cloaths for the Poor " ;—against superstition,—the story of the ghost in the church, or the dramatic Witch story of the Second Part ; and there are parallel examples of kindness and good sense.

A small child would make his first reading by the woodcuts (which are much like a child's drawings) : here, first, are little Margery and her brother, left, like the Children in the Wood " to the Wide World " ; here is Tommy Two-Shoes (at an incredibly tender age) dressed like a little sailor—" *Pray look at him* ",—and there again, wiping off Margery's tears with the end of his jacket—" *thus* "—and bidding her cry no more, for that he will come to her again when he returns from sea. He is much blurred in this picture—perhaps with tears.

At this point the story goes back to the frontispiece : by far the best picture of Margery, in a setting of trees and fields, with a little house on one side of her and a church in the distance. She is wearing her *two shoes* for the first time (for until a charitable good man gave her a pair, she had but one) : " stroking down her ragged Apron *thus* ", and crying out : " *Two Shoes, Mame, see two Shoes* ".

Next comes that serious business of Letters and Syllables.

But Somebody (with a Basket of Rattle-traps) is at the door.

"Tap, tap, tap, who's there?" (It might have been Red Riding-Hood! "*Toc, toc! Qui est là?*") But it is only little Goody Two-Shoes, greeting her new scholar in the same childish voice.

Thus the little one gets through the lessons and proverbs of the next few pages, and at Chapter VI, which tells " How the whole Parish was frighted ", knows the triumph and delight of reading.

" Babies do not want to hear about babies ", said Dr. Johnson ; but he was never, like Goldsmith, intimate with the Nursery in all its moods, and it did not occur to him that his favourite Tom Thumb was but a child seen through the diminishing-glass of a woodcut.

This, moreover, is a story that *grows up* in the reading. At Chapter VI, there is no more baby-talk. These are mature, even elderly villagers who are so " frighted " at the idea of a ghost in the church : the argument is between the Parson, the Clerk and the Clerk's Wife :

" I go, Sir, says William, why the Ghost would frighten me out of my Wits.—Mrs. Dobbins too cried, and laying hold of her Husband said, he should not be eat up by the Ghost. A Ghost, you Blockheads, says Mr. Long in a Pet, did either of you ever see a Ghost, or know any Body that did ? Yes, says the Clerk, my Father did once in the Shape of a Windmill, and it walked all round the Church in a white Sheet, with Jack Boots on, and had a Gun by its Side instead of a Sword. A fine Picture of a Ghost truly, says Mr. Long, give me the Key of the Church, you Monkey ; for I tell you there is no such Thing now, whatever may have been formerly.—Then taking the Key, he went to the Church, all the People following him. As soon as he had opened the Door, what Sort of a Ghost do you think appeared ? Why little *Two-shoes*, who being weary, had fallen asleep in one of the Pews during the Funeral Service, and was shut in all Night——".

Such incidents would make even a grown-up reader forget the Lilliputian context.

Nor is the Second Part (as in other " Histories ") of less interest, although it presents the dutiful contriving little Two-shoes as " Principal of a Country College—for instructing little Gentlemen and Ladies in the Science of A.B.C ". A formidable theme, if her inventive genius could not produce any number of variations upon Mr. Locke's method of playing at schools.

A reference to the *Spectator* at the close of Part I would make Mistress Two-Shoes a predecessor of Shenstone's Schoolmistress ; but this is clearly an anachronism. The village Dame as Shenstone studies her, still sits

> " disguised in look profound
> And eyes her fairy-Throng, and turns her Wheel around " ;

whereas Goody Two-Shoes, knowing that " Nature intended Children should be always in Action ", places her letters and alphabets all round the school, so that everyone in turn is obliged to get up to fetch a letter or to spell a word.

Her children have forgotten the hornbook, and with it, doubtless, " St. George's high Achievements " which used to decorate the back. It was Shenstone's Dame who kept "tway birchen Sprays" to reclaim her pupils' wandering attention from St. George. But Mrs. Margery ruled " by Reasoning and mild Discipline ", and could dispense with these.

" Her Tenderness extended not only to all Mankind, but even to all Animals that were not noxious ". Such humanity alone (notwithstanding the reservation) sets her above the poet's heroine, to whose credit he could only place

> " One ancient Hen she took Delight to feed
> The plodding Pattern of this busy Dame,
> Which ever and anon as she had need
> Into her School begirt with Chickens came."

Indeed, Mrs. Margery surpasses Æsop and Tommy Trip in her manner of pressing Beasts and Birds into the service of Education.

Locke, whose imagination had stopped short at pictures of animals, would have detected the insidious workings of romance in a school where the ushers were birds, where a dog acted as door-keeper and a pet lamb carried home the books of the good children in turn.

Yet in another place, the youthful Dame shows herself a mistress of utilitarian argument :

" Does not the Horse and the Ass carry you and your burthens ? Don't the Ox plough your Ground, the Cow give you Milk, the Sheep cloath your Back, the Dog watch your House, the Goose find you in Quills to write with, the Hen bring Eggs for your Custards and Puddings, and the Cock call you up in the Morning——? If so, how can you be so cruel to them, and abuse God Almighty's good Creatures ? "

Thus the creatures are protected chiefly for their services ; Nature, as yet, is no more than a useful and necessary background. It is still Humanity that counts.

As to Romance, the writer's attitude must be judged by default. There is but one reference to Fortunatus and Friar Bacon to indicate a preference for works of Reason and Ingenuity.

This follows one of those quaint interludes that prove the quick wit and hide the laughter of Mistress Two-Shoes. In her character of village peacemaker, she contrives a " Considering Cap ", " almost as large as a Grenadier's, but of three equal Sides ; on the first of which was written, I may be wrong ; on the second, It is fifty to one but you are ; and on the third, I'll consider of it. The other Parts on the out-side, were filled with odd Characters, as unintelligible as the Writings of the old Egyptians ; but within Side there was a Direction for its Use, of the utmost Consequence; for it strictly enjoined the Possessor to put on the Cap whenever he found his Passions begin to grow turbulent, and not to deliver a Word whilst it was on, but with great Coolness and Moderation.

*   *   *   *   *

They were bought by Husbands and Wives, who had themselves frequent Occasion for them, and sometimes lent them to their Children. They were also purchased in large Quantities by Masters and Servants ; by young Folks who were intent on Matrimony, by Judges, Jurymen, and even Physicians and Divines : nay, if we may believe History, the Legislators of the Land did not disdain the Use of them ; and we are told, that when any important Debate arose, *Cap was the Word*, and each House looked like a grand Synod of Egyptian Priests ".

After this, lest the old spells should work upon some unguarded child, Friar Bacon is called in, to advertise this " Charm for the Passions " in a letter of advice :

" What was Fortunatus' Wishing Cap when compared to this ? . . . Remember what was said by my Brazen Head, *Time is, Time was, Time is past :* now the *Time is*, therefore buy the Cap immediately, and make a proper Use of it, and be happy before the *Time is past* ".

The Learned Friar has burnt his books, and there is an end of Magic. Mrs. Margery has no dealings in a " Gothick Mythology of Elves and Fairies " ; her Familiars are the tame creatures of her household, she does her conjuring by the legitimate powers of Science. And when, through her cleverness in contriving a weather-glass to save her neighbours' hay, she is accused of witchcraft by the people of other parishes, her advocate, like a true Lilliputian, defends her with the arguments of Addison and Goldsmith.[1]

This witch-story is the climax (if such a haphazard little

---

[1] *Spectator*, 117, July 14, 1711 ; and Goldsmith, " On Deceit and Falsehood ", The Bee, No. 8, Nov. 24, 1759.

plot can have a climax) and it gives a masterly last touch to the heroine's portrait.

She is standing with all her pets about her, when Gaffer Goosecap (full of the weather-glass mystery) comes to spy upon her :

" This so surprised the Man that he cried out a Witch ! a Witch ! upon this she laughing, answered, a Conjurer ! a Conjurer ! and so they parted ; but it did not end thus, for a Warrant was issued out against Mrs. Margery, and she was carried to a Meeting of the Justices, whither all the Neighbours followed her ".

At the trial her triumph is complete. Even her judges join in the laughter when she produces the weather-glass and cries : " If I am a Witch, this is my Charm ".

The writer, whoever he was, had little to learn from Rousseau. Miss Edgeworth herself could not have invented a more reasonable and intelligent heroine.

It is easy to see why Charles Lamb put *Goody Two-Shoes* among " the old classics of the Nursery " [1], and no matter for wonder that it should be set down to Goldsmith.

For apart from that hint of *The Deserted Village* in the " Introduction ", it has living characters, natural speech and incidents of genuine comedy. The playful tenderness of the first chapters suggests Goldsmith's treatment of children, and the whole theme is near enough to his idea of a story " like the old one of Whittington *were his Cat left out* " [2]. For if he ever had written such a story and managed to keep the cat out of it, he would certainly have repented and introduced some other animal in its place, or with native inconsistency, might have multiplied it into a menagerie such as Goody Two-Shoes kept. The idea of talking animals had once attracted him, and if he could write a good Fable, why not a " History " ?

[1] See below. Chap. VII.
[2] *The Bee.* Nov. 10, 1759—" On Education."

Forster records Godwin's "strong persuasion" that Goldsmith wrote *Goody Two-Shoes*, and Godwin, himself a publisher of children's books, may have had good reason for his belief; yet there is no certain evidence to confirm it, nor will the book, as a whole, bear all the claims of its admirers.

Nichols, in his *Literary Anecdotes*,[1] associates this and other "Lilliputian Histories" with the brothers Griffiths and Giles Jones, and family tradition credits Giles with *Goody Two-Shoes* as well as *Giles Gingerbread* and *Tommy Trip*; but if, as Goldsmith would have it, Mr. Newbery was the real author of *Tommy Trip*, there is no reason why he should not have had a hand in the rest. *Goody Two-Shoes*, in fact, has several turns of speech and grammatical slips which occur in John Newbery's journal;[2] nor is it at all unlikely that Goldsmith, the friend of Giles Jones and Newbery, contributed such lively matter as the ghost and witch stories, or so quaint a fancy as the "Considering Cap".

John Newbery's successors[3] carried on the tradition, but at his death the great period of "Lilliputian Histories" was past. Their numbers were always increasing, but they were mostly imitations and moralised echoes of folklore like *Tom Thumb's Exhibition* or *The Enchanted Castle*.

Yet there are a few late "Lilliputians" that have the true Newbery touch, and even a fresh spice of satire. *The Lilliputian Masquerade*,[4] though it goes back to *Gulliver*, belongs to the age of the Pantheon and Almack's, and its gay "Masks" (all "Lilliputians of Repute") include two romantic surprises. For in the company of Sir William

[1] See Note in Appendix A. III.

[2] Examples in Appendix A. III.

[3] Some account of them, and of the later "Lilliputian" books is given in Appendix A. III.

[4] Mentioned in Carnan's list of 1787. For details see Appendix A. III.

Wise and Sir Francis Featherbrain of Butterfly Hall, there
is the unexpected figure of a Beggar " singing merrily ",
and one undoubted harbinger of the New Age—a little hero
of Blake and of Charles Lamb,—the Chimney Sweeper,
new as yet to the mystery of his " cloth ".

In the meantime, a whole section of the dwarf library was
devoted to the Wyse Chylde in a variety of rôles.   Following that " Rise and Progress of Learning in Lilliput ",
there came a formidable crowd of little Philosophers, little
Statesmen, little Judges, little Divines and (to keep an
accurate record of their careers) little Historians and Bio-
graphers.

" Self-Government " in the Schoolroom (by no means, as
some may suppose, a present-day innovation) made its
first appearance in *Juvenile Trials*,[1] the acknowledged
device of a Tutor and Governess who prescribe it as a
" Regimen " for their " unruly Pupils ", and thus, profiting
by the wisdom of Cato, induce the authors of great evils to
remove them.

This is the first hint of a Lilliputian Republic : the logical
outcome of Locke's principles in a revolutionary age.
The Lilliputians give their best support to the new Govern-
ment and throw themselves with zest into their parts.

Little Judge Meanwell who, though but twelve years old,
has " all the Appearance of Gravity and Magistracy ", in a
long robe and full-bottomed wig, anticipates parental
criticism by reminding the public that " neither Vanity,
nor Ambition, nor the Desire of governing Others at an
Age in which he stands so much in Need of being governed
himself, has raised him to this Office, which he cannot exe-
cute but with Regret ".

He adds (doubtless after consultation with his Leaders)

[1] *Juvenile Trials* " for robbing orchards, telling fibs and other
heinous offences—Embellished with Cuts. By Master Tommy
Lyttleton, Secretary to the Court ".   T. Carnan, 1781.   Another
edition—Lond. for T. Carnan, 1786.

that the Trials, as the result of their " wisest Deliberation ",
are by no means to be treated as " the Sport of Boys and
Girls ".

The Tutor and Governess take full advantage of the
scheme, and after the royal ceremony of inauguration,
leave the unruly ones to the judgment of their peers.   Perhaps it is this unwonted freedom which lets loose a stream
of live and humorous dialogue ; for no sooner do the
" Trials " begin than these Lilliputians betray the natural
propensities and dramatic instincts of real children.

Mr. Newbery himself could hardly have drawn better
pictures of country life, or spoken better dialect than the
Farmer in one of these " trials ".   In another (which
suggests the ordeal of the Knave of Hearts) the evidence is
not unworthy of Defoe,—the Prosecution putting in a plan
of the kitchen where the stolen plum-cake was baked ;
and a third,—the case of Miss Stirling *versus* Miss Delia,
" for raising Strife and Contention among her Schoolfellows ",—is wholly " conveyed " from Sarah Fielding's
Governess,[1] a source that may explain many unexpected
features in the book.

But the old standards of Authority are restored in *The
Juvenile Biographer*,[2] a collection of " characters " in
moral contrast, with a " Bust of the little Author " as
frontispiece.   Some account of him at the end, had it been
prefatory, would have prepared the reader for much of his
philosophy.   Throughout the book he speaks plain Prig,—
a development that might be foreseen in one who " when
he came to be breeched, laid aside all juvenile Sports ".
His playfellows think him " a dull heavy little Fellow ",

[1] See below, Chapter VI.

[2] *The Juvenile Biographer*, " containing the lives of little Masters
and Misses, both good and naughty.   Price three-pence ".   E.
Newbery's list, 1789.   The first edition must have been earlier,
since a New England edition was published in 1787.   See Appendix
A. III.

he is " a very poor Hand at Marbles, Trap Ball or Cricket, and little attentive to Play " ; when other boys are engaged in strife, he retires into a corner with some little Book.

No doubt he is a very proper person to record those juvenile virtues and foibles that might escape a natural child,— to discern the " Thought, Prudence and admirable Needlecraft " of Miss Betsey Allgood, to speculate upon the literary ancestry of Master Francis Bacon, or to deprecate the failings of that " genteel Child," Miss Fiddle-Faddle, who " at seven Years of Age, could spend a whole Forenoon at her Glass, and devote an Hour to pitching upon the proper Part of her Face to stick that Patch on ". This " little Author " is, in fact, a reincarnation of the Baby Spectator.

There is a year or two between these " Lives " and the first book of Lilliputian " Letters ". No children's novel followed Richardson so closely as to adopt the letter form ; but Locke had expressly advised that children should write letters " wherein they should not be put upon any Strains of Wit or Compliment, but taught to express their own plain easy Sense ", and had further recommended that when they were perfect in this, they might, " to raise their Thoughts ", have Voiture's letters set before them as models.[1]

The Lilliputian editor, loth to await the child's readiness for Voiture, adapted Locke in his own fashion, and devised new models for the Nursery, which should admit the usual " Characters " and " Reflections " of the miscellanies, and at the same time give a suggestion of reality to formal dialogues.

However full these letters might be of grown-up sentiment, their very directions and signatures gave proof (convincing to a child) of the editor's good faith.

[1] Vincent Voiture (1598–1648). See *Some Thoughts Concerning Education*, § 189. Pope also praised Voiture.

The Letters between Master Tommy and Miss Nancy Goodwill, published by Carnan and Newbery in 1770, was revised in 1786 with " the Parts not altogether properly adapted to the Improvement and Entertainment of little Masters and Misses expunged ".[1] What remains, however, shows no change in style or substance ; the Lilliputian features are intact. As the editor observed : " The epistolatory Style here adopted is that which little Masters and Misses should use in their Correspondence with each other " (not that which they naturally would fall into) and it is designed " to regulate their Judgments, to give them an early Taste for true Politeness and inspire them with a Love of Virtue ".

The " Holiday Amusements " described in the letters seem to be " regulated " on the same plan (the editor had obviously forgotten his own) ; and it is something of a relief to find Master Tommy (whose relationship to the Juvenile Biographer is close) warning his sister and her schoolfellows against the cult of nursery bluestockings.[2] He hopes they are " not going to turn Philosophers " ; if they are, he will put them in mind of their needles, their pins and their thread papers. " Leave these Subjects " advises this lordly midget, " to us Boys (I was going to say Men) and we may perhaps now and then condescend to give you some short Lectures upon those Matters ".

Miss Nancy, schooled in the sisterly virtues, responds with Persian stories, references to Mr. Addison, quotations from Pope, and (to clear herself of any suspicion of the bluestocking heresy) a present of worked ruffles. Upon this, he, with restored confidence, imparts an allegorical dream, an instructive story and a " Dissertation on the Value of Time " which closes on this characteristic note :

" But of all the Diversions of Life, there is none so

[1] Printed for T. Carnan in St. Paul's Churchyard, 1786.

[2] This advice suggests a sly hit at the conversation-parties of the bluestockings, some of whom became writers of children's books.

proper to fill up its empty Spaces as the reading useful and entertaining Authors. For this Reason, my dear Nancy, you will receive by the next Coach, Mr. Newbery's *Circle of the Sciences*, and such other of his Books as I apprehend could anyway contribute to your Instruction and Amusement."

There is one letter, and one only, in which Master Tommy forgets his Philosophy and lets the Child in him escape :

" O, my dear Nancy, how shall I tell you that my sweet Kite which boasted of the two finest glass Eyes perhaps ever seen, which was so crowded with Stars and which cost me such immense Labour, is lost."

The revised edition was doubtless an attempt to keep pace with the rival firm of John Marshall ; for between the two issues (about 1777) they had printed a new collection under the title of *Juvenile Correspondence*,[1] which in some ways was better adapted to Locke's original plan, as well as to the theories of Rousseau.

The very fact that these letters are " suited to Children from four to above ten Years of Age ", and that their aim is to encourage " a natural Way of Writing ", implies a change in the general view of education ; yet it would be rash to assume that the writer had more than a passing acquaintance with Rousseau, or that she (this writer is almost certainly a woman) drew any clear distinction between childhood and youth. The whole design of *Juvenile Correspondence* is Lilliputian ; its aim is expressed almost in the exact phrase of the Royal Society, and its origin (apart from the Goodwill " Letters ") can be traced to a remark of Pope's (quoted in the book) that he " should have Pleasure in reading the Thoughts of an Infant, could it commit them to Writing as they arose in its little Mind ".

---

[1] *Juvenile Correspondence ; or letters suited to Children from four to above ten Years of Age.* In three Sets. 2nd edition, London, John Marshall, n.d. (*c.* 1777). For details of another collection by Lucy Aikin (1816), see Appendix A. III.

Moreover the children who write the letters, instead of developing on Rousseau's lines, become more Lilliputian with each year of growth.[1] All the natural touches are in the letters of the younger ones ; from five to seven, they would pass for living children. Indeed, the first letter " from Miss Goodchild, a little more than seven Years of Age to her Brother nearly five " suggests that the next generation of Lilliputians will refuse to grow up so soon :

" Would you think it ? I am sitting in a little Room full of Books, with a Desk for Reading and my Papers round me, as if I were a Woman ! *But I am not so silly as to forget that I am but a little Girl,*

and, my dear Brother,

Your loving Sister, JANE GOODCHILD."

This is the first sign of revolution. The puppets are still content to play their parts, but they refuse to believe in them. Instead, they begin to assert their own " Gothick Mythology ", and are no longer so " subservient to the Rules of Reason " as to despise the name of Fairies.

Miss Goodchild " could talk all day of the Play " (Mr. Garrick's " Fairy Tale " from Shakespeare.[2] She actually quotes the song beginning : " Come follow, follow me, ye fairy Elves that be " from an Entertainment " full of Fairies ", and confesses that she and Jenny were ready to jump up and join in the chorus, singing :

" Hand in Hand we'll dance around
For this Place is Fairy Ground."

But the book is full of contradictions ; nothing in it bears out the promise of those early letters. Master Gentle,

[1] The letters of real children were even more mature. See Appendix A. III.

[2] Called here " *A Midsummer Night's Dream* ". This must have been Garrick's *Fairy Tale in Two Acts, taken from Shakespeare,* played at the Haymarket in 1777. " The young Princes and Princesses " mentioned as having been at the play, were the children of George III, then between the ages of three and fourteen.

at the age of seven, is delivered into the hands of Mr. Birch who, as his name forebodes, believes neither in Reasoning nor mild Discipline ; and at ten, Mr. Birch's pupils become little monsters of virtue and precocity. They are Lilliputians of a larger growth, but they certainly are not boys. This book, moreover, lacks the Newbery touch of comedy. Its humour is mostly unconscious, as in the account of a father who asks permission to read his son's letters, where the boy confides to a friend that he feels " like the Swain in Shenstone : ' *fearful, but not averse* ' ".

Among the numberless books for children printed between 1780 and 1810, there were three which, although they discarded the nursery badge of " Flowery and Gilt ", and had little in common with the Newbery miscellanies, followed Lilliputian precedent in form and title.

These were the *Juvenile Tatler* (1783), the *Fairy Spectator* (1789) and the *Juvenile Spectator* (1810).[1] The first two are among the earliest books that show the influence of Marmontel and Madame de Beaumont ; they therefore are no true Lilliputians : the third mimics Addison's method with absolute fidelity, and sparkles with the satirical spirit of its original ; yet this too breaks loose from Lilliputian convention ; it has almost enough sanity and wit to be called a nursery Jane Austen.

These three will be seen to better advantage with others of their kind.

A strong revival of romance in children's books would have driven out the Lilliputians at the close of the eighteenth century ; but the progress of Theory prevented it, and produced, with a fresh crop of moral tales, innumerable reprints.

Canning's amusing paper in the *Eton Microcosm* (June 11, 1787),[2] did more than mark the vogue of those tiny

---

[1] See below—Chapters V and VI.
[2] See further—Appendix A. III.

" 16 mo's " at Mr. Newbery's and " the Bouncing B, Shoe Lane " : it was also a tempting advertisement ; and in the early nineteenth century small Londoners who could not rise to the splendours of " twopence Gilt " might buy their own New Year and Easter Gifts at Catnach's or the " Toy and Marble Warehouse " in Seven Dials, for a half-penny, or even (with covers of rough blue sugar-paper) for a farthing.[1]

In 1779 Saint, the north-country Newbery, had printed a Newcastle edition of *Tommy Trip*, and between 1790 and 1812, the entire Lilliputian library was revived in the York chap-books by Wilson and Spence.   Other provincial booksellers, following these, began to improve their stocks of school-books and battledores with pirated " Newberys " ;   and some, like Rusher of Banbury, retouched old rhymes and tales with local colour.   It was Rusher who restored the tradition of *Giles Gingerbread* with the *History of a Banbury Cake* ;[2] and in the childhood of Queen Victoria, his little shop was still famous for toy-books.

[1] For nursery-books printed by Catnach and Pitts, see Appendix A. III.
[2] *The History of a Banbury Cake*, " An entertaining Book for Children ". Banbury, printed and sold by J. G. Rusher, Bridge Street, 1d., n.d.

CHAPTER IV

ROUSSEAU AND THE MORAL TALE

Locke and Rousseau—A New Conception of Childhood— Rousseau's Theory of Education—Parent and Tutor, Artificial Experiences, Books, Handicrafts, Attitude to Nature and Humanity— The Infallible Parent—Marmontel's *Contes Moraux*—Berquin's *L'Ami des Enfans*—*The Looking Glass for the Mind*—Madame d'Epinay's *Conversations d'Emilie*—Madame de Genlis and her Books—French Lilliputians : *Le Petit Grandison* and *Le Petit La Bruyère.*

ROUSSEAU, even when he repeated Locke's precepts, caught the ear of a wider public because he appealed not so much to reason as to feeling, and instead of commending his doctrines by argument, charged them with warmth and eloquence.

Locke had been before him in exposing the shams and pedantry of schoolmasters, as in striving for a more natural method of education ; but he carried out his task in a quiet professional way, regarding the child as a patient in need of a new regimen, but never setting him on a pedestal.

It was Rousseau's inspiration to take the beauty and promise of childhood for his text, to make the child stand forth as the hope of the race, the centre of all its aspirations, the proof of its powers.[1] Thus his philosophy acquired the dignity of a new faith ; and yet the child lost nothing of his personal and human interest, for in Rousseau's scheme, he was the very core of a new conception of family life. There could be no better setting for a natural education than the family, no simpler unit of fellowship ;

[1] Rousseau's *Emile* was published in 1762. Translated into English, 1763.

and Rousseau drew persuasive pictures of the child at successive stages of his growth,—pictures which writers of moral tales reproduced with modifications of their own, and a greater or less amount of theory.

For there was this great difference between Locke and Rousseau, in their effect on children's books : that Locke, beyond encouraging Fables, did no more than furnish a toy library with his *Thoughts* ; whereas Rousseau taught two generations of writers to substitute living examples for maxims.

In making Emile an orphan, Rousseau was guarding against interference with his experiment ; it is no part of his doctrine that a child should be brought up by any but his parents, unless they are unable or unwilling to do their duty. Then, indeed, a Tutor must be found, though he will never be required, after the manner of tutors, to instruct. A child needs no other teacher than Experience, no schoolroom but the open country which is also his playground ; all that the tutor need do is to enter into his interests and amusements as an equal, and watch over him while he educates himself. This marks a revolutionary change in the attitude of the Philosopher to the Child. Locke's theory of habit, his practice of reasoning with children, have no place in the new scheme. Rousseau would as soon have a child be five feet in height as to have judgment at the age of ten. Children, he declares, are incapable of reason, Nature meant them to be children before they become men. To forget this is to force a fruit that has neither ripeness nor savour, to produce old infants and child-philosophers.

Rousseau hits hard and straight at the pedantic mania for instruction that filled the early miscellanies with Geography, Chronology and other studies " remote from man and especially from the child ". Emile must never be allowed to cheat himself with words. He shall learn nothing by heart, not even Fables ; for these he is sure to misinterpret. And how is a child to grow up with any respect for truth, if his first book teach him that *Foxes speak and speak the same language as Ravens* ?

With Words and Fables, Rousseau dismisses all the inventions of primitive imagination that find their natural place in a child's mind.

At twelve, Emile hardly knows what a book is. He has spent his whole life in the country, with a tutor whom he regards as a playfellow. In climbing among rocks and trees and leaping over brooks, he has learnt to measure himself with his surroundings and has lost all sense of danger. No human will has ever opposed him, and since it is useless to fight against circumstance, he submits to necessary evils, and bears pain without complaining.

Emile is stronger and more capable than other children ; yet conscious of his dependence on others, of his need of protection. Abstract terms, such as duty and obligation, mean nothing to him, nor will he practise the empty forms of courtesy ; but he has the basis of all good breeding, being candid and fearless, but neither arrogant nor self-conscious.

From twelve to fifteen, Emile's education is equally practical. Curiosity moves him to experiment and discovery, and thus he learns the simple truths of science without teaching. Locke's belief in utility was not greater than Rousseau's. The word "useful", he says, is the key to the whole situation. Emile is always to test his discoveries by the question " What is this good for ? " and things which do not satisfy this test are of no account. The tutor still attends the boy like his shadow, never seeming to influence the course of events ; but since Nature cannot be trusted to adapt herself to his scheme, he now finds it necessary to contrive artificial experiences which Emile accepts as natural.

Rousseau sees nothing inconsistent in this use of artifice

by which the Child of Nature, though wholly dependent on the will of his tutor, thinks he is governing himself ; yet everything is so planned and so foreseen that he does nothing of his own choice.

It is here that Rousseau grudgingly admits the need of books ; but he takes care to restrict his Emile to a single book which deals chiefly with practical affairs. " What is this wonderful Book ? is it Aristotle ? is it Pliny ? is it Buffon ?   No, it is *Robinson Crusoe*."

Here at any rate, Rousseau made no mistake. Had Emile been free to choose, this is precisely the book he would have chosen, though for less philosophical reasons ; and the very fact that it fits Rousseau's scheme of educa- tion is a proof that the scheme is sound. Robinson Crusoe, alone on his island, with neither house nor tools, gradually providing for his needs ; it is Rousseau's allegory of the triumph of man, and failure of civilisation. Emile cannot understand this yet, but the book will be a touch- stone for his taste and judgment, and serve him and his tutor as a text for all their talk on the natural sciences. The boy's interest is wholly practical ; but it stimulates " the *real* castle-building of that happy age when we know no other happiness than necessity and freedom ". Of free and imaginative castle-building, Rousseau has no notion, but Emile will know his Robinson Crusoe all the better, if he is allowed to act the story.

" I would have his head turned by it," says Rousseau, " and have him always busy about his Castle, his goats and his plantation. . . .   I would have him imagine he is Robinson himself."

It is the reality of drama that appeals to the educator ; the hint was not lost upon writers of children's books.

And now, since Emile cannot remain always in his island, it is time to recall him to everyday life. His natural interest in handicrafts will smooth the transition.

The tutor goes with him from shop to shop, that he may understand the division of labour among men. Thus he learns more in an hour than from a whole day's explanation. And lest this should be only surface knowledge, he must learn some trade (for choice a carpenter's) which will guard him against common prejudice, and make him independent of fortune.

Rousseau keeps the road so clear for his young traveller that he is not afraid of chance encounters. In these years, Emile is to learn nothing of the relations of man to man. His heart is not to be touched by suffering nor his imagination kindled by the " living spectacle of Nature " which Rousseau himself paints in such glowing colours. Eloquence and poetry are wasted on a child. Moral and spiritual teaching can safely be left till his sixteenth year. Up to that point Emile has studied nothing but the natural world. He has little knowledge, but what he has is real and complete.   Simple surroundings have taught him to be content with what he has and to despise luxury, which, according to Rousseau, is the secret of true happiness. His body is strong and active, his mind unprejudiced; he has courage, industry, self-control,—all the virtues proper to his age.

Rousseau's disciples had some excuse for disregarding one of his chief discoveries : the distinction between childhood and youth. It was obviously impossible to draw a hard and fast line between the two stages, and Rousseau would not give an inch to individual difference. Thus his followers were either forced back upon precedent, or had to trust to their own experience of children. On the one hand, they clung to the old encyclopædic methods ; on the other, they transferred Rousseau's provisions for youth and manhood to an earlier stage. Experience taught them that a child could be stirred by other motives besides prudence and self-love, that moral and spiritual influences in early childhood were not to be ignored, that there were such things as childish imagination and sympathy.

The greater number of moral tales owe their very existence to Rousseau's inconsistency; for although he had exposed the fallacy of maxims and fables, he found no better substitute than the Example of a perfect Parent or Tutor—a man without passion or prejudice, detached and colourless, who, without seeming to guide or correct, should watch the child's every movement and on occasion teach Nature herself how to go about her business.

The first generation of Emile, which proved Rousseau's theory of Childhood, disposed, once for all, of the Infallible Parent in real life. A child might suspect that it was a literary rather than a practical idea, and the few parents who, after a vigorous course of self-discipline, felt equal to the part, would find it easier to sustain by proxy in a moral tale. They decided, at any rate, to ignore Rousseau's veto upon books for children under twelve, and writers quickly rose to the demand for a new sort of Fables, wherein the Child of Nature, walking in the shadow of the Perfect Parent, acquired a measure of wisdom and philanthropy beyond his years. Such tales, inspired by the Emile, are a satirical comment on the writing of books to prove that books are useless.

Marmontel, though he did not write for children, was an admirable guide for lesser moralists. His vivid character-contrasts, dramatic incidents and humorous treatment of every-day life taught them that art might not be thrown away upon a child's book, if it only served to keep alive interest and curiosity. The " Good Mother " and " Bad Mother " of the *Contes Moraux*[1] supplied useful variants of the good and bad child, and the " School for

[1] Contributed to *Le Mercure* (c. 1758). Translated into English " by a Lady " (Miss Roberts), 1763. Translated by Mrs. Pilkington and illustrated by Bewick, 1799.

Fathers " encouraged the writers of little books to venture satirical comments on the faults of parents.

It is true that Marmontel's types are less convincing when reduced for the nursery and coloured by Rousseau. " The School for Fathers " turned out a uniform pattern of the Infallible Parent, and " The Good Mother ", " *La femme comme il y en a peu* ", assuming the proportions of her virtues, cast a monstrous shadow over two generations ; yet there were books that reflected Marmontel's wise moderation, his sympathy with youthful follies, all that was implied in the motto of his bon Curé, " *Moins de prudence et plus de bonté* ".

The Nursery had its Marmontel in Armand Berquin, better known by the name of his most famous book, *L'Ami des Enfans*,[1] an addition that no man deserved better then he. Like Perrault, Berquin owed his reputation to a book that he wrote for children ; but times had changed : education had now become of so much consequence that the writer of children's books was regarded as a public bene-factor. Perrault the Academician had never openly acknow-ledged the *Contes* of 1697; but in 1784, Berquin's *L'Ami des Enfans* was crowned by the French Academy.

Perhaps it was well for Berquin that by this time fairies were discredited in France, and Perrault was gone from his old shelf, so that no child could choose between them. As it was, children of all sizes and conditions, with and without tutors, but all equally ignorant of magic, read Berquin's stories and read them again. Something of his own sweetness and humour got into his book ; they felt that he loved and understood them, and those who lived near him used to crowd round him, eager for a word or a handshake, whenever he came out of his house.

[1] *L'Ami des Enfans*. Published monthly " *avec approbation et privilège du roi* ", January, 1782–December, 1783. First English translation (24 vols.) by M. A. Meilan, 1783. See Appendix A, IV. Note on Armand Berquin.

Berquin's book owes something to Weisse's *Der Kinder-freund*, from which he took some of the stories, as well as to the writings of Campe and Salzmann ; but no German ever pointed a moral with such playful grace.

There is hardly a point in Rousseau's argument that Berquin does not illustrate ; but he does it in a perfectly natural way, drawing the events out of simple situations, and showing delightful glimpses of childish character.

Marmontel's " Bad Mother ", with her blind and cruel preference for one of her two children, is easily recognised in the story of " *Philippine et Maximin* ". His device of moral contrast appears in every variation of Rousseau's theme.

These are mostly little studies in black and white : Industry opposed to Idleness in " The Two Apple Trees " ; a rational education preferred to riches in the story of Narcisse and Hippolyte ; the character-contrast grafted on fable in a similar study of two dogs.

Emile's gentle consciousness of his dependence on others (one of his more amiable traits) is shown in the docility of Prosper, who, by accepting the gardener's advice, finds in due season ripe strawberries of an exquisite flavour hanging from his plants. " Ah, had I only planted some in my garden," cries the brother who jeered at him. Whereupon the generous one replies : " You can eat them as if they were your own."

M. Sage, who might be Emile's tutor, believes that if he can make his boy Philippe content with what he has, instead of longing for things which he cannot get, he will do more for his happiness than by leaving him untold wealth.

When the boy envies a rich man's garden, his father says that he himself possesses a finer one. Taking Philippe by the hand, he leads him to the top of a hill that over-looks the open country. " Shall we soon come to our garden, papa ? " the boy asks eagerly.   " We are already there ! " answers M. Sage.

Rousseau himself was not a greater lover of gardens than Berquin.   Gardening is the theme of half his stories : " *Le rosier à cent feuilles et le genêt d'Espagne* " ;   " *Les cerises* " ;   " *Les tulipes* " ;   " *Les fraises et les grosseilles* " ;   " *Les deux pommiers* " ;   the greater number deal with country life and have their setting in the family.

The tale of the farmer who brings a jar of candied fruits to his landlord's children, is an eloquent sermon against ill-breeding and prejudice.

This is a sequence of moral contrasts.   First, the insolent treatment of the farmer by the two boys is set against their little sister's courtesy, then contrasted with the simple friendliness of their father ;   and the corresponding scene of their entertainment at the farm is drawn with the same delicate point.   The two boys are compared with the farmer's sons, more capable, even more accomplished than themselves ;   and stung to shame by the generosity and natural courtesy of their host.

Farming, according to Rousseau, is the most honourable of industries.   After farmers he places blacksmiths and carpenters.   Berquin brings his children into a natural contact with men of various crafts, the farmer, the blacksmith, the mason.   They watch the building of a house and learn the need for division of labour.   He can dispense with Rousseau's artifice.   He never hampers himself with theory, but allows Emile's virtues to appear in common adventures with men and birds and animals.

Clementine, who loads the little peasant girl with useless gifts, learns, in a dialogue with her mother, to serve the real needs of her protegée ;   the dentist's visit to Laurette and Marcellin is a test of courage ;   " *Le menteur corrigé par lui-même* " becomes a champion of truth.

Foolish wishes and false judgments are corrected

according to Rousseau's plan. Little Fleuri, who, as each
new season arrives, would have it last for ever, is made to
set down his fickle desires on his father's tablets, and, faced
in Autumn with his Winter, Spring and Summer wishes,
decides that all the seasons of the year are good. Armand
would cut away the brambles that take toll of the sheep's
wool, but in the nesting season, discovers how the wool is
used.

Berquin cannot bring himself to judge the things that
are merely beautiful by Rousseau's standard of utility.
Lucette, when she finds gay flowers in a place where her
father planted those " *tristes oignons* ", learns with astonish-
ment that these were tulip-roots ; and Berquin allows her
to rejoice where a rigid Rousseauist would have compared
the uses of flowers and vegetables.

" The time of faults is the time for fables," said Rousseau ;
but he put it late, when Emile was no longer a child.
Berquin knows what happens in nurseries : that Josephine
will forget to feed her canary, that Firmin and Julie will
eat forbidden cherries, that Ferdinand, all frankness and
generosity, if he cannot control his temper, will be a danger
to his friends, and Camille if they give her the chance, will
tyrannise over the whole family.

The remedies are mostly found in the natural consequences of these things ; but Berquin brushes aside
Rousseau's strict law of necessity with a light mischievous
touch ; nor does he ever sanction the plan of governing
a child by letting him suppose he is the master.

" The Children who wanted to govern themselves ",
having tried it, do not wish to repeat the experiment ; and
Camille is completely reduced by the officer who advises
her Mother to give her *a uniform and a pair of moustaches*,
in which she can more appropriately indulge her fancy
for ordering people about.

These children of Berquin's are less hard and self-reliant than Emile. Even the good ones are not unnatural. There is little Alexis on a showery day in June, running first down to the garden to look at the sky, and then back, three steps at a time, to the barometer—only to find that the two are in league against him ; and the eight-years-old Marthonie, a delicious picture in her white linen dress, a pair of morocco shoes on her " dear little feet ", and her hair, dark as ebony, hanging in loose curls on her shoulders ; Marthonie, who insisted on being dressed for a picnic in a frock of the prettiest apple-green taffetas, with rose-coloured ribbons and shoes—and came home hatless and draggled, a tearful Cinderella with one shoe left in the mud. The Mother who met her thus and only said, " Would you like me to have another silk frock made up for you to-morrow ? " owes her wisdom to Rousseau, but her playful irony to Berquin and Marmontel.

Berquin's parents are nearly infallible, but he does not give them every point in an argument. In the affair of Charlotte and the watch, for example, it is not always M. de Fonrose who scores.

Charlotte invents a dozen reasons for wanting a watch, and her inexorable parent disposes of them all, till she is forced back on Rousseau's final position. A watch must needs be a *useful* possession, since her Papa, philosopher as he is, cannot do without it. This, obviously, is a point to Charlotte. If she wants the thing for its *usefulness*, it is hers. The sudden capitulation is too much for Charlotte. She suspects her Papa of badinage. Not at all; he is perfectly serious. She will find the watch hanging from the tapestry by the side of his bed.

Charlotte :   What ! that ancient thing, that King Dagobert perhaps used for a pot to feed his dogs ?
M. de Fonrose : It is a very good one, I assure you. They were all made like that in your grandfather's time. I regard it as an heirloom. But in giving it to you,

> I shall not let it go out of the family, nor shall I lose sight of it when I see you wearing it.
>
> *Charlotte :*   But what will other people say, who are not my grandpapa's descendants ?

Few English children could buy the first translation of Berquin, in twenty-four volumes.   A selection, including many little dramas for three or four persons, appeared later under the title of *The Children's Friend* ; but the true English version was the admirable *Looking Glass for the Mind*[1] adapted by Mr. Cooper for E. Newbery and illustrated by John Bewick's inimitable cuts.   Alexis transfers his best grace to Bewick's "little Anthony", standing a-tiptoe on a chair to read the barometer ; Caroline walks as proudly as Marthonie in her finery; and the four little pupils of Mademoiselle Boulon are not less French for their English names.

It is odd, considering Rousseau's attitude to the education of girls (for in his account of Sophie he reverses the whole method of Emile's training) that the trilogy of educational romance, begun with Emile, should have been completed by two women.

Madame d'Epinay, Rousseau's friend and benefactress, published her *Conversations d'Emilie*[2] at his request, and Madame de Genlis, in *Adèle et Théodore*,[3] worked out her own scheme of practical education on his principles.

Of the two, Madame d'Epinay is more faithful to Rousseau, and so great was the interest aroused by the

[1] *The Looking Glass for the Mind ; or, Intellectual Mirror* ; " being an elegant collection of the Most Delightful little Stories, and Interesting Tales : chiefly translated from that much admired Work, L'Ami des Enfans.   With seventy-four Cuts, designed and engraved on Wood, by J. Bewick." First published 1787.   E. Newbery's list, 1789.   Reprinted in 1885, with an introduction by Charles Welsh.

[2] *Les Conversations d'Emilie*, crowned by the French Academy in 1783.   Translated into English.   London, John Marshall, 1787.

[3] *Adèle et Théodore* (3 tomes), Paris, 1782.   Translated (3 vols.), London, 1783.

Emile, that she was awarded the French Academy prize for " a work of the greatest benefit to humanity ".

She herself declared that her book contained " neither a plan of education, nor any connection in the ideas " ; yet it is plain that Emilie follows Emile like an obedient younger sister.

An age that believed in freedom and equality could not long stand by the privilege of sex, and Emilie, although she suffers some of the restrictions imposed on Sophie, shares the natural education of Emile, and is taught to practise most of his virtues. She gains her knowledge, as he does, from experience ; Nature is the wise Mistress who refuses her request for more lessons, and had Emilie's mother followed her own inclination, it is likely that the little girl at ten years old " Would not yet have known how to read."

As it is, she is allowed to spend ten years (for Emile's twelve) in jumping and running, and her enlightened Parent (the counterpart of Emile's guardian) believes that the time has not been wasted. Not that Emilie is ever allowed to forget Rousseau's Salic Law concerning obedience and restraint. She is sternly snubbed for romping with her brothers, and after a disastrous adventure with a beautiful green ladder, admonished that " the modesty of her sex requires a decorum which should restrain the giddiness and warmth even of childhood ". This sends her back to her doll, the care of which has so far exercised her ingenuity that her mother " will not oppose a continuation of it for some time to come ". And to Sophie's sewing and embroidery, Emilie adds a new amusement : that of passing these instructive conversations on to her doll.

Thus even " moments of relaxation " are to be employed by a vigilant mother in order to form the understanding of her child. There is no escape for little Emilie, she must be educated every minute of the day. Her play is always

7

under supervision, always liable to interference and criticism. Her mother, usually her sole companion, is present at all interviews between Emilie and other human creatures.

The book is, in one sense, a simplified *Emile*, intended for children as well as parents ; but Madame d'Epinay has not a vestige of Berquin's humour to help her along the " paths of pleasure and amusement ". These repeated portraits of Emilie and her mother look dull indeed beside Berquin's dainty groups, and her insistent doctrine almost hides the one beauty of the book : the character of Emilie.

There is no merit in Madame d'Epinay's fancy portrait of herself as the Perfect Parent, but Emilie is lifelike, and holds out for a number of years in her stronghold of childhood. It is only on the eve of her tenth birthday that she remarks resignedly, " To-morrow will be an important day. When I rise, *I shall no longer be a child* ".

The tyranny of reason had, in fact, begun much sooner, when Emilie, curious about her own small part in the Universe, learnt that *in time* she would become a Reasonable Being.

Emilie : But what am I now, being but a child ?
Mother : How ! You are *five years old* and have not yet reflected
       on what you are ! Endeavour to find out yourself.
Emile : I cannot think of anything !

This is a priceless opportunity to impress the lesson of dependence,—to prove that it is only by mildness, docility and attention that she can hope for a continuation of help and protection.

Punishment, says the Maternal Governess, is proper only for intractable and servile dispositions ; but she is willing, before Rousseau, to correct faults by means of Fables.

This is how she deals with her pupil after a courageous burst of naughtiness :

Mother : Take a book from that shelf : that which you see at the end of the second lowest shelf.

Emilie : Is it this, Mamma ?

Mother : Yes, bring it to me.

Emilie : Mamma, it is Moral Tales.

Mother : So much the better ; it will amuse us.

Emilie : Which shall I read ?

Mother : The first.

Emilie : Oh ! Mamma.

Mother : What now ?

Emilie : It is—Let us read the second, Mamma.

Mother : Why not the first ?

Emilie : Mamma, it is " The Naughty Girl " !

Mother : Well, we shall see if it bring to our recollection any of our acquaintance.

Emilie : Must I read it aloud ?

Mother : Without doubt ; and pronounce distinctly.

(The very snap of the consonants can be heard.)

Madame d'Epinay was too true a disciple of Rousseau to follow him slavishly.   Not only did she ignore his strictures upon reading, through the fear of being singular, and still more that of making an unfortunate experiment, but she was even ready to tolerate myths for the sake of morality, and to compare them with modern instances ; on the other hand, it must be confessed that she only once talked of fairies, and regretted it afterwards.

Emilie herself has a child's love of fairies ; but she is made to reason about them :

" Mamma, you will make me umpire between you and the fairies," says the intelligent little person, making the most of her dull game ; and she obediently works it out against herself : " They were, perhaps, two fairies and a genii I met this morning.   Well, no matter, Heaven bless them, I say, you are the fairy Luminous and have *disenchanted me* ! "

The Mother never shrinks from this grave responsibility.   Berquin, though he made war upon ghosts, was wise enough to let the fairies alone.   At least he could laugh like one of them.   But Madame d'Epinay, in her first Conversation with Emilie, finds it hard to be amused, and in the twelfth, the little girl declares : " *In my whole life I never saw you play at anything* ".

This, indeed, is a mother that sends Love himself to school :

Emilie :   Mamma ! Mamma ! Let me come and kiss you.
Mamma : Most willingly ; *but you will tell me upon what account !*

Madame de Genlis's *Adèle et Théodore*, published in the same year as *Emilie*, gives her interpretation of Rousseau in the form of correspondence with a mother who desires to be enlightened, but as yet clings to the ordinary customs of Society :

" You prevent your children till the age of thirteen from reading Telemachus, Fontaine's Fables and all such books, yet you would inspire them with a taste for reading ! What books would you give them instead of those I have mentioned ? Are they only to read the Arabian Nights and Fairy Tales till they are thirteen ? "

The answer gives the author's convictions about children's books :

" I neither give my children Fairy Tales to read nor Arabian Nights ; not even Madame d'Aulnoy's Fables, which were composed for this purpose. *There is scarcely one of them which has a moral tendency.*"

To provide works " proper for infancy " she wrote *Les Veillées du Château,* [1] tales which carry Rousseau's theories along a facile stream of conversation and incident. Adèle, until she is seven, is allowed to read no other books. " I shall then", says Madame de Genlis, "give her the Conversations of Emilie, a book you have often heard me praise, and this will employ her till she is eight."

The apparent generosity to her rival, however, did not

[1] *Les Veillées du Château.* 1784. Translated by T. Holcroft, Dublin, 1785. See Appendix, A. IV, for an account of Mrs. Pilkington's *Tales of the Cottage,* 1799.

prevent the writer of *Adèle et Théodore* from attributing the success of *Emilie* to the good will of the Encyclopædists. " Madame d'Epinay was a philosopher," she remarks, " and took good care not to talk of religion to her Emilie."

It is certainly true that Madame de Genlis had many qualifications for her task which Madame d'Epinay lacked ; and when for a moment she allows herself to forget her theories, there are glimpses of autobiography in her books. Her own life, in fact, was the most interesting of her tales, and the rest are interesting chiefly for reflections of it.

No child could have reproached Madame de Genlis with never playing at anything. She had an extraordinary childhood, and her early years in the quiet Château of St. Aubin were filled with unusual interests.[1] At eight years old she dictated little romances and comedies to her governess, and amused herself by playing schoolmistress to some Burgundian peasant children who came to cut rushes under her window ; at eleven she was the chief attraction of her mother's theatrical fêtes. It was characteristic of the society of the day to seek refuge in private theatres from political and social realities ; most owners of country houses had their own companies composed of friends and neighbours, and thus Félicie, before her twelfth year, had mixed freely with gentlefolk and villagers, and had shown the aptitude for teaching and acting which marked her whole career. Her dramatic talent, indeed, might be said to cover all her other activities, for with her, teaching was little more than a favourite and particularly successful rôle. She was active, curious and enterprising as any child ; before her marriage she was an accomplished harpist and fluent writer ; afterwards she acquired a knowledge

[1] See Mr. Austin Dobson's account of Madame de Genlis in *Four Frenchwomen*. London, 1890.

of literature, anatomy, music and flower-painting ; but there were other occupations which fitted her even better to be the exponent of Rousseau's theories. Writing in the *Memoirs* of her early married life, " I endeavoured ", she says, " to gain some insight into field-labour and gardening. I went to see the cider made. I went to watch all the workmen in the village at work, the carpenter, the weaver, the basket maker ".

Rousseau thought her the most natural and cheerful girl he had ever met. Their friendship was short, but she never wavered in her loyalty to his teaching, and could say at the age of seventy, " What I pride myself on, is knowing twenty trades, by all of which I could earn my bread."

In 1777, Madame de Genlis was made governess to the daughters of the Duchess of Chartres, for whom, with her own children, she established a school at the Convent of Belle Chasse. Her success was so great that, in 1782, the Duke of Orleans took the unusual step of appointing her as " governor " to his three sons. The result fully justified his courage and silenced the critics who ridiculed this new method of using revolutionary theory to educate princes.

The Duke purchased a country estate at St. Leu, and here the boys made experiments in chemistry, studied botany, practised gardening, carpentry, and other forms of handwork. But Madame de Genlis did more than play the part of Rousseau with three Emiles. She handed on to her pupils the delights of her own childhood. These boys could laugh at Emile marooned in his island. They played out a dozen different Voyages in the park of St. Leu ; and had a theatre of their own in which they acted moral plays from the *Théâtre d'Education*.[1]

Madame de Genlis had long ago added authorship to

---

[1] *Le Théâtre d'Education*, published, 1779. Translated (4 vols.) 2nd edition, London, 1781. See Appendix A. IV, Educational Dramas.

her list of trades and had written stories for the children of Belle Chasse. It was easy enough to invent new ones for St. Leu. " There is no great wisdom required in the composition," she declared, " but only Nature and common sense."

Doubtless her books deserved Madame Guizot's criticism, " *toujours bien et jamais mieux* ". She is discursive, even garrulous, and often loses the thread of the story in moral dialogues ; but there are tales in the *Veillées du Château* that suggest her own enjoyment of the " delicious life " with her children ; and if none of them betray her love of mischief and adventure, it is but a fresh proof that she was acting a part, that she could not move freely under the cloak of the Infallible Parent. For in actual life she could take either side in a moral contrast, bear her part in the maddest pranks, assume every virtue of a heroine and hide with complete success a thousand faults.

Her books, after all, were simply properties reserved for her parts of Moralist and Schoolmistress. She dramatised the theories of Rousseau, and although her wonderful energy hardly atoned for her lack of depth and soundness, she left a rich legacy of device and suggestion to those who could use it better.

Rousseau's affinity to Locke on the side of theory, and to Richardson in sentiment may account for some common features of French and English tales, but it does not explain the writing of " Lilliputian " books by two such authors as Berquin and Madame de Genlis.

There is, of course, no great difference between " writing down " Rousseau's doctrine for children, and making miniature versions of Richardson and La Bruyère ; but Berquin's humour should have saved him from *Le Petit Grandison*,[1] and Madame de Genlis might have reflected

[1] Translated into English as *The History of Little Grandison.* " By M. Berquin, Author of *The Children's Friend*." London, printed for John Stockdale, 1791. (Price one shilling.) Frontispiece by John Bewick.

on the undramatic qualities of *Le Petit La Bruyère*.[1]
Berquin's Lilliputian hero reveals himself in letters to his
mother as a perfect miniature of Sir Charles Grandison,
not less insufferable for his youth ; and the little *La
Bruyère* is made up of conventional homilies : " Of Reading, Study and Application " ; " Of Personal Merit " ;
" Of the Heart " (introduced by a quotation from Marmontel) ; " Of Insipidity " (perhaps evoked by the other
platitudes).

It was Rousseau himself who saw that the subject of
education was entirely new, even after Locke's treatise,
and would be new after his own. The closest of his
followers overlooked his chief discovery.

---

[1] *Le Petit La Bruyère ; ou, Caractères et Moeurs des Enfans de ce
Siècle. Nouvelle édition, Paris,* 1801. Translated as *La Bruyère
the Less,* Dublin, 1801.

CHAPTER V

THE ENGLISH SCHOOL OF ROUSSEAU

Effects of Rousseau's teaching in England—Henry Brooke's *Fool of Quality*, the English *Emile*—Thomas Day: his connection with the Edgeworths—*Sandford and Merton*—*Little Jack*—Theory and Romance: Philip Quarll as a Rousseauist—*The New Robinson Crusoe*—Madame d'Epinay and Mary Wollstonecraft: The *Original Stories*—Blake's illustrations—Traces of Marmontel and Madame le Prince de Beaumont in *The Juvenile Tatler* and *The Fairy Spectator*.

IN England, Rousseau's teaching had more effect on the actual life of the family than on books. Children, no longer cramped by the old pedantries, began to show unexpected powers of action and self-control, and parents, relieved of their harsher duties, chose to make friends rather than philosophers of their children.

It was only in books that theorists could represent this genuine progress by the make-believe of impossible children and perfect parents. Most writers of children's books were theorists of one sort or another, and now that they had begun to draw from life, they tried to make it fit their theories. Thus the new books were hardly less didactic than the old.

Some reflect Johnson's hostility to Rousseau, others support the new ideas with definite religious teaching, and many that present the Child of Nature as an existing type, endow him with the precocious wisdom of a Lilliputian. There is hardly a book among them, even among the many adaptations of French stories, in which the setting and characters are not plainly English.

The most consistent of all Rousseauists was Thomas

Day,[1] the author of *Sandford and Merton*,[2] and he owed the success of his book at least as much to his own observations and experiments, as to Rousseau.

Much of its interest, moreover, can be traced to the example of an English novelist ; for in choosing some pieces for children from Henry Brooke's *Fool of Quality*, Mr. Day had been so struck by its simple and vivid style as to regret that Brooke himself had not written books for children ; and it is clear that, while the theory of *Sandford and Merton* came direct from Rousseau, many dramatic situations, which are the life of the story, were suggested by *The Fool of Quality*.[3]

This, indeed, was a book after Rousseau's own heart. The hero, Henry Earl of Moreland, is an English Emile quickened out of knowledge by more natural and livelier adventures. Brought up by a foster-mother among village children, he stands for the virtues of a natural education, against a brother bred at home in the luxurious fashion of the time. The scene of his first visit (at five years old) to his parents, is a satire on Society, and the farcical turn of his adventures brings the romance of theory into touch with the novel of life and humour. This little Harry is the most natural child of fiction ; like Emile at a later stage, he knows nothing of the respect due to people of rank, and is quite unmoved by his unusual surroundings ; but as yet he has no philosophy ; he values things as children do, for what they mean to him. A laced hat is useless as a head-covering, but an effective missile for playing ducks and drakes among the wine-glasses ; when

---

[1] See Appendix A. V.

[2] *The History of Sandford and Merton*, " A work intended for the use of children ". London. For L. Stockdale, 1783–6–9 (3 vols.). The book was reprinted all through the nineteenth century.

[3] The first volumes were published in 1766, the fifth not till 1770, when an abridged chap-book version also appeared. Charles Kingsley edited a reprint in 1872

he gets astride a Spanish pointer and rides him among the company, he sees no reason to dismount because the dog, growing outrageous, rushes into a group of little masters and misses and overthrows them like ninepins ; and when he has crowned the adventure by throwing down a fat elderly lady and three men, he arises and strolls leisurely about the room " with as unconcerned an aspect as if nothing had happened amiss, and as though he had neither art nor part in this frightful discomfiture ".

Emile, a much older boy, at his dinner party, received a hint from his mentor, and for the rest of the meal " philosophised all alone in his corner " about luxury, superior all to the grown-up guests. The little Harry, merely unhappy at having to hold his knife and fork " just so " and say so many " my lords and my ladies ", very naturally cries, " I wish I was with my mammy in the kitchen." Neither then nor at any other time does he seem conscious of superior wisdom ; but Theory hangs upon the foolishness of his mother. An uncle, whimsical rather than didactic, but none the less a moralist, fills the place of Rousseau's tutor, and later, when the boy appears in clothes " trimmed like those of your beau insects vulgarly called butterflies," this humorist so impresses him with the comparison of that " good and clever boy called Hercules " who was given a poisoned coat to wear, that Harry rips and rends the lacings of his suit and runs down to obey a summons " with half the trimmings hanging in fritters and tatters about him."

Where Emile was controlled and self-centred, Harry is all impulse and warmth of heart. He fights like a little tiger to avenge his brother or to punish some young scamp, and cares little for the opinion of his fellows ; yet he shows the greatest tenderness to animals or persons in distress. His mother, seeking proof of his wits and finding him ready to give away all his clothes except his shirt, decides that " there is but the thickness of a bit of linen between this child and a downright fool ", and so leaves him to his more discerning father.

At times, the author, preoccupied with social and political ideals, so neglects the story that even his lively humour can scarce restore it ; yet he can forget Rousseau's theories in scenes that he invents to illustrate them ; nor does he ever accept a theory without proof. To the philosopher's contention " that self-love is the motive to all human actions ", Brooke answers in the words of the estimable Mr. Meekly, " Virtue forbid " ; and his own philosophy is the sounder for a trustworthy ballast of religion and patriotism.

Among minor digressions are a dialogue about toys, another on ghosts, and some of the " thousand little fables " by which Harry's uncle, " with the most winning and insinuating address, endeavoured to open his mind and cultivate his morals ". One of these, " The Fable of the Little Silver Trouts ", has a tenderness that sets it apart from common fables. It reads like an Irish folk-tale moralised by some good priest.

If Henry Brooke could have passed on his gifts of humour and sympathy to the writers of children's books, they would have known better than to tie life down to theory. As it was, they were mostly obsessed by the desire to teach, and preferred Mr. Day's model of a fault- less hero to one like the Fool of Quality, who actually discovered two boys within him, one " proud, scornful, ostentatious and revengeful ", the other " humble, gentle, generous, loving and forgiving ".

This English Emile was a moral contrast in himself, an anomaly that might weaken every "Example" in moral tales.

Thomas Day would have no such compromise between good and evil. Moral truths were best expressed by distinct types. To combine these in one person was to confuse the issue. Mr. Day lived, as he wrote, to prove his theories, and whenever the unknown quantity of human nature thwarted him, went back to them with unshaken confidence. A great part of his life was given to works of active benevolence, and his death was no less consistent than his life ; for he died in trying to prove that a young horse could be tamed by kindness.

Only once he seems to have acted in what must have seemed to him an irrational way, and that was at the request of the lady (Miss Elizabeth Sneyd) whom at that time he hoped to make his wife. With his natural propensity to improve and educate, he had asked her, in preparation for their future life, to forgo many pleasant and harmless diversions which seemed to him useless or unreasonable. Miss Sneyd, with proper spirit, suggested that a French dancing-master might help Mr. Day to overcome certain faults of deportment which displeased her, and so nice was his sense of justice, that he actually crossed to France and spent some time in a hopeless experiment. Nobody could have taught Mr. Day to dance ; perhaps the lady knew it. Such graces as he managed to acquire only provoked her to say that she liked him better as he was before, and he retired to console himself with philosophy.

His next venture promised better success. He resolved to educate two orphan girls upon Rousseau's plan, so that, in time, one of them might fill the place he had intended for Miss Sneyd. But Nature again proved herself too strong for Philosophy. The children quarrelled, refused to be educated " in Reason's plain and simple way ", and could not be cured of shrieking when their guardian frightened them to test their courage. As they grew up, he was forced to admit another failure ; but he clung to his theories, and oddly enough lost nothing of his belief in the reasonableness of " female character ". A later pupil of his more than justified this confidence. Richard Lovell

Edgeworth, although he had been Day's successful rival in love, was still his friend, and used to send his little daughter Maria to spend her holidays with him. By that time Mr. Day had found a lady who could endure his ways, and was settled in Essex, busy with schemes for the benefit of his poor neighbours.

Maria Edgeworth, fresh from a conventional boarding school, was quick to appreciate his odd humours and philosophic mind. She obediently swallowed his doses of tar-water, submitted to the severest tests in exact reasoning, and under his influence, acquired that intense regard for truth which stamped all her later writings. Yet it was not through any theories derived from him or from her father that she became the greatest writer of Moral Tales, but through her own experience of life and character ; and her work for children must be considered apart from her Rousseauist principles. Mr. Day, indeed, whose ideal of womanhood was in some ways little in advance of Rousseau's, did his best to crush her first effort (the translation of *Adèle et Théodore*) by expostulating with her father for encouraging it ; but Maria was too much his pupil to give way to a prejudice based solely on his horror of " female authorship ".

Mr. Day was fully alive to the want of good books for children ; not only did he put his own talents at their service, by contributing to Mr. Edgeworth's instructive serial *Harry and Lucy*,[1] but he found the task so interesting that it grew into an independent volume, three parts dissertation and experiment, and the fourth a fresh effort to express life in terms of theory.

Doubtless he found it a relief to work out in a book the experiments which he had found so disconcerting in practice : to show, as the result of his system, a super-Fool of Quality,—a farmer's son, instead of a nobleman's,—and to

[1] See below, Chapter VIII.

make his foil the spoilt child of rich parents. These are
the two children, Harry Sandford and Tommy Merton,
" introduced as the actors " to give interest and coherence to
Mr. Day's collection of lessons and stories.

When he says they are " made to speak and behave
according to the order of Nature," " Nature " must be
understood to mean the "natural " result of Theory ; for it
is only the Bad Boy who, in his naughtiness, is a real child
of Nature. The Good Boy of the Moralist is a stock figure
of allegory, but the Bad Boy lives ; a hundred models will
serve for his portrait. He is the real hero of *Sandford and
Merton*, as Satan is of *Paradise Lost*.

Thus, even in a book, human nature was too much for
Mr. Day ; and yet his Good Boy, Harry Sandford, is something more than the good half of the Fool of Quality.
His virtues, although superhuman, are not unlike those of
the youthful Thomas Day ; but under the guidance of Mr.
Barlow, that insufferable model of the Perfect Tutor, he
exhibits the mature head of Mr. Day on young shoulders,
and so becomes the mouthpiece of Rousseau, the lay-
preacher of Mr. Barlow's sermons, and the chief instrument
of the Bad Boy's reformation.

There is a note of English severity in Mr. Day's reading
of Rousseau. His notion of self-control is stricter than
anything in the *Emile :* " Mr. Barlow says we must only
eat when we are hungry and drink when we are dry " ;
he is utterly intolerant of wealth : " The rich do nothing
and produce nothing, the poor everything that is really
useful ". Mr. Barlow, Harry Sandford and the amiable
Miss Simmons take it in turns to express Mr. Day's opinions
of the idle and frivolous pastimes of Society. Mr. Barlow
was " an odd kind of man who never went to assemblies
and played upon no kind of instrument," he was " not
fond of cards " and preferred relating moral histories.
Harry Sandford found the theatre " full of nothing but

cheating and dissimulation ; " and when the youthful guests of Tommy's house-party were preparing for a Ball, " Miss Simmons alone appeared to consider the approaching *solemnity* with perfect indifference ".

Much of this is autobiography. Under the figure of Miss Simmons's uncle, Mr. Day, in fact, discloses himself : " a man of sense and benevolence, but a very great humorist ". It is his humour to look at the world as his poor boy looks at the rich man's house :

" To the great surprise of everybody, he neither appeared pleased nor surprised at anything he saw."

Many incidents of the story, which, like the fight between Harry and Master Mash, owe little to Henry Brooke, may be taken as reminiscent of Mr. Day's boyhood ; for although he has a true instinct for drama, he is incapable of pure invention.

" The originality of the author " he says " is a point of the least consequence in the execution of such a work as this ". Harry Sandford refusing to betray the hare to the huntsman, or at loggerheads with the " little gentry ", is the Fool of Quality ; but when he discusses the World with Miss Simmons, he is a brother of the philosophic Emile.

Mr. Day borrows many of his instructive details from Rousseau : the juggler, who taught Emile the use of magnets by means of an artificial duck, conspires with Mr. Barlow and Harry to teach the uninformed Tommy Merton ; but there are other experiments more practical than Rousseau's, which suggest actual experience and the co-operation of Mr. Edgeworth. These alternate with short tales introduced according to what Mr. Day calls the " natural order of association " ; but their effect is to weaken the genuine interest of the enveloping story. " The Gentleman and the Basket Maker "[1] gains nothing

[1] This story had appeared in *The Twelfth Day Gift*, and was very popular in pre-revolutionary days.

by the Good Boy's elocution; Leonidas shakes himself free from Mr. Barlow's patronage.

Yet, with all these digressions, children found matter of interest in *Sandford and Merton* for another century. The most didactic parents could not have controlled the choice of so many nurseries, nor would Mr. Day accept a grown-up verdict without the children's assent. " If they are uninterested in the work ", he wrote in his preface, " the praises of a hundred reviewers will not console me for my failure ".

The truth is that persons who stand no higher than Mr. Barlow's knee can go through the book without seeing much of him.

The simple story of " Little Jack ", no less characteristic of Day, appeared in *The Children's Miscellany :* (1787),[1] but may have been written earlier. The moral is quite explicit ; " that it is of little consequence how a man comes into the world, provided he behaves well and discharges his duty when he is in it " ; but Jack's life begins at the edge of experience, when he is suckled by a goat ; and later, his duty leads him into many adventures which, although they appear true, happen in a romantic setting of foreign countries.

Thus theorists, without acknowledging romance, may use it for their own purposes. Robinson Crusoe's island lent enchantment to Emile's most practical employments, and Rousseau's followers chose two wholly romantic figures to point their arguments against society. The negro, cut off from his own people, freed from his oppressors, is a striking and pathetic mark in the midst of his white brothers. He now becomes a type of the Natural Man, and a hero of children's books.[2] The second witness against social institutions is that first friend of children, the shipwrecked

[1] *The Children's Miscellany*. London, printed for John Stockdale, 1787. It included " The Gentleman and the Basket Maker ". " Little Jack ", printed separately, became a favourite chap-book.
[2] See Appendix A. V.

8

sailor-man in his island, who still holds them by the spell
of circumstance, even while he repeats the strange jargon
of revolutionary doctrines.

Mr. Day had transcribed, along with extracts from *The
Fool of Quality*, " some part of Robinson Crusoe ", without
any serious additions ; but Philip Quarll the Hermit, one of
Crusoe's earliest successors, appeared in *The Children's
Miscellany* as a Rousseauist philosopher.

The original chap-book of 1727[1] has no suggestion of
theory, but it points out one vital difference between
Philip Quarll and Crusoe.   Quarll actually comes to love
his solitude and loses all desire to return to his own country.

To the theorist, this proved him a forerunner of Rousseau,
and the editor of 1787 could furnish him with the latest
version of the creed.   He begins by reflecting (as Rousseau
did with *Robinson Crusoe*) on the edifying spectacle of
shipwrecked men, " deprived in an instant of all the advantage and support which are derived from mutual assistance
. . . obliged to call forth all the latent resources of their
own minds " ; and then remarks that the story " whether real
or fictitious, is admirably adapted to the illustration of
the subject ".

The poetical language of this hermit, so unlike Crusoe's
plain story, suggests the influence of Saint Pièrre, whose
descriptions of scenery were more elaborate but less
vigorous than Rousseau's.   " Feathered Choristers " entertain him " with melodious harmony ; " Nature " puts on
her gay enamelled garb and out of her rich wardrobe
supplies all vegetables with new vesture."

In such phrases, the philosophic hermit exalts Solitude
at the expense of Society.

There is much unconscious humour in the account of

[1] *The Hermit ; or, the Unparalled (sic) sufferings and surprising
adventures of Mr. Philip Quarll, an Englishman, who was lately
discovered by Mr. D—— upon an uninhabited island in the South Sea,*
etc.   London, 1727.   For other editions see Appendix A. V.

the hermit's efforts to overcome Nature, for although he has some of Crusoe's practical ability, he trusts rather to theory. Depressed at the persistent hatred of a tribe of monkeys, for whom he has dug roots, he meditates on its cause, and deciding that he must have forfeited their respect " by hiding the beauty of his fabric under a gaudy disguise ", he discards the irrational garments which distinguish men from monkeys, and presents in his own person Rousseau's Natural Man.

A friendly monkey, " Beau Fidèle ", plays the part of Friday, and the " surprising tractability and good nature " of this beast, contrasted with the ingratitude of a ship-wrecked sailor, strengthen the general argument.

This is how the Philosopher, after fifteen years in his island, apostrophises a ship that suddenly appears :

" Unlucky invention ! That thou shouldst ever come into men's thoughts ! The Ark which gave the first notion of a floating habitation, was ordered for the preservation of man, but its fatal copies daily expose him to destruction " ; and when the sailors fail to take him off, " despite a sudden impulse to return ", he reflects upon his good fortune in having escaped the world, and counts his own situation happier than theirs. There is, of course, no Footprint in the Sand ; yet the tale has romantic features. A child might skip most of the descriptions, but he would remember the white-bearded hermit and his monkey-servant in their hut built of growing trees. Crusoe had no such leaf-tapestry on his walls ; and there is a map of Philip Quarll's island which is a formulary of romantic truth ; for in it may be seen (at A) the place where the Hermit was cast away, and at B, the place where Mr. Dorrington (who discovered him) landed ; at E, the Hermit's Lodge, and at K, the lake between the Rock and the Island.

The new *Philip Quarll* with all its absurdities was better

reading for Children than *The New Robinson Crusoe*
(Campe's *Robinson der Jüngere*, translated into English
from the French in 1788).[1] Crusoe's ship never carried a
heavier cargo than Campe's tiresome family, who break up
the story with their dull colloquies ; but the book is a
fresh proof that these philosophers had to call in the old
masters to enforce their lessons, and could discover no
more attractive theme than the old one of voyages and
islands.

The English *Conversations of Emily* appeared in the same
year as *The Children's Miscellany*. Four years later,
Mary Wollstonecraft, full of theories for the better education of girls, assumed the mantle of Madame d'Epinay,
or rather placed it on the shoulders of a Representative
whom no touch of human weakness could redeem from the
hard grip of Reason : Mrs. Mason, a monstrous creation
of her own.[2] It would be impossible to paint Mrs. Mason's
portrait. Nothing softer than granite could suggest her
outline. Compared with her, Emily's Mother is all kindness and indulgence. Her two charges, Mary and Caroline,
are mere wax tablets whereon she records her impressions
of virtue. Their very faults are placed upon them like
labels, for Mrs. Mason to remove. Emily, though she was
her mother's " friend ", was a real child, pleased and
amused by formal Nature lessons and unimaginative
stories, since nothing better might be had ; playing with
dolls, " jumping, running about and making a noise ".

Mary, in the *Original Stories*, has to prove that she can
" regulate her appetites ", before Mrs. Mason says : " I
called her my friend, and she deserved the name, *for she*

[1] *The New Robinson Crusoe*, 4 vols. London, 1788.
[2] *Original Stories from Real Life*, " with Conversations calculated
to Regulate the Affections and Form the Mind to Truth and Goodness ". By Mary Wollstonecraft. London. Printed for J.
Johnson, 1791 (Illustrated by William Blake). Reprinted, Oxford,
1906, with five of Blake's illustrations. Intro. Mr. E. V. Lucas.

was no longer a child." Mary and Caroline have no mother ; Mary Wollstonecraft had no confidence in parents. She called in Mrs. Mason, a sort of moral physician, to make good the defects of a casual up-bringing. Mrs. Mason, true to the *tradition d'Epinay,* " never suffered them to be out of her sight ". She exhibited every excellence that she exhorted them to attain ; and that none of her perfections should escape their notice, she discoursed upon these at intervals. Her success is inevitable and complete. She conducts her pupils through carefully selected experiences ; she conducts the reader through the book. She never hesitates or doubts ; she never betrays surprise.

The Tales were written " to illustrate the Moral " : it is thus that Mrs. Mason answers " the Ænigma of Creation ". She sees everything, understands everything, explains everything.

" ' I declare I cannot go to sleep ', said Mary, ' I am *afraid of Mrs. Mason's eyes '."*

Mrs. Mason conforms and makes everybody else conform to her moral formulæ : " Do you know the meaning of the word Goodness ? " she asks. " I see you are unwilling to answer. I will tell you. It is, first, to avoid hurting anything ; and then to continue to give as much pleasure as you can."

Three chapters are given to " the treatment of animals ". The children are allowed to read Mrs. Trimmer's *Fabulous Histories,*[1] and to read it " over again " to a little friend, if they can make her understand that *birds never talk.*

In the *Original Stories,* pleasure is administered like medicine. Benevolence is a chief part of Mrs. Mason's Theory ; she is resolutely, almost sternly benevolent. Joy is never admitted without a dispensation from Reason. When the children have acted " like rational creatures ", Mrs. Mason allows them two lines of joy :

[1] See below—Chapter VI.

" Look, what a fine morning it is. Insects, birds, and animals, are all enjoying this sweet day."

Blake snatched the words eagerly for his frontispiece. His " illustrations " are a touchstone for Mary Wollstonecraft's imagination. *He could not draw Mrs. Mason.* In her place he introduces a central figure of his own, meditative, sweet, and firm ; spiritual, even decorative, as Mrs. Mason never was. Yet he, like the rest, was dominated by the monstrous original ; his Masonic Symbol appears in every picture. The children are his own ; he dresses them to order, but makes haloes of their little round straw hats.

This author has an effective manner of disposing landscape to correspond with her sombre or determinedly joyful moods. Blake does not attempt the moonlight scene that moves Mrs. Mason to discourse upon her gloomy past, and present resignation. " I am weaned from the world, but not disgusted," she observes. Such a state of mind would be unintelligible to Blake. But he manages to convey something of the formal desolation of the ruined Mansion-house, to which Mrs. Mason brings the children " to tell them the history of the last inhabitants ". They cling about her, and one looks back in a vain hope of escape, for " when they spoke, the sound seemed to return again, as if unable to penetrate the thick stagnated air. The sun could not dart its purifying rays through the thick gloom, and the fallen leaves contributed to choke up the way and render the air more noxious ". A heavy atmosphere is characteristic of the book ; it suggests the German *Elements of Morality*, which Mary Wollstonecraft translated two years later. The promise of romance in the settings of Mrs. Mason's stories is never fulfilled.

Blake was oppressed by her realistic solution of the mystery of the unseen harper. He followed the " pleasing sound " in his own way, and discovered the player for himself : not Mrs. Mason's explicit and tangible old man, but a spirit harping under a starry sky.

Neither Thomas Day nor Mary Wollstonecraft could have written a " Lilliputian " book ; and even the author of the *Juvenile Tatler* and *Fairy Spectator*, whose titles suggest the old traditions, turns back only to copy the types of Marmontel, the moral fairy tales of Madame le Prince de Beaumont.

The Juvenile Tatler,[1] by Mrs. Teachwell (Lady Fenn) is a collection of moral dialogues and dramas : " The Foolish Mother ", " The Prudent Daughter ", " The Innocent Romp ", and others suggested by Marmontel. But the characters are wholly English. The Innocent Romp is a feminine counterpart of the Bad Boy.

The other persons of this drama (real people too) are Mr. Briskly, a Widower, whom Marmontel would have called " The Foolish Father " ; Mrs. Freeman, his sister, " The Wise Aunt " ; Miss Prudence Freeman, her daughter, " The Good Cousin ".

Lady Fenn's humour is English, like her characters : she invents amusing pranks for her heroine, and is original in admitting a girl to the masculine pastime of mischief.

A very natural dialogue between the Foolish Father and the Wise Aunt prepares the reader for the entrance of the Romp. Her latest offence has lost her an eligible suitor. Chasing the housemaid with a rotten apple, she has just thrown it full in the face of Lord Prim, alighting from his coach to pay his compliments to her, on her return from school. Thus announced, she enters, fresh from an excursion into a neighbour's garden by way of the wall. Questioned about the visible traces of this adventure, she confesses that she fell from the top of the wall, and adds

[1] Dated (1783) by a reference to " the invention of Air Balloons ", quoted below. Earliest edition seen : *The Juvenile Tatler*, " by a Society of Young Ladies under the Tuition of Mrs. Teachwell." London, J. Marshall. 1789.

that she would like to fall twenty times if she could be sure she was not seen, and *to make her cousin Prudence fall too*. " La ! Cousin," she cries, with seductive enjoyment," 'tis delightful ! Just like flying." (A cautious foot-note explains : " This was written before the invention of Air Balloons.")

When the author has a doubt about the moral influence of her heroine, she inserts a corrective foot-note.

The Romp, it is disclosed by her Aunt, not content with dressing the cat in baby-linen to play at a mock-christening, disguised herself as an old woman, and carried it to Mr. Starchbland, the Curate. Upon this there are three separate comments : The Foolish Father's " *A profane trick* " ; The Wise Aunt's " She thought no further than the surprise it would be to the person who should lift up the mantle and possibly "—— Oh, excellent Wise Aunt ! —" *possibly*, the roguery of getting the parson scratched." And, last, the foot-note, to avert parental criticism : " *Let it not be supposed that Miss B would suffer the Sacred Rite to begin* ".

The author's sympathies are with the Aunt (she was an aunt herself). So the Wise Aunt carries off her niece to undergo a moderate process of conversion. The Foolish Father, who " dotes " upon his daughter " when she is neatly dressed and tolerably sedate ", is obviously drawn from life.

The Fairy Spectator,[1] " By Mrs. Teachwell and Her Family ", is Mrs. Argus transformed into the Benevolent Educational Fairy of Madame de Beaumont. Here is a characteristic bit of dialogue :

Mrs. Teachwell : You know that stories of Fairies are all fabulous ?

---

[1] *The Fairy Spectator ; or, The Invisible Monitor.* By Mrs. Teachwell and her Family (Eleanor, Lady Fenn). London. J. Marshall. 1789.

Miss Sprightly :   Oh, yes ! Madam.
Mrs. Teachwell :   Do you wish for such a Fairy Guardian ?
Miss Sprightly :   Very much, Madam.
Mrs. Teachwell :   Why, my dear ?
Miss Sprightly :   *Because she would teach me to be good.*

A world where all fairies are " fabulous " is, of course, a world without dreams.   When Miss Sprightly weeps on rising, because she cannot banish the thought of " the most pleasing dream which she ever had in her life ", the inexorable Mrs. Teachwell meets the situation with a simple formula : " Idle girl, make haste ! "   The Fabulous Beings whom she admits on sufferance are not more fairylike than " the smallest wax doll."

Two lines from *The Fairy Spectator* betray the Rousseauist's attitude to Fairyland :

" I will write you a Dialogue in which the Fairy shall converse, and *I will give you a Moral for your Dream.*"

CHAPTER VI

DEVICES OF THE MORALIST

THE great writers for children were neither Lilliputian nor Rousseauist. They emerged from a good company of aunts and mothers who, with a sprinkling of fathers, were driven into anonymous authorship by the demands of their own families: minor moralists, without any special gifts of art or imagination, who managed to draw live pictures from their own little world, and hit upon simple devices for holding attention and exciting interest.

They were mostly innocent of Theory, but an intimate acquaintance with the Child of Nature taught them in one way or another to avoid the unpardonable sin of dulness.

Little novels, following their grown-up prototypes with unequal steps, had their own limitations of setting and character. A nursery or a schoolroom is always a nursery or a schoolroom, and varies only according to particular houses and inhabitants. The few ways of escape (by a window, a chimney or a keyhole) into fairyland, were blocked in most eighteenth century houses, and the persons of moral tales, however lifelike, were apt, from contact with a narrow circle, to assume familiar characters.

Adventures of the milder sort might happen on the road to school, but the only changes of scene were from parlour to schoolroom, or from town to country. Any effort to exceed these by travels abroad landed the unsophisticated author in a hopeless confusion of unknown tongues and half-remembered directions.

And yet there was something in these English settings to compensate a child for the loss of fairyland, if not to set his feet in the track of it. Authors chiefly concerned with character were apt to give the briefest indication of a background; but before 1780, there were woodcuts that implied more than the words of the story.

Thomas Bewick had cut his first blocks for the York and Newcastle chap-books, and although he soon passed on from these to a wider study of Nature, they were enough to seal the fate of the old slovenly pictures in children's books.

As a boy, Bewick had filled the margins of his school-books and covered the hearthstones of his mother's cottage with drawings of the men and beasts that he knew about his native village[1]; and these he reproduced later in the cuts for chap-books and fables.

He could never draw fairies. The " Pigmy Sprite " in Gay's *Fables*[2] is not half so fairy-like as the little spinning-wheels and brooms of the corner-pieces; but his drawings of trees and meadows, rocks and pools, show the " fairy ground " of his own happy childhood.

It was thus that he gave a new meaning to the country setting which was now a recognised feature of moral tales. A writer might demand no more of Nature than that she

[1] See the *Memoir of Thomas Bewick* (1862). See also Mr. Austin Dobson's account in *Thomas Bewick and His Pupils* (1884)

[2] *Fables, by the late Mr. Gay.* In one Volume complete. Newcastle, T. Saint, etc., 1779.

should provide the Industrious Boy with fruit in season ; but Bewick caught her among the corn ricks or at the corner of a lane, and she herself took up the parable.

The younger brother, John, who began by adapting some of Bewick's drawings, is better known as an illustrator of children's books. Between 1790 and 1820, there are few cuts that do not show some trace of his influence, and many of those in the smaller chap-books,—*The Adventures of a Pincushion*, for example, and *The Life and Adventures of a Fly*,[1]—have been attributed to him.

In a sense, John was more imaginative than his brother, quicker to appreciate subtleties of character and expression. There is hardly less truth of detail in the Lime-walks and rose-gardens of *The Looking Glass for the Mind* than in Thomas Bewick's village scenes ; but the little figures are more graceful and courtly, the backgrounds more delicate.

John Bewick's illustrations to *The New Robinson Crusoe* gave shape to Rousseau's vague ideal ; but his pictures of English children in their natural surroundings were a literal return to Nature. And although they were in complete accord with the changed attitude of the story-writers, they proved (to the confusion of Theorists) that the new Philosophy had made little impression on the familiar moods of Nature and childhood.

The School-setting, however cramped, was a source of wider interest than the alternative parlour or nursery. It varied, according to the fortunes of the persons concerned, from the Village School (commonly built on the *Two-Shoes* foundation, but without its Lilliputian features) to the Academy for young Ladies or Gentlemen : an exclusive community which had received its traditions from Sarah Fieldings's notable little book *The Governess* ;

[1] See below—Appendix A. VI.

or, *The Little Female Academy*[1] published some fourteen years before Rousseau's *Emile*.

Writing in the first decade of Lilliputian books, the author of *David Simple* anticipated Rousseau with a gallery of children's portraits, and showed that the Child of Nature could survive pedantic forms as well as theories.

Madame le Prince de Beaumont chose the same framework for her *Misses' Magazine* ;[2] Charles and Mary Lamb used it to connect the separate stories of *Mrs. Leicester's School*; Mrs. Sherwood seized upon the book itself and revised it ruthlessly, and a host of anonymous writers copied Miss Fielding's method and envied her genius.

Half periodical, half novel, *The Governess* was a perfect medium for " Instruction and Amusement ". It contains sermons, fables, Oriental-Classic stories and a moralised romance in the style of the *Cabinet des Fées*.

Of the Governess herself, whose name of Mrs. Teachum became a popular pseudonym for instructive writers, it must be confessed that she is a Presence hardly less dominating than Mrs. Mason. To the mature reader, who is uncomfortably conscious of having met her in real life, she is more formidable than any lay-figure of a theorist. Her husband, described as " a very sensible Man who took great Delight in improving his Wife," having completed his task, disappears from the story and leaves her to pass on his improvements, to the " nine young Ladies commited to her Care." She is " about forty Years old, tall

---

[1] *The Governess ; or the Little Female Academy*, 'calculated for the entertainment and Instruction of Young Ladies in their Education. By the Author of *David Simple*." London, printed for A. Millar, over against Catharine Street in the Strand. The Third Edition, Revised and Corrected, 1751.

A second edition had been printed in 1749. Miss Fielding's novel, *David Simple*, had appeared in 1744.

[2] *Le Magasin des Enfans, par Madame le Prince de Beaumont.* 2nd ed. 1757. Translated into English in 1767 as *The Young Misses' Magazine.* See Appendix A. VI.

and genteel in her Person, though somewhat inclined to
Fat," and her " lively and commanding Eye " (more human,
if less hypnotic than Mrs. Mason's) " created an Awe in
all her little Scholars, except when she condescended to
smile and talk familiarly with them."

Theorists, working upon this Paragon, extracted the
more human elements ; but the children escaped, like
Hop o' my Thumb out of the Ogre's house.

The long line of authentic portraits that extends from
Miss Fielding to Miss Edgeworth is of one family, and it
is doubtful whether any amount of " practical education "
could have improved some of Mrs. Teachum's pupils,
restricted as these were to " Reading, Writing, Working
and all proper Forms of Behaviour ".

The naughty children in books, as in life, can take
care of themselves, but it needs a writer of unusual tact
to make the good ones live. Miss Fielding's good children
are more to her credit than the " Rogues " who figure in
some of her best scenes ; but there is nothing in the book
quite so amusing as her " Account of a Fray begun and
carried on for the Sake of an Apple, in which are shown the
sad Effects of Rage and Anger."

Mrs. Teachum, entering unexpectedly, produces a sudden
calm in which the losses on all sides can be counted :

" Each of the Misses held in her right hand, fast clenched,
some Marks of Victory. One of them held a little Lock
of Hair, torn from the Head of Her Enemy, another grasped
a Piece of a Cap which, in aiming at her Rival's Hair, had
deceived her Hand and was all the Spoils she could gain,
a third clenched a Piece of an Apron, a fourth of a Frock.
In short, everyone unfortunately held in her Hand a Proof
of having been engaged in the Battle. And the Ground
was spread with Rags and Tatters torn from the Backs of
the *little inveterate Combatants* ".

Here is a satirical scene not unworthy of Fielding's

sister, yet not too subtle for her audience. (The Ladies Caroline and Fanny, new to their titles, are visiting Miss Jenny Peace.) :

" Lady Caroline, who was dressed in a pink Robe embroidered thick with Gold and adorned with very fine Jewels and the finest Mechlin lace, addressed most of her Discourse to her Sister, that she might have the Pleasure every Minute, of uttering ' Your Ladyship ', in order to show what she herself expected. Miss Jenny, amused by their insolent Affectation, addressed herself to Lady Caroline with so many Ladyships and Praises of fine Clothes as she hoped would have made her ashamed ".

Nobody who reads the book can suspect Miss Fielding of more than a distant admiration for Mrs. Teachum. Her own sympathies are clearly with the old dairywoman who, when the children were rebuked for a want of tact in their remarks to her, replied : " O, let the dear Rogues alone, I like their Prattle," and taking Miss Polly (the youngest) by the hand, added : " Come, my Dear, we will go into the Dairy and skim the Milk pans."

There is a kind of story-telling, touched with the same wise playfulness, which is not beyond the talents of average aunts. Two such there were, sisters-in-law, Dorothy and Mary Jane Kilner, whose stories, published in Dutch flowered covers, were as popular after 1780 as the earlier Newberys. There is some doubt about their respective pseudonyms, but the family records ascribe the signature " M. P." to Dorothy and " S. S." to her sister, which establishes Dorothy as the author of *The Village School*.[1]

[1] *The Village School*, "interspersed with entertaining stories." By M. P. 2 vols. Price 1/-. From a list of " New Books for the Instruction and Amusement of Children ". London, J. Marshall *c.* 1788. (At the back of a copy of *Primrose Prettyface*, inscribed " Thomas Preston," with date March 22nd, 1788). See Appendix A. VI.

Her stories grew naturally out of a happy and uneventful life spent in the little Essex Village of Maryland Point, and her best critics were the nephews and nieces for whom she wrote.   But she was in the habit of sending her books to " the Good Mrs. Trimmer " for criticism, and it seems likely that she wrote *The Village School* to help that lady in her work of teaching poor children to read.

" M. P." (she borrowed the initials of her village) is in some sort a nursery Crabbe.   There is not an incident in her story outside a country child's experience : no Babes-in-the Wood opening, no clever animals, no romance of improbable good fortune.   This is the " clean pleasant village " of every-day life.   The schoolmistress, Mrs. Bell, believes in simple virtues, but has no theories.   Boys and girls learn to read, and girls to spin, knit stockings and sew.   They are grouped quite simply, as in some old-fashioned print, and M. P., having borrowed Miss Fielding's device of labelling them with symbolic names, uses it to avoid the complexities of character.   Jacob Steadfast and Kitty Spruce are predestined to carry off the prizes which Betsy Giddy, Master Crafty and Jack Sneak inevitably lose ; and a child is content with the main distinctions of Good and Bad.

The story, slight as it is, reveals M. P. as an aunt who is not indifferent to " Flowers picked out of the Hedges, Daisies and Butter Flowers " ; who can make garlands and enjoy a singing-game,—the right sort of game for village schools :

> " What we have to do is this
> *All bow, all courtesy and all kiss ;*
> And first we are our Heads to bow
> As we, my Dear, must all do now ;
> Then courtesy down unto the Ground,
> Then rise again and all jump round."

" You cannot think " she concludes, " how pretty it is when they mind to sing and dance in the right time."

This was an aunt who, in her own century, deserved some such tribute as Stevenson's :

> " Chief of our Aunts—not only I
> But all your dozen of nurslings cry—
> What did other children do
> And what were Childhood, wanting you ? "

Jemima Placid,[1] variously ascribed to Dorothy and Mary Jane, is woven of the same simple stuff. George Frere, writing in 1816 to his brother Bartle[2], bore witness to its practical effect on one nursery. They evidently came to it in turn, at a particular age. " You ", he wrote, " are more of a philosopher than I am and can bear these things better, and yet I have read *Jemima Placid* since you have, but you have made the best use of it ".

A Rousseauist might have overlooked the philosophy in this little book,—the annals of a parsonage family, in which all the characters are individuals and friends of the writer ; for there is not an ounce of theory in it. Jemima herself is neither a pedant nor an infant prodigy. She is never expected to reason about her own development. Her philosophy is of the older sort that comes of gentle discipline, and she is " placid " not through pleasing no one but herself, but in spite of other people's unjust or exacting ways. It is doubtful whether she would have been very different under the Eye of Mrs. Mason, but assuredly she would have been less happy. No theoretic Child of Nature ever was so happy as Jemima with her brothers.

The scene of parting, when the little girl (six years old) goes to London, is an introduction to these three :

" I wish you were not going " says Charles, " for

[1] *Jemima Placid ; or, the Advantage of Good-Nature*, etc. By S. S.   Price 6d.   Marshall's List, *c.* 1788.

[2] See *John Hookham Frere and his Friends*, by Gabrielle Festing. Nisbet, 1899.   Jemima Placid is ascribed in a foot-note to " *Miss Dorothy* Kilner."

9

I put this box and drove in these nails on purpose for you to hang up your doll's clothes, and now they will be no further use to us." William bids her not cry, and promises to write about the young rabbits. "And, Jemima," adds Charles more tactfully, "I wish I was going with you to London, for I should like to see it, 'tis such a large place, a great deal bigger than any village which we have seen; and they say the houses stand close together for a great way and there are no fields or trees . . ."

It is the same village, seen from a different standpoint, narrowed on the one hand to the record of a particular house, on the other, varied by journeys and visits to town.

Old customs survive with the flowered covers of the book, and the next few lines bring *Jemima Placid* into touch with her predecessors. For in London there is a great number of shops, and to be sure, among other things, Jemima must bring back "Some little books which we can understand, and which . . . may be bought at Mr. Marshall's *somewhere in some churchyard*, but Jemima must inquire about it."

The little things that make up a child's life happen with natural inconsequence. What gives the book a hold is the author's unaffected truth and tenderness, the modest philosophy which hides under simple speeches or incidents.

Who but Jemima Placid, the unhappy guest of two spoilt London cousins, could comfort herself under unjust reproof with "the rough drawing of a little horse, which Charles had given her on the day of her departure and which she had since carefully preserved."

It is no wonder that her brothers are loth to welcome the Londoners on their return visit; but "S. S." can make her own "Book of Courtesy", and she refreshes it with the comments of real boys. William answers his father's rebuke with disconcerting logic: "You always tell me that the naughtiest thing I can do is to tell lies, and I am sure I am very sorry they are come, for I like Jemima to ourselves : so pray, Sir, what would you choose I should do ? "

There is not a trace of the " Juvenile Correspondent " in Charles's letters to Jemima ; but the sentiment of humanitarians is mere vapouring compared with this boy's account of how they found the dog shot by a game-keeper and buried him under the Laylock tree.

" ' Poor Hector ! I shall hate Ben Hunt as Long as I live for it ! '

' Fy Charles ' said my father. ' *Hector is dead, Sir,*' said I, and I did not stay to hear any further."

Elizabeth Sandham, who wrote somewhat later " for the Children of former Schoolfellows ", claimed a wider influence for the story of school life. " A school ", she says, " may be styled the world in miniature. There the passions which actuate the man may be seen on a smaller scale."

On this assumption, she ventured into the unknown microcosm of a boys' school,[1] where even Miss Edgeworth came to grief ; but her book was a model for some hundreds of school stories in which ambitious, studious or mischievous boys play impossible parts. She was more at home in a later study of schoolgirls[2] : careful sketches, brightened by satirical remarks ; but the moral is too obvious. Miss Sandham's sense of humour was too slight for effective relief.

An admirable miscellany, which brings genuine adventure and comedy into the school setting, is *The Academy ;*

[1] *The Boys' School ; or, Traits of Character in Early Life.* A Moral Tale by Miss Sandham. London, printed for John Souter at the School Library, 73 St. Paul's Churchyard, 1800. See Appendix, A. VI.

[2] *The Schoolfellows, a Moral Tale.* By the author of *The Twin Sisters*, etc. 1818.

or, a Picture of Youth,[1] published in 1808 by a Scottish schoolmaster who, in his preface, claims to have taught " all ranks, from the peer's son to the children of the lower orders." His taste is hardly less catholic than his experience, for he not only adds satirical and dramatic scenes to the old fables and admonitions, but adapts Berquin to an English atmosphere, and is ready to sympathise with the shepherd, the labourer, the old man and his horse. The book is a medley of old manners and new sentiments, in which the characters, although they stand for familiar types, earn some rights of personality by individual acts and speeches.

This author is indebted to Smollett for a trick of making his characters talk in the language of their callings. Young Tradewell's father consigns him to the Rector's care " per the bearer," as if he were a bale of merchandise ; and a nautical father advises a son who has " gone a little out of his course " to " sail clear of faults ", but if at any time he is driven into them, to " be a brave boy and steer honourably off."

Satire in Children's books is apt to miss its mark. Some parents who bought this *Picture of Youth* must have felt like the old gentleman of the story, who was furious at a clever caricature of himself until somebody assured him that it was intended for his neighbour. Restored to good humour by similar means, they would doubtless enjoy these burlesques : the foolish indulgent mother, the sporting squire who laughs at his son's escapades, the parents who teach their boy " to recite passages with tragic effect from our best poets ".

The Rector's rational methods recall *Sandford and Merton* ; but the book is for older lads. The Bad Boy of *The Academy* is more like a hero of Picaresque romance,

[1] *The Academy ; or, a Picture of Youth.* London, G. Harris, and Darton and Harvey. Edinburgh, W. Bury, 1808.

and the Good Boy (the son of a naval officer, destined for the Service) is a new figure in moral tales ; a pupil " highly acceptable to the Rector " for his own sake ; the more so, perhaps, for the fresh memory of Trafalgar.

English people have an inherent power of reconciling opposites, which perhaps comes of their being a mixed race.   The most revolutionary writers were held back by some thread of ancient custom, and those who clung to the older modes of thought were not without some broadening influence.   " Nature " and " Truth " were still the accepted ideals of literature, although the meaning of both had changed ; and *The Juvenile Spectator,*[1] which applied Addison's method of character-drawing to the nursery, used it with a new understanding of childhood.

Mrs. Arabella Argus,[2] its author, adds piquancy to her general scheme by introducing herself as a Grandmother. Doubtless she was old enough to remember Lilliputian traditions ; but she was also too young to forget the newer counsels of sanity and freedom.   Like Addison, she begins by describing herself and her aims, but so far is she from admiring the model of the Baby Spectator, that she directs her brightest satire against " little prodigies " and child-philosophers.

She is " an old woman, but not an old witch nor yet a fairy " ;   and without resorting to anything so irrational as magic, she is able to set forth secret information upon " Nursery Anecdotes, Parlour Foibles, Garden Mischief and Hyde Park Romps ".

Now, a Newbery writer might have dealt with the first two of these items ; but he never could have countenanced

[1] *The Juvenile Spectator,* " Being observations on the Tempers Manners and Foibles of Various Young Persons.   Interspersed with such lively matter as it is presumed will amuse as well as instruct." By Arabella Argus.   London, W. & T. Darton, 1810.
[2] For other books by Mrs. Argus, see Appendix A. VI.

such portents of revolution as " Garden Mischief " and
" Hyde Park Romps ".

The letters which Mrs. Argus receives from children
show nothing like the decorum of the Goodwill Correspondence.

Here is one from a typical Bad Boy (which however,
Mrs. Argus contrasts with another, " couched in terms of
becoming timidity ", from a girl) :

" To Mrs. Argus,

" A friend of Mamma's says that you are very clever
at finding out the faults of children, pray tell me mine,
for if you are as cunning as she says you are, I need not
mention them to you. I am certain I know you ; don't
you walk in the Park sometimes ? I am sure you do,
though, and you have a very long nose ; my sister Charlotte and I hope you will answer this directly, for we are
in a great hurry to be satisfied about you.

" Your's
CHARLES OSBORN."

Mrs. Argus gives sound and pleasantly pointed advice
in her replies, though she loses more than one laugh to
modern readers in her care for propriety.

" Will you be so good " she writes in one postscript " as
to tell your brother that the word *Thump* which occurred
in his letter appears to me an expression unworthy of a
well-educated child."

Yet she surprises a pugnacious grandson with the novel
argument that so few things are worth fighting about ;
and shows a genuine sympathy with boyish pranks.

Her remarks upon fairy tales are a juvenile version of
Addison on the " Lady's Library ". She knows exactly
what sort of writing pleases some children ; how " the
eager eyes of a little story-loving dame glisten with delight "
at a promising opening, and the lover of fairy tales " wishes,

just to gratify her curiosity, that there were really such creatures as fairies ". Yet she is so far persuaded that " an early course of light reading is very prejudicial to sound acquirement ", that she rejects any story without the hall-mark of a " Moral ".

A favourite device for connecting the haphazard events of ordinary life (and one that embellished the bare truth) was borrowed from current satires. *The History of Pompey the Little ; or, the Life and Adventures of a Lap-Dog*[1] became a model for stories in which an animal, telling the story of its life, acts as an observer and critic of human conduct.

Humanitarians and lovers of nature, taking up this form, produced more or less faithful studies of birds and animals ; and critics who objected to fables, or thought satire dangerous had nothing to say against this mixture of Natural History and Morality.

Doubtless the stricter guardians of youth looked askance at such a defiance of Reason ; but the " Creatures " had an immense influence in the Nursery : their morals were vouched for by Æsop and all his tribe. After all, it was only a new way of presenting the old lessons, and the sternest parent could hardly reject so engaging a tutor as a Robin or a Mouse.

Miss Fielding's *Governess* had not a larger following of School Stories than Mrs. Trimmer's *Fabulous Histories*[2] produced in moral tales of birds and beasts. This little book, better known by its later title, *The History of the Robins*, was suggested by Mrs. Trimmer's children, which

[1] A satire on well-known persons of the day, by F. Coventry, 1751.
[2] *Fabulous Histories*, " Designed for the Instruction of Children, Respecting their Treatment of Animals ". By Mrs. Trimmer. London, Printed for J. Johnson, etc., J. Harris and others.   1786. Eighth edition (dedicated to " H.R.H. Princess Sophia ", then a child of nine), 1807.

may account for its being her only imaginative work. The children, taught during walks in the fields and gardens " to take particular notice of *every object* that presented itself to their view ", were able, by a natural process of elimination, to develop a chief interest in animals, and " used often to express a wish that their Birds, Cats, Dogs etc., could talk, that they might hold conversations with them ". Their mother, instead of rebuking them for so irrational a desire, adapted the idea of talking birds to her own theories of morality and for once managed to see things from a child's point of view.

Her own childhood had never been anything but middle-aged. At ten she wrote like a grown-up person, and her youth was spent in the company of people much older then herself. Dr. Johnson, meeting her as a girl of fifteen at Reynolds's, was so much struck by her behaviour that he invited her to his house next day, and presented her with a copy of *The Rambler*.[1] This may have had its effect upon a style developed in formal " correspondence " under her father's direction ; at any rate, her diction remained pompous and conventional. Mrs. Trimmer " composed " works as she " indited " letters. In " composing " *Fabulous Histories*, she " seemed to fancy herself conversing with her own children in her accustomed manner " ; but that was because she was accustomed to converse, not talk.

The children, secure in the possession of a " kind pussy Mamma ", never noticed it ; to them it was the most natural thing in the world that birds should converse in the same way.

In their family relations, the robins are passable under-studies of the excellent Mr. and Mrs. Trimmer and their children ; but the introduction of a human family as their

---

[1] *See Some Account of the Life and Writings of Mrs. T.* Further details in Appendix A. VI.

patrons and protectors restores them to the shape of birds. For the first time in the history of children's books, the real centre of interest is transferred from the conduct of children to such matters as living in a nest and learning to fly.

Here is a good example of Mrs. Trimmer's style :

" When Miss Harriet first appeared, the winged suppliants approached with eager expectation of the daily handful which their kind benefactress made it a custom to distribute ".

On the human side, Mrs. Benson, a kind of domestic Mrs. Teachum, presides over the morals of a son and daughter. Her interest in education is almost equal to Mrs. Trimmer's, who " wearied her friends by making it so frequently the subject of conversation " ; but benevolence softens her utilitarian morality. When Master Frederick rushes to the window to feed his birds and forgets to bid his Mamma good-morning, she admonishes him thus :

" Remember, my dear, that you depend as much on your Papa and me for everything you want, as these little birds do on you ; nay, more so, for they could find food in other places ; but children can do nothing towards their own support ; they should therefore be dutiful and respectful to those whose tenderness and care they constantly experience."

The Robin family is more than half human. Nestlings, distinguished by the expressive names of Robin, Dicky, Flapsy and Pecksy, exhibit all the faults of children. But there is a world of difference between Mrs. Trimmer's treatment and that of the fabulist. She has learned to look at a nest of birds from a child's point of view ; what is infinitely more novel and surprising, she actually shifts her ground and considers the Benson household *from the standpoint of a bird*. It is here that so many of her imitators lost the trail ; and thus it is that their books were soon forgotten, while hers was read with delight for a century.

The adventure of the nestlings and the gardener has something of the fascination of *Gulliver*. This is Robin's description of the " Monster " who visited them in their mother's absence :

" . . . . Suddenly we heard a noise against the wall, and presently a great round red face appeared before the nest, with a pair of enormous staring eyes, a very large *beak*, and below that a wide mouth with *two rows of bones* that looked as if they could grind us all to pieces in an instant. About the top of this round face, and down the sides, hung something black, but *not like feathers* ".

The children dragged Mrs. Trimmer from her didactic throne : they even made her talk their language. Her own style is reserved for the parent birds, and in discussing important matters, the young ones imitate them.

" This great increase of family ", says the Robin to his mate, " renders it prudent to make use of every means for supplying our necessities. I myself must take a larger circuit." The Mother bird thus addresses her penitent son : " I have listened to your lamentations, and since you seem convinced of your error, I will not add to your sufferings by my reproaches."

All this can be endured for the sake of so many delightful incidents. For a child can climb up the ivy and creep under the wing of the mother bird. He can join the nestlings in their first singing-lesson, follow them in their first flight, and best of all, he can look at the great world beyond the nest with their wondering eyes :

" *The orchard itself appeared to them a world.* For some time each remained silent, gazing around, first at one thing, then at another ; at length Flapsy cried out : ' What a charming place the world is ! I had no conception that it was half so big ! ' "

The Life and Perambulation of a Mouse[1] was Dorothy Kilner's contribution to the literature of talking beasts. The author is discovered in a frontispiece, seated at a little round table, in a mob-cap and kerchief. Her quill has just reached the end of the second line. Erect in a box of wafers, the Mouse, with extended paw, is dictating the story of his life.

This " chief of aunts," snow-bound in a country house with many " young folk," takes up her pen at their request, to attempt her autobiography.

" I took up my pen, it is true ", she writes, " but not one word toward my appointed task could I proceed . . .

' Then write mine, which may be more diverting ', said a little squeaking voice."

Few " Introductions " were so promising, and the story (apart from inevitable lessons) keeps its promise.

Four mice, Nimble (the narrator) and his brothers Longtail, Softdown and Brighteyes, correspond to Mrs. Trimmer's nestlings ; over whom, to a child's mind, they have one advantage :   they are *outlaws*, repeating in miniature the adventures of Robin Hood.

To be sure, they lack the outlaw's chief virtues, for they fly at the approach of an enemy, and rob rich and poor alike. And although such creatures could always be excused in the words of Dr. Watts :

" *For 'tis their Nature too,*"

a problem remains to puzzle the wit of a little philosopher : how it happens that creatures so keenly alive to human errors are blind to the iniquity of eating a poor woman's cake, a present from her foster-son, or the solitary candle that lights a poor man to bed.   For indeed, these mice are unsparing critics of cowardly, cruel and overbearing children ; they have a full repertory of moral and cautionary

[1] *The Life and Perambulation of a Mouse.* By M. P. 2 vols. Price 1/-. *c.* 1788.

tales ; they preach sermons on human courage and honour.

The child of action puts aside all questioning, jumps nimbly into a mouse's skin and makes a fifth on these marauding expeditions. He scuttles along behind the wainscot, buries himself in the most delicious of plum cakes, outwits the footman, narrowly escapes the trap and thrills at his first sight of the cat.

In a mischievous mood, he can hide in a lady's shoe, or wake the children and hear them wonder what it was. There are Eastern adventures to be had among " spacious and elegant apartments ", where he can choose from " a carpet of various colours " a flower that will hide him, and crouch motionless at a passing footstep ; and when there is a price upon his head, or the house catches fire, there are still more thrilling adventures of escape.

Should a critic remark that these things do not make up one quarter of the book, a child may tell him that he does not mind sermons and, for that matter, can preach them himself.

In 1798, one of the most realistic animal stories appeared : *Keeper's Travels in Search of his Master*,[1] the adventures of a dog. Its author, Mr. Kendall, wrote other books, mostly about birds ;[2] but *Keeper's Travels* was the only serious rival to *Fabulous Histories*.

If any parent had scruples about talking beasts, here was a book that could be put into a child's hand with perfect safety. No eighteenth century writer could help making an animal reason as if he were human ; but this is a real dog, wagging and whimpering his way

[1] *Keeper's Travels in Search of his Master.* By Edward Augustus Kendall. London, E. Newbery, 1798.
[2] See Appendix A. VI.

through the book, and if he does not speak, the story is not a whit less interesting for that.

From the time that he loses sight of his master on a market-day by being " so attentive to half a dozen fowls that were in a basket ", his adventures are entirely natural and probable.

Keeper is never too human for belief : he does nothing that any dog might not do ; yet he makes a good hero, —sticking to his quest in spite of pain and hunger, refusing comforts and saving the lives of children.   Mr. Kendall sums up his hero's virtues in a quotation from Cowper, for those who are " not too proud to stoop to quadruped instructors ".   He was not the only lover of animals to quote a humanitarian poet.   The author of *The Juvenile Spectator* in her quaint *Adventures of a Donkey*,[1] has these lines from Coleridge below the frontispiece :

> " Poor little foal of an oppressed race !
> I love the languid patience of thy face :
> And oft with gentle hand I give thee bread,
> And clap thy ragged coat and pat thy head."

The Autobiography of a Cat was a more delicate task. a psychologist could not explain the workings of its mind, although a careful observer might record its more intelligible movements ; but since every cat is a critic of human character, there was nothing in the way of sermon or satire that it could not achieve.

Elizabeth Sandham's *Adventures of Poor Puss*[2] is a very literal story, setting off the philosophy of " two four-footed moralisers " on a sunny wall ; but the anonymous author of *Felissa ; or, the Life and Opinions of a Kitten of Sentiment*[3] produced a masterpiece in this kind.

[1] *The Adventures of a Donkey.* By Arabella Argus, Author of *The Juvenile Spectator.* London, W. Darton, 1815.

[2] London. J. Harris, 1809.   See Appendix A. VI.

[3] *Felissa ; or, the Life and Opinions of a Kitten of Sentiment.* J. Harris, 1811. Reprinted, Methuen, 1903.

Felissa is a Kitten of Satire as well as of Sentiment. This Author adopted the form of *Pompey the Little* in order to ridicule cant and affectation in general, and Rousseau's doctrine in particular ; yet the chief aim of the book (as the title-page shows) is to turn a child's thoughts from the hackneyed problems of juvenile conduct :

> " We'll have our Mottoes and our Chapters too,
> And brave the Thunders of the dread Review :
> *Misses no more o'er Misses' Woes shall wail,*
> *But list attentive to a Kitten's Tale."*

The heroine's pedigree goes back to Perrault ; she actually claims descent from " that noble, excellent and exceeding wise Cat . . . who owed his honours to the liberality and gratitude of the celebrated nobleman the Lord Marquis of Carabas " ; and indeed she resembles her ancestor as much in " Genius and Discretion " as she excels him in Morals. She is one that might have sat on Dr. Johnson's knee ; her remarks upon Rousseau would have delighted him. Describing the Countess of Dashley, her little mistress's mother, she says that this lady " had been advised by a French gentleman, one Mr. Rousseau, to suffer her children to remain foolish till seven or eight years of age, when, he said, they would grow wise of their own accord ", a plan " so easy and delightful " that she immediately adopted it.

Felissa's satire has the prettiest effect of innocence. One moment she is all kittenish mischief, the next, lost in wonder at the lady of fashion who spares half a moment on the way to her carriage to peep in at her little girl.

" For my part," declares the Kitten, " my eyes were so dazzled by her dress and her diamonds, and so alarmed by some feathers that grew out of her head, in a manner which I had never witnessed before, but in my old master's cockatoo at the Castle (and she never wore hers so high), that it was some minutes before I could recover myself."

The episode of a mock-christening, which recalls the *Juvenile Tatler*, serves to change the scene. Felissa, provoked to scratch, is sent down in disgrace to a country Rectory, where she enjoys a quiet interval; but before long, the Bad Nephew gets the better of the Good Midshipman, and the kitten runs away.

She now seeks a refuge in the house of " the most charitable woman living ", where, taking up her old part of unconscious critic, she discovers that charity may be a mere cloak for display; and coming thence to another house, ventures into the library of a Man of Sentiment whose portrait would have pleased Rousseau's enemies.

" I crept behind a huge folio to recover my fright and, as usual, set about rendering my person neat and attractive, in expectation of soon becoming visible. My new master, it was evident, could never have been instructed on this subject; for as I peeped at him from behind my folio, I thought that he was the dirtiest and most disagreeable man I had ever seen in my life; and wished from my heart, that my nice clean father and mother had had the education of him. He was short and thick, and by no means pretty; of an ill complexion, and his face very far from clean; *all his skins*, likewise, were of a bad colour, *both his shirt skin and his outer-skin*, which seemed much out of repair. . . ."

She is irresistible, this Felissa: reassured to find the sentimentalist writing an *Ode to Mercy*; listening " with her ears pricked up, *as if she had been watching for a mouse*," while he reads it to his daughter; puzzled by the extraordinary fact that " the more she appeared distressed, the more pleased her father seemed to be." It is even more unaccountable that a young lady of so much sensibility should turn a starved kitten out of doors. " But kittens are easily puzzled ", and Felissa runs into fresh adventures on her way to a happy ending.

Her fortune is almost too modest for a descendant of Puss in Boots : no more than the blessings of an Establishment and many friends ; but the chief of these is the daughter of an officer " who lost his invaluable life in the memorable battle which deprived our country of the gallant and lamented Nelson."

She, of course, marries the promoted Midshipman, and the Kitten, having attained a certain seniority, and finding little scope for her sly wit, devotes herself to the instruction and amusement of little *Felissae*. If a story could end better, let the Wyse Chylde show how.

Adventures of things, a variation of the same idea, were mostly derived from Charles Johnstone's novel, *Chrysal; or, the Adventures of a Guinea.*[1]

If small coins might be supposed to talk as well as great ones (and moralists saw no reason against it), a silver Threepence,[2] the equivalent of a guinea in juvenile commerce, could relate transactions at the Village Shop or at the corner of St. Paul's Churchyard which, if less thrilling than the Guinea's, were more creditable to those concerned.

Other subjects of these stories had a greater fascination for unworldly youth.   These were things that a child would play with or carry about : a Doll, a Pegtop or a Pincushion, which, from their intimate association with the family, were in a position to discuss its affairs.

" S. S." designed her *Adventures of a Pincushion*[3] " chiefly for the use of young ladies," little thinking that

[1] *Chrysal ; or, the Adventures of a Guinea.* By Charles Johnstone (1760).

[2] *The Adventures of a Silver Threepence,* " containing much Amusement and many Characters with which young Gentlemen and Ladies ought to be acquainted ".   Adorned with cuts. Burslem, J. Tregortha, n.d. (Dutch flowered bds.) For other " adventures " of things, see Appendix A. VI.

[3] *The Adventures of a Pincushion,* " Designed chiefly for the Use of Young Ladies ".   By S. S.   Price 6d., Marshall's list, *c.* 1788.

old ones would turn back with delight to these records of domestic life in their great-grandmothers' time.

It seems that the proper place for a pincushion (that essentially feminine possession) was the pocket ; but there were occasions, making for adventure, when it was put into a workbag by mistake, or " lent to Miss Meekly to fasten her Bib ", and then it was sure to be carried off in another pocket to another house.

One effect of the book, unforeseen by its gentle author, was doubtless to increase the number of lost pincushions ; for never, until it was published, had little Misses suspected what secret critics and inveterate gossips they carried about with them, disguised in harmless taffetas.

Rarely indeed is this watchful companion at a loss for information, but once (when S. S. decides to skip a scene) it remarks :

" The ladies now retired to dinner, but I am ignorant of what passed there, as I was left upon a piece of embroidery."

As for the woodcuts, they may well be John Bewick's ; they follow each turn of the author's quiet humour. Any little Miss could tell at a glance that Martha was personating the Music Master and Charlotte teaching the rest to dance. These pictures show everything but the colours, and for that matter, nobody shrank from painting the Green Parlour, when the pincushion declared that " the furniture was all of that colour ". Bewick Collectors have never understood the fatal attraction of " plain " cuts.

" S. S.", justifying her simple narrative in a preface (and thinking, perhaps, of *Chrysal*), admits that " the pointed satire of ridicule might have added zest to her story ", but thinks it unfit for children.

" To exhibit their superiors in a ridiculous view is not the proper method to engage the youthful mind to respect.

10

To represent their equals as objects of contemptuous mirth is by no means favourable to the interest of good nature. And to treat the characters of their inferiors with levity, the author thought, was inconsistent with the sacred rights of humanity."

The criticism is a thought too serious. Ridicule is not always a bad method of dealing with children's faults ; " S. S." herself could use it on occasion. Had she forgotten the Wagstaffs' party in *Jemima Placid*, or the delightful mischief of the dressing of Sally Flaunt, in which the Pincushion played a chief part ?

It is really a question of treatment ; a wooden sword is sharp enough for the nursery. If children are simply tickled by incongruities or miss the point altogether, it is because the satirist has an eye on the grown-up part of his audience. But, as " S. S." points out, there is a danger that incidents will be dragged in for satirical ends " without any cause to produce them " ; and, true to her own simple canon of art, she decides " to make them arise naturally from the subject ", though it increase the difficulties of her task.

The Preface shows a concern for form which is rare in these modest writers ; and the method justifies itself.

It is extraordinary that so much food for profit and enjoyment could be stored in the shelves of old-fashioned houses.

CHAPTER VII

SOME GREAT WRITERS OF LITTLE BOOKS

The fallacy of Disguise—Qualities of the " great " writers—
Mrs. Barbauld's literary lessons : *Hymns in Prose*—*Evenings at
Home*—A new vein of romance—Charles Lamb's attack on the
Schoolroom: Science and Poetry—The *Tales from Shakespeare*—
"Lilliputian " attitude of the Lambs—*The Adventures of Ulysses*—
Mrs. Leicester's School—The Taylors of Ongar: Imagination and
spiritual life—Method of work—*The Contributions of Q. Q.*—" The
Life of a Looking Glass "—Mrs. Sherwood : the struggle between
imagination and dogma—*The Infant's Progress*—*The History of the
Fairchild Family.*

DISGUISE is of little advantage to a writer, least of
all to a writer of children's books.   For although
he has many invisible cloaks to choose from,
Sharp-Eyes and Fine-Ear are hot upon his track.   They
recognise the pedant under his " Mask of Amusement ", they
judge the Moralist by the standard of his own Bad Boy, and
are no more impressed by the Perfect Parent or Tutor than
birds by a scarecrow, when once they have found out that
it is not alive.

A writer may be just as sincere in acknowledging the
reality of wonders as in finding matter of interest in every-
day things, if he express his own point of view ; but the
maker of puppets or bogeys has given up his personality
and disguised his voice.   He may be forgiven if he can
reveal himself at odd moments by individual gestures, as
the whimsical editor of a Lilliputian " Gift " would sometimes peep out in his preface ; no single lapse will be remembered against him : the " Children's Friend " atoned for
one little Grandison by many lifelike portraits.

But the great writers were those that lived most fully
in their stories.   It was no more essential that they should

write nothing else but children's books than that a mother should never go outside her nursery ; for as every man (unless he be a pedant or a monster) has something of the child in him, so every child likes to enter into the talk and business of men. There never was a good child's book that a grown-up person could not enjoy ; and the habit of " talking-down " to children, whether in books or in life, is more fatal to understanding and friendship than the abstract reasoning of the Lilliputians. When Johnson praised Dr. Watts for his condescension in writing children's verses, he did him an injustice, for no man could have taken a little task more seriously. As to Mrs. Barbauld,[1] had she deserved half the abuse of her critics, she never would have found favour in so many nurseries.

De Quincey, who was evidently well-disposed towards the " Queen of all the Blue-stockings " (in spite of her misguided preference for Sinbad) says that she " occupied the place from about 1780 to 1805 which from 1805 to 1835 was occupied by Miss Edgeworth." At any rate she was a pioneer in the art of writing for children, and Miss Edgeworth had a genuine admiration for her work.

But although there was a certain likeness in the aims and ideas of these two, each had her own qualities, which were the outcome of essential differences in character.

Mrs. Barbauld had grown up among the boys of her father's school, and in her youth was as active and mischievous as a boy. There is a story told of how she escaped an importunate suitor by climbing an apple-tree in the garden and dropping over the wall into a lane. Miss Edgeworth, in the same situation, would have walked out by the gate.

It is true that none of Mrs. Barbauld's stories show this

[1] Anna Laetitia Aikin (afterwards Mrs. B.). See the Memoir by A. L. Le Breton, 1874. Her sister Lucy was the author of *Juvenile Correspondence* and other children's books.

spirit of mischief : she was playful only in light verse or talk or letters ; but she made her personality felt in a romantic attitude to life and Nature, which, although it did not much affect her choice of subjects, made her style unusually free and moving.

She had no children of her own, but adopted a nephew, " little Charles ", for whom she wrote most of her stories ; and at Palgrave, where she and her husband had a school, she was the mother, tutor and playfellow of the boys.

The tutor, indeed, comes out in all her stories ; the playfellow and the mother are not always there. Yet she was dominated neither by facts nor theories. A deep sense of spiritual truth underlay her teaching, and her feeling for the poetry of Nature was the nearest approach to a Renaissance of Wonder in children's books.

It may be doubted whether the famous *Hymns in Prose* [1] ever appealed to children as it did to their parents. Mrs. Barbauld entirely disagreed with Rousseau's principle that there should be no religious teaching in early life, and that a young child cannot appreciate natural beauties ; but she also rejected Paley's crude idea of the Creator as a sort of Divine Mechanic,[2] which some writers preferred to the neutral deism of Rousseau.

She held that children's thoughts should be led from the beauty of the flower to the wonder of creation.

" A child ", she says, " to feel the full force of the idea of God, ought never to remember when he had no such idea." It must come early, with no insistence upon dogma, in association with " all that a child sees, all that he hears, all *that affects his mind with wonder or delight.*"

" Wonder " was a word unknown to educational theorists, who believed that everything could be discovered or

[1] *Hymns in Prose for Children,* 1781. This was preceded by Mrs. B.'s *Lessons for Children,* a first reading-book. (1780).

[2] *Harry Beaufoy ; or, The Pupil of Nature,* by Maria Hack (1821), was written to illustrate Paley's doctrine.

explained. It is her use of those words " wonder " and " delight " which sets Mrs. Barbauld apart from other writers of little books, for it shows something like the spirit of romantic poetry.

The revealing power of the poet was never hers. She feels, but cannot show a child as many wonders as he could find for himself in the nearest hedgerow. The *Hymns* are a kind of compromise between " Emblems " and pictures of Nature. There are no far-fetched analogies : the parable of of the Chrysalis anticipates Mrs. Gatty; [1] and the language, though rhythmic, is free from the conventional phrases which spoil some of Mrs. Barbauld's " prose-poetry."

Any mother might use the same images to give her child a first idea of the love of God :

" As the mother moveth about the house with her fingers on her lips, and stilleth every little noise that her infant be not disturbed ; as she draweth the curtains around its bed and shutteth out the light from its tender eyes ; so God draweth the curtains of darkness around us, so He maketh all things to be hushed and still that His large family may sleep in peace."

But it was the Tutor in Mrs. Barbauld that made her choose prose ; for although she was a facile verse-writer, she was better acquainted with Latin hexameters than with ballads, and doubted whether children should be allowed to read verse " before they could judge of its merit ".

Her best work is certainly in *Evenings at Home* [2], the popular miscellany which she and her brother, Dr. Aikin, brought out in parts between 1792 and 1796.

" Sneyd is delighted with the four volumes of *Evenings at Home* ", wrote Miss Edgeworth in 1796, " and has pitched

[1] Mrs. G., the mother of Mrs. Ewing, published her *Parables from Nature* between 1855 and 1871.

[2] Published in six volumes (1792–1796) and frequently reprinted during the nineteenth century.

upon the best stories—' Perseverance against Fortune,'
' The Price of a Victory ', ' Capriole ' ".

It would take an Edgeworth boy to amuse himself with
" The Price of a Victory ", a logical exposition which robs
soldiering of its romance ; or with " Capriole ", the tale
of a little girl and her pet goat ; but " Perseverance against
Fortune " fills a whole " Evening " with adventures that
most boys would read.   The hero is sold as a slave, pressed
into the Navy and suffers many other hardships before he
succeeds as a farmer.   Yet he is a mere type of the persever-
ing man.   The story amounts to little more than a clear
statement of what happened, with pictures of what was
there.   It was the matter of these tales that chiefly interested Miss Edgeworth.   She approved of arguments
against the cruelties of war, she wept with the little girl
over her lost pet, she heartily admired the good farmer for
his patient industry and liked to picture his fields, fenced off
from the " wild common ", his " orchards of fine young
fruit trees ", his hives and his garden.

Sneyd Edgeworth had had a " practical education " and
kept the family traditions.   Another boy, perhaps, would
have chosen " Travellers' Wonders," though the traveller
confessed that he never met with Lilliputians, nor saw the
black loadstone mountains nor the valley of diamonds ;
or, if these " voyages " were too tame, there were " The
Transmigrations of Indur ", adventures of a man, an
antelope, a dormouse, a whale,—centred in one person by
the mystery of transmigration.

Mrs. Barbauld wrote without apology of " the time when
Fairies and Genii possessed the powers which they have now
lost ".   Nobody reading " Indur " would suspect her of a
design to teach Natural History ; but she never forgot her
profession and there are more lessons than stories in her
books.

The average boy would submit to a talk about Earth and

Sun, or Metals, or the manufacture of Paper, rather than read " Order and Disorder, a *Fairy Tale* ", and doubtless, in those days, boys were less impatient of Instruction ; but a lesson never can be a story. A hundred stories could be written on Stevenson's text :

> "The world is so full of a number of things.
> I'm sure we should all be as happy as kings " ;

but the authors of *Evenings at Home* chose instead the encyclopædic ideal of " Eyes and no Eyes ", and produced a series of object lessons. What was worse, Mrs. Barbauld, in her anxiety to be clear, made the fatal mistake of " talking down ".

Charles Lamb, writing to Coleridge in 1802, bitterly resents her popularity : " Goody Two Shoes " he says, " is almost out of print. Mrs. Barbauld's stuff has banished all the old classics of the nursery, and the shopman at Newbery's hardly deigned to reach them off an old exploded corner of the shelf when Mary asked for them. Mrs. Barbauld's and Mrs. Trimmer's nonsense lay in piles about. Knowledge, insignificant and vapid as Mrs. Barbauld's books convey, it seems must come to a child in the shape of knowledge ; and his empty noddle must be turned with conceit of his own powers when he has learnt that a horse is an animal, and Billy is better than a horse, and such like, instead of *that beautiful interest in wild tales*, which made the child a man, while all the time he suspected himself to be no bigger than a child. Science has succeeded to poetry no less in the little walks of children than with men. Is there no possibility of averting this sore evil ? Think what you would have been now, if instead of being fed with tales and old wives' fables in childhood, you had been crammed with Geography and Natural History ! "

Lamb is so clear upon the main issue that he cannot be

just to the "instructive" children's book. He loved the tales of his own childhood, with their "flowery and gilt" and all their delightful oddities.

For that, and because he understood the gentle humour of the "Lilliputians", he forgot whole pages of "instruction" in *Goody Two Shoes*, and placed it on a level with the "wild tales" of romance and adventure.

Had Mary and he read *Fabulous Histories* together, or "The Transmigrations of Indur", he might have allowed some "old exploded corner of a shelf" to the schoolroom authors; at any rate he would not have written:

"Hang them! I mean the cursed Barbauld crew, those blights and blasts of all that is human in man and child!"

Science had succeeded to poetry. "The little walks of children" ran through Botanical Gardens; but there is no doubt at all that children, those amphibious breathers of romance and realism, enjoyed it.

Lamb's quarrel with the Schoolroom was something of a paradox. He took the side of the Romantics against the Scientists; and yet wrote children's books at the suggestion of the arch-theorist Godwin, who, as his publisher, naturally had some influence upon his choice. It was doubtless through Godwin that, instead of following the traditions he admired, he began by "adapting" greater works, and went on to write about children from a grown-up point of view.

The greater number of the *Tales from Shakespear*[1] are Mary's; but she and Charles lived and wrote in such accord, that there is no marked difference in the style. His, of course, are freer and more graceful.

"I have done Othello and Macbeth," he writes to Manning (May 10th, 1806), "and mean to do all the tragedies. I think it will be popular among the little people, besides money. It's to bring in sixty guineas."

[1] Written 1805–1806. Published by M. J. Godwin, at the Juvenile Library, Skinner Street, 1807. 2nd Edition, 1809.

Now it is one thing to turn a child loose in an old library,
—he will forage for himself and will seldom choose any
but wholesome fare. It is quite another to provide him
with such stories as "Measure for Measure", "Othello"
and "Cymbeline"; to simplify the philosophy of *Hamlet*
and weaken the grim magnificence of *Lear*.

The raw material of the plays would not attract many
children, and those who were ready for Lamb's *Tales* might
have gone to Shakespeare himself.

It is clear, then, that the Lambs were Lilliputian in
their attitude to children. Yet they were wise in their
generation; for in 1805 (when they began to write the
Tales) a boy of twelve was playing Romeo, Hamlet and
Macbeth to crowded houses at Covent Garden and Drury
Lane.[1]

The "little people" of the day were incredibly mature.
To know them, in the delicate studies of Charles and Mary
Lamb, is to find the limits of Rousseau's influence. For in
spite of the pioneer work of Mr. Day, and the activities of
the whole "Barbauld crew", these were Lilliputians, the
children of Lilliputians. Lamb's *Tales* must have been
infinitely more diverting than most of the books they read;
and if some, more childlike than the rest, flinched at the
tragedies, they could turn to the magician Prospero, the
fairies of *A Midsummer Night's Dream*, or the trial between
the Merchant and the Jew.

After all, the Lambs understood the vital qualities of
the stuff they used. Who would not choose these tales
rather than "The Price of a Victory"? They are not
lessons, but literature, and that is why children are still
reading them.

Lamb's next venture was surer.

[1] William Betty, "the celebrated Young Roscius", appeared in
Belfast, Dublin and London, between 1803 and 1805. A "Bio-
graphical Sketch" of him, by G. D. Harley, appeared in 1804.

" Did you ever read my Adventures of Ulysses,[1] founded on Chapman's old translation of it ? " he asks in a letter to Barton, " for children or men. Chapman is divine, and my abridgment has not quite emptied him of his divinity."

A prose version of Homer, if he had gone straight to the Greek, would have been still better ; there was no good reason for turning Chapman into prose, although Lamb could do it gently.

But Mrs. Barbauld's " nonsense " fades into insignificance beside the matter of this book, and her remarks about "wonder and delight " have not half the meaning of Lamb's phrase " *for children or men.*"

These were " adventures " that had been told in the childhood of the Greek people. Lamb knew they were a natural food for children, trusted his instinct and defied his publisher.

In the matter of catering for children, Godwin was constrained on the one side by his theories, on the other by the parents who bought the books.

Not every parent professed his hard and cold philosophy, but they were mostly concerned for morals, and if any lacked interest in the more serious problems of education, they were the more likely to be caught by some prevailing pose of " Sensibility ". It did not follow, if they allowed their children to read " Othello ", that they would approve of the primitive survivals in Homer ; nor did these in the least agree with Godwin's exalted theories of the uncivilised mind. He would have had Lamb soften his account of the Cyclops devouring his victims, and the putting out of the monster's eye, which Lamb called " lively images of shocking things ". This is the point where Art and Theory must part company.

[1] Published by M. J. Godwin, at the Juvenile Library, Skinner Street, 1808. Mentioned in the European Magazine for November, 1808. See Appendix A. VII.

" If you want a book which is not occasionally to shock ",
wrote Lamb, " you should not have thought of a tale
which was so full of anthropophagi and wonders. I
cannot alter these things without enervating the book,
and I will not alter them if the penalty should be that you
and all the London Booksellers should refuse it."

Lamb had good reason to trust his sister's judgment
where children were concerned.   Their partnership in the
making of little books was one-sided, and in a letter to
Barton, Charles confessed that he wrote only three of the
stories in *Mrs. Leicester's School* : [1] " I wrote only the
Witch Aunt, the First Going to Church and the final story
about a little Indian girl in a ship ".   But there are many
subtle touches in the rest which suggest his hand, and if
one may hazard a guess at their manner of working, Mary
wrote little that they did not first discuss together, and
revised much with his help.   The framework of the book
is all that connects it with Miss Fielding's *Governess* ;
there is nothing of her bright objective treatment.

This, indeed, is not a child's book at all, but a book of
child-thought and experience, full of insight and tenderness,
revealing everywhere the pathos of childhood.

Charles and Mary lived their childish days over again
in these stories.   They forgot that as children they had
not seen things in the same light.   They forgot (those days
had been short for them) that children, however precocious,
are not concerned with their own thought-process, but with
life and movement and adventure.   And so their stories
are really essays about children : essays that let the grown-
up reader into some of the little people's secrets.   If it
were possible for children to see themselves with the eyes
of men and women, then *Mrs. Leicester's School* might be

[1] *Mrs. Leicester's School ; or, the History of Several Young Ladies,
Related by Themselves.*
   Written 1808.   Published 1809.   2nd edition, 1809.   Mentioned
in the *Critical Review* for December, 1808.   See Appendix A. VII.

to them what the *Essays of Elia* are to their parents. As it is, no child could appreciate the irony of innocence which runs through the book like a refrain.

A suggestion of Wordsworth, in the story of " Elizabeth Villiers ", can hardly be accidental. The little girl has learnt to read from her mother's epitaph, and her sailor uncle, just home from sea, finds her in the churchyard rehearsing her lesson.

" ' Who has taught you to spell so prettily, my little maid ? ' . . . ' Mamma,' I replied ; for I had an idea that the words on the tombstone were somehow a part of mamma, and that she had taught me ." The uncle, who knows nothing of his sister's death, asks for her and turns in the direction of the house. " You do not know the way, I will show you," says the child, and she leads him to the grave.

There is a similar pathos, not less beyond the insight of most children, in Elinor Forester's account of her father's wedding-day :

" When I was dressed in my new frock, I wished poor Mamma was alive to see how fine I was on Papa's wedding-day, and I ran to my favourite station at her bedroom-door."

But there is another motif in the book which, although its chief appeal is to grown-up sympathies, might satisfy a child's love of contrast and surprise : the strangeness of familiar things ; the romance of the unromantic.

Emily Barton is a little Cinderella, carried off by her father (whom she has forgotten) from the house of relations who have neglected her. A postchaise takes the place of the pumpkin-coach, a new coat and bonnet do humble duty for a ball-dress.

Thus equipped, she jumps into the chaise " *as warm and lively as a little bird* ". Mary Lamb has a store of such tender phrases.

The home that most children take as a matter of course, is a palace of delight to this little girl.   Tea is a feast.

" Whenever I happen to like my tea very much, I always think of the delicious cup of tea Mamma gave us after our journey."

The father and mother, loved by other children without thought, are a King and Queen of romance :

" Mamma, to my fancy, looked very handsome.   She was very nicely dressed, quite like a fine lady.   I held up my head and felt very proud that I had such a papa and mamma."

A ride through the London streets becomes a royal progress.   In her exile, the child has had no toys : " the playthings were all the property of one or other of my cousins ".   Now she appreciates the joy of ownership. Not toys alone, but little books are purchased, and by a mischievous turn, Mr. Newbery's old device is turned against his successors : " Shall we order the coachman to the corner of St. Paul's Churchyard, or shall we go to the Juvenile Library in Skinner Street ? "

This is far removed from the dramatic realism of the Edgeworth School.   It is the difference between the facts and the poetry of everyday life.

There is more poetry (but less that a child would take) in Charles Lamb's story of the little four-years-old girl in Lincolnshire and her " first going to church ".

The house is too far from a village for the family to attend church, until they are able to set up " a sort of carriage ". But the child is attracted by " the fine music " from the bells of St. Mary's, which they sometimes hear in the air. " I had somehow conceived that the noise which I heard was occasioned by birds up in the air, or that it was made by the angels, whom (so ignorant I was till that time) I had always considered to be *a sort of bird.*"

The bells calling Susan to church give the story a

spiritualised Whittington touch. The ride to church and
the child's first impressions are wonderfully described.

" I was wound up to the highest pitch of delight at having
visibly presented to me the spot from which had proceeded
that unknown friendly music : and when it began to peal,
just as we approached the village, it seemed to speak *Susan
is come*, as plainly as it used to invite me *to come*, when I
heard it over the moor."

Here again, things that most children disregard, from
thoughtless familiarity, appear strange and delightful to
the lonely child. " All was new and surprising to me on
that day ; the long windows with little panes, the pillars,
the pews made of oak, the little hassocks for the people to
kneel on, the form of the pulpit with the sounding board
over it, gracefully carved in flower work."

Akin to this is the theme of changed fortune : privileges
only recognised when lost. It is the moral (never pointed
in these tales) of " Charlotte Wilmot " and " The Changeling ". The child of the ruined merchant describes her
first night in the house of his poor clerk. The moon, often
watched in happier days, is now a symbol of misfortune :

" There was only one window in the room, a small case-
ment, through which the bright moon shone, and it seemed
to me the most melancholy sight I ever beheld."

Poetry, not fact, is again the chief element in the story
of the " little Indian girl in a ship ". Her gentle, imaginative sailor-nurse gives her no Natural History or Geography.
He turns her thoughts to " the dolphins and porpoises
that came before a storm, and all the colours which the sea
changed to " ; she is never troubled about the genus of the
one or the causes of the other. If Lamb had set down this
sailor's tales, as no doubt he would have told them to a
child, he could have made a real children's book, of " the
sea monsters that lay hid at the bottom, and were seldom
seen by man ; and what a glorious sight it would be, if our

eyes could be sharpened to behold all the inhabitants of the sea at once swimming in the great deeps, as plain as we see the gold and silver fish in a bowl of glass ".

In the same way a visit to the country is not made the subject of lessons on rural occupations or botany. As a matter of fact, Grandmamma's orchard is a fairy place where pear-trees and cherry-trees blossom together, and bluebells come out with daffodils. The profusion of these flowers and the sound of their names might attract a child that yet would miss the best touches :

" Sarah was much wiser than me, and *she taught me which to prefer*. . . . I was very careful to love best the flowers which Sarah praised most, yet sometimes, I confess, I have even picked a daisy, though I knew it was the very worst flower, because it reminded me of London and the Drapers' Garden ! "

Here Mary might have aimed a gentle shaft at the hated instructive writers, who taught children " which to prefer " ; but there is no double intention in Sarah.

Only one story, " The Changeling ", has really dramatic moments. There is a miniature *Hamlet* scene in this, a " little interlude " played by children, which causes the wicked nurse to betray herself. A child would enjoy it better than the *Tales from Shakespear*. But the little girl who frightens herself into believing that her aunt is a witch is best understood by readers of " Witches and Other Night-Fears " ; little Margaret, reading herself into Mahometism and a fever would be less interesting to small folk than the book, *Mahometism Explained*, which she found in the old library, " as entertaining as a fairy-tale ". The humour is too subtle for children, they would enjoy the picture of Harlow Fair better than that quaint account of the grave physician puzzled over an extraordinary case, " he never having attended a little Mahometan before ".

And so it is with the pictures of child-life. The grown-up reader has the best memory for Emily Barton (very young indeed) at her first play. Emily herself remembered that it was *The Mourning Bride* ; but she was so far confused between this " very moving Tragedy " and " the most diverting Pantomime " which followed it, that she made a strange blunder the next day.

" I told Papa that Almeria was married to Harlequin at last, but I assure you I meant to say Columbine, for I knew very well that Almeria was married to Alphonso ; for she said she was in the first scene."

At the back of the grown-up mind, besides, there are pictures to help in the reading. Charles and Mary, instead of Emily Barton, reading the tomb-stones, looking up at the great iron figures of St. Dunstan's Church,[1] or talking over their first visit to Mackery End (too long ago for Charles to remember) ; Mary at Blakesmoor with the old lady who had " no other chronology to reckon by than in the recollection of what carpet, what sofa cover, what set of chairs were in the frame at that time ". Or John Lamb, the father, taking a walk to the Lincolnshire village, " just to see how *goodness thrived.*[2]

Ann and Jane Taylor cherished ideals clearer and much simpler than the Lambs. They had no tragedy to darken their youth ; the struggle with poverty (very real at first) was lightened by the cheerful co-operation of a whole family. They were all engaged upon the father's craft of engraving ; they all (father, brothers, sisters, even the mother) wrote.[3] They were " directed " (a phrase of their own) by an unquestioning religious faith which simplified and solved all the problems of life. The narrowing

[1] See the note in " Emily Barton ", Vol. III of the *Works of Charles and Mary Lamb*, edited by Mr. E. V. Lucas.

[2] See Appendix A. VII.

[3] See *The Family Pen*, edited by Isaac Taylor, Jun., 1867. See further, Appendix A. VII.

influence of the village was counteracted by breadth of intellect and by individual genius. There was, of course, nothing to supply the generous education of London life, or the exquisite literary discernment of the Lambs ; but Jane Taylor showed, even in her books for children, a power of enjoyment and a sense of humour that is sometimes associated with intensely serious beliefs. She was untouched by popular philosophy, and adhered to the literary traditions of the school of Pope ; but the world of the spirit was more real to her than earth itself ; her work has rare qualities of spiritual insight and imagination.

This does not apply, of course, to the simple rhymes which were the sisters' first literary venture. Mary Lamb could make waistcoats while she was " plotting new work to succeed the Tales ". The intricate process of engraving demanded more attention. They were not free till eight o'clock, and had household duties besides ; but, as Ann says, "a flying thought could be caught even in the midst of work, or a fancy ' pinioned ' to a piece of waste paper."

Some of the rhymes (there is more to be said of them) were written too easily or too hastily to be of much account, but there are points in favour of a method that makes writing a relaxation, and allows no time for second thoughts.

The *Original Poems*[1] have a spontaneity and freshness that take a small child at once. The sisters never lost the secret of writing for children, because they could always think with them. Ann, the eldest, had mothered the family, and afterwards brought up a family of her own ; yet she wrote at *eighty* : " The feeling of being a grown woman, to say nothing of an *old* woman, does not come naturally to me ".

Many writers (especially moralists) try to hold a child's

[1] See below, Chapter IX.

attention beyond its power. Jane Taylor in this, as in other matters, understands her audience.

" I try to conjure up some child into my presence, address her suitably, as well as I am able, and when I begin to flag, I say to her, ' *There, love, now you may go.*' "

Jane was the genius of the family. " Dear Jane had no need to borrow, what I could ill afford to lose," said the gentle Ann, of some good thing which had been attributed to her brilliant sister.

The habit of " castle-building " caused Jane many heart-searchings. She was as stern with herself as Bunyan ; she magnified all her little failings (or supposed failings) into sins. " I know I have sometimes lived so much in a *castle* as almost to forget that I lived in a *house,* and while I have been carefully arranging aerial matters *there,* have left all my solid business in disorder *here.*"

It was absurd, of course, to accuse a Taylor of disorder ; but the distrust of imagination was characteristic. She valued imagination only so far as it interpreted spiritual truth. The great difference between Jane Taylor and the realists was that her reality had no connection with materialism. To her, the life of the spirit was the greatest reality. A thing was real or unreal according to its intrinsic worth. Her sharpest satire was poured upon the material benevolence of philosophy, " *the light of Nature-boasting man* ", or the poet who could

> " Pluck a wild Daisy, moralise on that
> And drop a tear for an expiring gnat."

True benevolence, so her creed ran,

> " . . . . . rises energetic to perform
> The hardest task, or face the rudest storm."

Duty and sacrifice are her watchwords. The search for happiness brings only " The lessons taught at Disappointment's knee." Earth is wonderful, but men misuse it, seeking worthless things in their madness ; yet :

> " The soul—perhaps in silence of the night
> Has flashes, transient intervals of light ;
> When things to come without a shade of doubt
> In terrible reality stand out.
>
> .   .   .   .
>
> These are the moments when the mind is sane."

The Essays in Rhyme[1] are for grown-up readers, but they state with perfect clearness the ideals that inspired her work for children.

Under the pseudonym of "Q. Q.", Jane Taylor contributed for six years to the *Youths' Magazine*,[2] and her best pieces (afterwards collected) were " for children or men."

" *The young are new to themselves ; and all that surrounds them is novel.*"

"Q. Q." gives them short moral tales, full of point and humour : really " entertaining " moral tales, and brilliant little character-studies. They read, and begin to know themselves. She introduces them to " Persons of Consequence " (one, " little Betsy Bond, daughter of John Bond, the journeyman Carpenter "). She sets forth a contrast : the old Philosopher, so wise that he is humble, and the Young Lady, just leaving School, who considers herself " not only perfectly accomplished but also thoroughly well-informed " ; or the two brothers, one of whom writes a clever essay on self-denial, while the other practises it. Youth is left to judge between them.

The most arresting of these " Contributions ", " How it strikes a Stranger ", inspired Browning's poem " The Star of my God Rephan." A stranger from another planet,

---

[1] Published June, 1816.

[2] From Feb., 1816, to the end of 1822. Collected as *The Contributions of Q. Q. to a Periodical Work* ", with some pieces not before published. By the late Jane Taylor. 2 vols. London. B. J. Holdsworth, St. Paul's Churchyard, 1824.

finding himself upon Earth, is filled with interest and wonder at what he sees. He enters readily into the pleasures of the new life, and remains thoughtlessly happy till he is faced with the unknown fact of death.

They refer him to the priests for an explanation. " How ! " he replies, " then I cannot have understood you ; do the priests only die ? Are not you to die also ? " When he understands, he regards death as a privilege and refuses to do anything " inconsistent with his *real interests.*" The Adventure is described with a wonderful force of imagination ; but the lesson strikes upon youthful ears like the voice in *Everyman* :

> " Everyman, stand still. Whither art thou going,
>   Thus gaily ? "

Some, not yet ripe for this encounter, would turn for comfort to the bright and imaginative " Life of a Looking Glass," and revive their more childish interest in the " adventures of things ".

The Glass, " being naturally of a reflecting cast," would catch, but not hold the restless attention of very little persons. It was for those past the stage of actual belief in talking things, who came back to it with a new perception of imaginative correspondences.

The tranquil passage of the story (so perfectly adapted to the " speaker ") is broken now and then by a flash of wit. There is nothing extraordinary about the incidents : that the writer admits ; but she never fails " to give the charm of novelty to things of everyday ", and chooses her pictures not so much for moral ends as because they would be likely to persist among the " reflections " of a looking-glass.

First, the large spider in the carver and gilder's workshop " which, after a vast deal of scampering about, began very deliberately to weave a curious web " all over the face of the glass, affording it " great amusement." There is something in the responsive brightness of the thing that gives immediate sanction to the idea of its being *amused*. Then, the lively apprentice who gave it " a very significant look ", which it took at the time for a compliment to itself. And then a succession of images in quick movement reflected from a London Street. " The good-looking people always seemed the best pleased with me ", it remarks, with a sly gleam, " which I attributed to their superior discernment."

After this, the scene changes to one of almost lifeless calm ; the " best parlour of a country house, whose Master and Mistress see no company except at Fair time and Christmas Day."

" Perhaps I should have experienced some dismay ", remarks the glass, " if I could have known that I was destined to spent *fifty years* in that spot."

The younger the reader, the more endless such an interval would seem ; yet if any had patience to follow the tale at its own pace, they might enjoy the fashion of that parlour : the old chairs and tables, the Dutch tiles with stories in them, that surrounded the grate, and the pattern of the paper hangings " which consisted alternately of a parrot, a poppy and a shepherdess—a parrot, a poppy and a shepherdess ". The repeated phrase suggests the length of days. " The room being so little used, the window-shutters were rarely opened ; but there were three holes cut in each, in the shape of a heart, through which, day after day and year after year, I used to watch the long dim dusty sunbeams streaming across the dark parlour."

Youth cannot wait for description, but these words translate themselves into light and shade.

Here is the mistress of that parlour, ready dressed for church on a Sunday morning, trotting in upon her high-heeled shoes, unfolding a leaf of the shutters and standing straight before the looking-glass. She turns half round to the right and left to see if the corner of her well-starched kerchief is pinned exactly in the middle. The glass has turned portrait painter. "I think I can see her now", it says, "in her favourite dove-coloured lustring (which she wore every Sunday in every Summer for seven years at the least) and her long full ruffles and worked apron". Then follows the master, who, though his visit was somewhat shorter, never failed to come and settle his Sunday wig before the glass.

Thus half a century goes by, with the imperceptible movement from youth to age. The glass is reset in a gilt frame to suit the fashion of new times ; once more it reflects young faces and vibrates with the laughter of youth.

Jane Taylor could be didactic on principle, but she was a true artist and knew that virtue is best recommended by its visible effects.

The looking-glass, "incapable of misrepresentation," cannot help showing errors and vanities ; but having acquired "considerable skill in physiognomy", discovers more than the mere outside. Its last study is almost a " Character " :

" There was, of course, in a few years, some little alteration, but although the bloom of youth began to fade, there was nothing less of sweetness, cheerfulness and contentment in her expression. She retained the same placid smile, the same unclouded brow, the same mildness in her eye (though it was somewhat less sparkling) as when it first beamed upon me ten years before."

This is the Princess of the Moral Tale. She gives a last glance at the looking-glass in her bridal dress, and leaves it to its memories.

" Sometimes my dear mistress's favourite cat will steal in as though in quest of her ; leap up upon the table and sweep her long tail across my face ; then, catching a glimpse of me, jump down again and run out as though she was frightened."

There is no " moral ", only this epilogue in dumb-show to repeat the theme of change.

The humour of the looking-glass has an undersense of pathos ; but this is not the pathos of *Mrs. Leicester's School*. It would touch a child directly, like a picture without words.

Books had no more to do with Jane Taylor's love of Nature than with her understanding of her fellow creatures. She looked out of a diamond-paned window upon quiet Essex fields and " a tract of sky ".[1] The sky, always the most beautiful thing in a flat country, was to her more productive than the soil of the realists. But she loved gardens too, and caught the individuality of flowers.   Ann's *Wedding Among the Flowers*[2] is less amusing than Jane's " fable " of the envious weed that shoots up till it overtops the fence, and then, provoked by the beauty of the flowers in the next garden, twists the chief beauty of each into a defect :

> " Well, 'tis enough to make one chilly
> To see that pale consumptive lily
> Among these painted folks.
> Miss Tulip, too, looks wondrous odd,
> She's gaping like a dying cod ;
> What a queer stick is Golden-Rod !
> And how the violet pokes ! "

Flowers are *persons* to Jane Taylor. She loves them as friends : " the good, gay and well-dressed company which a little flower garden displays ".

" Science has succeeded to poetry," said Lamb.   Jane Taylor did not think them incompatible.   Her " old retired gentleman " could look at his garden from two points of view :

[1] From a letter of J. T.'s, describing her room.
[2] *The Wedding Among the Flowers* (verse) by Ann Taylor, 1808.

" a part of the pleasure which now in my old age I
derive from my flowers arises, I am conscious, from the
distant yet vivid remembrance they recall of similar scenes
and pleasures of my childhood.   My paternal garden seems
still to me *like enchanted ground*, and its flowers like the
flowers of Paradise.   I shall never see the like again, vain
as I am of my gardening !   Those were *poetry*, these are
botany ! " [1]

Imaginative power in the Taylors illuminated their
religious conceptions.   In Mrs. Sherwood,[2] it struggled
against the formulæ of rigid doctrine.   From six to
thirteen, she learned her lessons standing in the stocks with
an *iron collar* round her neck.   When it was taken off
(seldom, she says, till late in the evening), she would run
for half a mile through the woods, as if trying to overtake
her lost playtime.   It says much for the quick recoveries
of youth that she was a happy child.   Stanford Rectory,
where she spent her " golden age ", was surrounded by
woods and hills that seem to have become a part of her
before the iron collar was imposed.   She built huts and
made garlands with her brother ;   they acted fairy tales
in the woods :   tales of " dragons, enchanters and queens ".
She remembered her mother teaching them to read from " a
book where there was a picture of a white horse feeding by
moonlight ", a print of pure romance.   She remembered the
wonder-tales told on dark winter evenings by " a person
vastly pleasant to children " who came across the park
" in a great bushy wig, a shovel hat, and a cravat tied like
King William's bib ".

And yet, when she began to write books for children,
after some years of married life in India, she put on an iron

[1] See " Spring Flowers ", No. XXX of *The Contributions of Q. Q.*
[2] Martha Mary Butt (afterwards Mrs. Sherwood), 1755–1851.
See *The Life and Times of Mrs. Sherwood*, edited by F. J. Harvey
Darton.   London, 1910.

collar of her own accord, to set forth the dire consequences of Original Sin. When (perhaps late in a chapter) she took it off, her imagination could conjure up no fairies ; but working upon the memories of her own childhood, it brought life into the tale.

Mrs. Sherwood wrote an extraordinary number of children's books ; many were published by Houlston the Quaker as chap-books.[1] The sternest and most uncompromising dogmatism cannot crush the life out of them, nor weaken the vivid pictures they contain. Her first journey across the hills to Lichfield, when she was a child of four, had made a deeper impression on her mind than all her Indian travels. She had fresher memories of the English hills than of " the Indian Caucasus hanging as brilliant clouds on the horizon ". The quiet inland life that is the chief matter of her autobiography[2] is reflected in most of her stories. She is not concerned with any wider interests ; great events pass unnoticed, as they do in some nurseries ; but whenever Mrs. Sherwood remembers her Doctrines, she goes back to the Warnings and Examples of the seventeenth century. There is a grim shadow on her nursery wall, and in the midst of the most innocent employments, her little people shrink and cower. This spectre stood over her when she tampered with a book which children of all ages understand and enjoy. She accepted *The Pilgrim's Progress* as a part of her creed ; her knowledge of it accounts for the fine simplicity of her style. Yet in her *Infant's Progress from the Valley of Destruction to Everlasting Glory*,[3] there is not a giant nor a castle to atone for her bane on " toys " which the strictest philosopher would pass as harmless and instructive. Her poor

[1] See Appendix A. VII.

[2] Reprinted by Mr. Darton in his *Life and Times of Mrs. S.*

The Infant's Progress from the Valley of Destruction to Everlasting Glory. By Mrs. Sherwood, author of *Little Henry and his Bearer*, etc., etc. Houlston, 1821. Composed in India, 1814.

little pilgrim suffers a martyrdom of denial in a juvenile
Vanity Fair :

" Then I saw that certain of these teachers of vanities
came and spread forth their toys before Humble Mind,
to wit, pencils, and paints, maps and drawings, *pagan
poems* and *fabulous histories*, musical instruments of various
kinds, with all the gaudy fripperies of modern learning."

Some of these things had been the delight of Mrs. Sherwood's youth ; but in her passion for dogma, she forgot
the white horse and the fairy tales, and persuaded herself
that an iron collar was the only protection against vanity.

Her adaptation of Sarah Fielding's *Governess*[1] shows the
same Puritan intolerance. The book had been in her own
nursery library, along with *Margery Two-Shoes*, *Robinson
Crusoe* and " two sets of fairy tales."   Yet she expurgated
all but one of the " moral " fairy tales allowed by Mrs.
Teachum, and inserted in their place " such appropriate
relations as seemed more likely to conduce to juvenile
edification."

It is likely (and for her children's sake to be hoped)
that Mrs. Sherwood's practice was kinder and more cheerful than her precepts.   *The Fairchild Family*,[2] the best
known, and the best of her books, is full of interest and
reality ; and in this, the setting is her home and the persons
are her own children.

To enjoy it, a child must skip solid pages of doctrine,
and would do well besides to skip most of the stories read
by the Fairchild Family out of little gilt books which " the
good-natured John " brought them from the Fair.

[1] *The Governess ; or, the Little Female Academy.* " By Mrs.
Sherwood."   See Appendix. A VII.
[2] *The History of the Fairchild Family ; or, the Child's Manual.*
" Being a Collection of Stories calculated to show the Importance
and Effects of a Religious Education ".   By Mrs. Sherwood.
London.   Printed for J. Hatchard and sold by F. Houlston & Son,
Wellington, 1818.

These were chap-books, but of a sort only less forbidding than those the pedlar carried in Puritan days.   John gave the largest to Lucy and the other to Emily.   " ' Here is two pennyworth, and there is three pennyworth,' said he.

' My book,' said Emily, ' is the History of the *Orphan Boy* !¹, and there are a great many pictures in it ; the first is the picture of a funeral.'

' Let me see, let me see ! ' said Henry, ' *oh, how pretty !* ' "

Late editors flinch at the inhumanity of the punishments, and usually omit the gibbet story which, at the outset, throws a horrible shadow on the book.   There has been a quarrel in the nursery ; the children are penitent, they have been forgiven ; but Mr. Fairchild deems it necessary to give them a concrete illustration of the fate of one who has failed to control his passions.   He takes them to " Blackwood " (so far off that little Henry has to be carried) and shows them the body of a murderer hanging from a gibbet. " *The face of the corpse was so shocking that the children could not look upon it* ".

It is to be supposed that children who survived this kind of treatment could be happy, since there was little left to excite their terror.   Henry, when he steals a forbidden apple, is threatened with fire and brimstone and locked up in a dark room.   The very frightfulness of all this would defeat its end, for if a child could live through it, and look up the next morning at an unclouded sky, or take his part in the cheerful concerns of men, the thing would come, in time, to have no meaning for him.   It is clear that this happened with the Fairchild Family.   They act and talk (save when they are made the mouthpieces of older persons) like healthy and ordinary children.   They even dare to be naughty in an ordinary way.   No sooner are Mr. and Mrs.

¹ *The Orphan Boy ; or, a Journey to Bath.* By **Mary Elliott.** See Appendix A. VII.

Fairchild called away from home, than original sin begins to assert itself. This chapter is " *On the Constant Bent of Man's Heart towards Sin* ".

Emily and Lucy play in bed instead of getting up : " Emily made babies of the pillows, and Lucy pulled off the sheets and tied them round her, in imitation of Lady Noble's long-trained gown." There is no encouragement for the dramatic games of children, any more than for dancing, in Mrs. Sherwood's books.

Then Henry announces hot buttered toast for breakfast ; they hurry down " without praying, washing themselves, combing their hair, making their bed, or doing any one thing they ought to have done."

After breakfast they take out their books, but they have eaten so much that they " cannot learn with any pleasure ". A quarrel is checked by Henry's discovery of a little pig in the garden. The three at once give chase. Another " juvenile " *Pilgrim's Progress*, this :

" Now, there was a place where a spring ran across the lane, over which was a narrow bridge, for the use of people walking that way. Now the pig did not stand to look for the bridge, but went splash, splash, through the midst of the water ; and after him went Henry, Lucy and Emily, though they were up to their knees in mud and dirt." Mrs. Sherwood had caught the live clearness of Bunyan's pictures.

A neighbour (one of the unregenerate, whom the children have been forbidden to visit) kindly dries their clothes ; she also regales them with cider, " and as they were never used to drink anything but water, it made them quite tipsy for a little while."

The good-natured John, discovering their condition, calls them " naughty rogues ". He gives them dinner and ties them to their chairs, but afterwards relents and allows them to play in the barn, where he thinks they can do no more mischief. Here they let down a swing which they are only supposed to play with when Papa is present ; Emily falls out of it and narrowly escapes being killed.

At this point Mr. and Mrs. Fairchild quite unexpectedly come home. The children fall upon their knees and fade once more into unreality.

Thus Mrs. Sherwood replaces the iron collar after her bursts of freedom. It is hardly a disguise. It does not change her personality, it simply keeps her rigid.

Even Mrs. Fairchild had enjoyed some interludes ; but that was when she was little and naughty. She actually confessed to her Family that " a little girl employed about the house " had tempted her on one occasion *to climb a cherry-tree.*

Afterwards her aunts talked to her whilst she cried very much. "Think of the shame and disgrace ", said they, " of climbing trees in such low company, after all the care and pains we have taken and the delicate manner in which we have reared you ! "

But she also remembered and quoted the words of that " little girl employed about the house " :

" Oh, Miss, Miss ! I can see from where I am all the town and both the churches, and here is such plenty of cherries ! Do come up ! "

This is a prose foretaste of *The Child's Garden.*

CHAPTER VIII

MISS EDGEWORTH'S TALES FOR CHILDREN

Life at Edgeworthstown—Educational adventures—*Practical Education*—First stories—*The Parent's Assistant*—New elements— " Waste Not, Want Not " : the Geometric plot—" Little plays "— Settings of the tales—Practical interests—Characters—" Little touches "—*Early Lessons*—" The Purple Jar "—*Harry and Lucy*— " Nonsense in season "—*Moral Tales*—Qualities of Miss Edgeworth's tales—" *La triste utilité* "—The Edgeworth fairy —Dr. Johnson as the fairies' champion—Miss Edgeworth and her predecessors—The magic of science and life.

MARIA EDGEWORTH was sixteen years old when her father brought her to his Irish estate of Edgeworthstown.[1] Her childhood had been full of quiet preoccupations, and it argues much for the impersonal methods of Mr. Day that, although he had grounded her in Rousseau's theory, she was in no way dominated by it.

At Edgeworthstown, her ideas were brought into wholesome touch with reality. The life was almost adventurous after those quiet years in Oxfordshire and London. Her father gave her a real share in managing the estate and she was soon acquainted with many sides of Irish character ; but all her affections and interests were centred in the family, and in this lay the secret of her power as a writer of children's books.

Mr. Edgeworth had brought up his eldest boy upon Rousseau's exact plan, a more unfortunate experiment than Mr. Day's ; for this child of Nature would neither teach himself nor learn from others ; but his brothers and sisters gained more than he lost by it : the system

[1] See Helen Zimmern's *Maria Edgeworth*, 1883.

175

was modified for them, and Emile's solitary employments found a place among the cheerful occupations of a big family.

The children were so happy and so busy that Mr. Edgeworth could say in a letter to Dr. Darwin :

" I do not think one tear per month is shed in this house, nor the voice of reproof heard, nor the hand of restraint felt ".

He encouraged Maria to record their educational adventures, and her own translation of *Adèle et Théodore*[1] may have suggested the idea of a book. The two volumes of *Practical Education*, published in 1798, with the names of Richard Lovell and Maria Edgeworth on the title page, mark the beginning of the long partnership which she called " the joy and pride of my life ".

What her books might have been without her father's influence may be conjectured from what they are ; this is truer of the children's books than of the novels. She had no need of theory. Clear intelligence, warm and ready sympathies, carried her straight to the centres of childish thought. A little brother, Henry, had been her especial charge, and from him she learned what might have escaped her in the general business of the family.

She scribbled her first stories on a slate, read them to the children and altered them to suit their taste. Those they liked best were printed in 1796 at Mr. Edgeworth's suggestion,[2] and when the little outside public called for more, fresh stories were produced on the same co-operative plan and published in the six volumes of 1800.

" The stories are printed and bound the same size as

[1] Never published, as Holcroft's translation appeared before it was ready (1785).

[2] *The Parent's Assistant ; or, Stories for Children.* By " M. E." London, Joseph Johnson, St. Paul's Churchyard. 3 vols. 12 mo. published in 2 parts. Announced in the *Monthly Review* for Sept., 1796. See Appendix A. VIII.

Evenings at Home," wrote Miss Edgeworth to her cousin (Feb. 27, 1796), " but I am afraid you will dislike the title ; my father had sent *The Parent's Friend,* but Mr. Johnson has degraded it into *The Parent's Assistant,* which I dislike particularly from association with an old book of Arithmetic called *The Tutor's Assistant."*

There is Geometry, if not Arithmetic, in the book. The pattern is symmetrical : the tales are constructed to fit the morals ; but the Edgeworths recognised the chief faults of didactic books for children, and made the first definite attempt to deal with them.

" To prevent the precepts of morality from tiring the ear and the mind ", says Mr. Edgeworth in the preface, " it was necessary to make the stories in which they are introduced in some measure dramatic ; to keep alive hope and fear and curiosity by some degree of intricacy."

This is the best that can be done where the moral is so explicit ; and the device of intricacy serves to divert attention from a too exact correspondence between cause and effect.

In Miss Edgeworth's clear and well-ordered world the results of choice and action are inevitable ; but her plots (she was the pioneer of plot in children's books) involve a puzzle, and in the solution there is always an element of surprise.

That Bristol merchant in " Waste Not, Want Not,"[1] who invited his two nephews to stay with him, in order to decide which of them he should adopt, bears more than a chance resemblance to Mr. Day. If the two boys had been girls, the story might have been his own ; but in literature, as in life, Mr. Day was prone to digress ; he never could have followed the relentless order of events from the untying of the two parcels by Hal and Benjamin (the

[1] " Waste Not, Want Not ; or, Two Strings to Your Bow." P. A. Vol. III.

Merton and Sandford of this drama) to its logical result. There is a cumulative fatality about this which puts it beyond question.

No sooner has the inconsequent Hal watched the careful untying of Ben's parcel, and cut the whipcord of his own " precipitately in sundry places " than the uncle gives them each a top.

"And now" (a child never could resist the interruption). " And now, *he won't have any string for his top !* "

The improvident one, however, finds a way out by spinning it with his hat-string (the consequence of this is deferred) ; and then, after whipping the banisters aimlessly with the cut string, drops it upon the stairs. Little Patty, his cousin, running downstairs with his pocket-handkerchief (which he is in too desperate a hurry to fetch himself), falls down a whole flight of stairs ; and the assiduous Ben, hunting for her lost shoe, finds it *sticking in a loop of whipcord.*

For a time, the string theme is allowed to drop, but it comes up again as a chief agent of the catastrophe. Hal, on his way to the Archery-meeting stoops to pick up his ball and loses his hat. ("The string, as we may recollect, our wasteful hero had used in spinning his top ".). Running down the hill after it, he falls prostrate in his green and white uniform into a treacherous bed of red mud, and becomes the laughing-stock of his companions.

Last and bitterest of all, he sees his prudent cousin replace a cracked bow-string and win the contest by drawing from his pocket " an excellent piece of whipcord ". Not a reader but echoes, with additions, the unfortunate Hal's exclamation : " *The everlasting whipcord, I declare !* "

This single strand goes in and out with the shuttle-motion of a nursery rhyme :

> *This is the string that Hal cut.*
> *These are the Stairs*

That lay under the String
That Hal cut.
This is the Child
That fell over the Stairs—etc.

With it are interwoven character-incidents that echo the title-motto and harp on the note of Rousseau and Henry Brooke : the choice of the two boys between a warm great-coat and a green and white uniform, which culminates with perfect logic in Ben's loan of the despised coat to cover Hal's spoilt finery ; and the minor choice between queen-cakes and keeping one's halfpence to give to a beggar.

It is the strong point of Miss Edgeworth's contrasts that her bad children are never attractive, and her good ones hardly ever impossible.

Hal is no villain ; but there is no glamour about his naughtiness : he is greedy and boastful as well as im-provident ; a child is not moved to emulate him. The real villains are dishonest or cruel or insolent, never simply thoughtless or self-willed.

But the good children are a positive triumph. Only Miss Edgeworth could make a boy live that untied knots to save string, chose an overcoat instead of a gay uniform and had money to spare for good works. This Ben is as natural as his pleasure-loving cousin.

The moral, for all its insistence, never hides a picture : the house, the Bristol streets and shops, the scene in the Cathedral, where they listen to a robin that has lived there for so many years ; and Ben and his uncle admire the stained-glass windows, but Hal looks bored. These are drawn to the life.

" Cannot one see a uniform and a Cathedral both in one morning ? "

Every other boy in the Edgeworth family was a Ben, and would endorse this catholicity of interest.

It is odd that Miss Edgeworth's " little plays "[1] should be among the least dramatic of her works. They were, in fact, stories dramatised to fit the family " *théâtre d'éducation*," and the dramatist, intent upon her lesson, trusted her little company to create their parts. The link with Madame de Genlis is of the slightest, for although the Edgeworth children were being educated more or less upon the model of St. Leu, their plays and stories were not in the least like any that Madame de Genlis had written.

To Miss Edgeworth, truth was the first law of writing, and she must have felt the want of sincerity that came between Madame de Genlis and her books.[2]

Her own stories are essentially dramatic ; there is life in every word of dialogue,—but the characters need no artificial light.   A painted background was a poor substitute for her usual settings, villages that rang with the sounds of honest labour, fields and orchards full of children : a realist's Arcadia.

The little town of Somerville (in " The White Pigeon "), which in a few years had " assumed the neat and cheerful appearance of an English village ", is in fact a picture of Edgeworthstown.   It is only when the writer allows her characters to stray outside the bounds of her own knowledge that the scenery begins to shake.   Her school stories would hardly convince an outsider ;[3] the Neapolitan setting of " The Little Merchants " is ludicrously out of keeping with so moral a community.

But all this is nothing to a child.   His interest centres

[1] " Old Poz " (P. A. Vol. II) was the only play published early. Others, written between 1808 and 1814, appeared in *Little Plays for Young People ;* " Warranted Harmless ". By Maria Edgeworth. London, Baldwin & Cradock. 1827. See Appendix A. VIII.

[2] A letter from Maria Edgeworth to Mary Sneyd (March 19, 1803) describing her visit to Madame de Genlis, suggests a want of sympathy between them. See Appendix A. VIII.

[3] See Appendix A. VIII.

round the objects that make pictures in the mind, the business he can imitate.

Berquin understood the practical interests of children, but he had not Miss Edgeworth's keen eye for things that " draw ". The purple jar in the chemists' window, the coloured sugar-plums of the little merchants, the green and white uniform. Berquin's children were never so independent as these. His orphans were adopted ; Miss Edgeworth's keep house by themselves in a ruined castle, and ply their trades of knitting and spinning and shoe-making with the rhythm of a singing game. The finding of a treasure among the ruins is a freak of romance that holds the imagination even while the coins are being weighed and marked.

Goody Grope, the old treasure-seeker who demands her share of the orphans' luck, is the only Irish study, but other characters would connect these stories, if they were not so frankly acknowledged, with the author of *Castle Rackrent* and *The Absentee :* Mrs. Pomfret, that lesser Malaprop, with her " *Villaintropic Society* " and " *drugs and refugees* " ; Mrs. Theresa Tattle ; Mademoiselle Panache, the milliner-governess, betrayed by her mouthful of pins.

Emma and Helen Temple,[1] drawn without reference to a System, and left to develop each in her own way, would pass for sedate and early types of " Sense and Sensibility "; it pleased Miss Edgeworth the better that she could allow a measure of sense to Sensibility.

She has many variants of these types : the wise sister and playful brother ; the well-informed brother with a thoughtless sister, the wise or thoughtless one with a foolish or a prudential family. Not one of them is quite like any other. Nobody could mistake Laura, Rosamond's

[1] The two sisters, contrasted with the frivolous Lady Augusta in " Mademoiselle Panache ".

good sister[1] for the equally sensible Sophy, sister to Frederick and Marianne.[2]

Rosamond, with her filigree basket, would have repeated the lesson of Charlotte and the watch, but unlike Charlotte, she made the useless thing as a birthday present for somebody else.   The worst that can be said of Miss Edgeworth's young people is that they sometimes (from the very reasonableness of their up-bringing) assume an attitude of " civil contempt" towards ordinary folk. They understand too soon the dangers that arise in education from a bad servant or a silly governess, and are too fond of arguments and encyclopædias.   These are annoying traits in otherwise natural and pleasant persons, for although they are prigs in matters of knowledge or conscience, they have a very sound sense of values and can even be merry when it is not unreasonable to laugh.

Sir Walter Scott said that Miss Edgeworth was " best in the little touches."[3]   Children always find this out. They love the robin that sings in the Cathedral, the child that shared her bread and milk with the pig, the " little breathless girl " who ran back to thank Simple Susan for the double cowslips and violets, crying, *" Kiss me quick, for I shall be left behind."*

The smallest parts are played in character, in spite of the didactic purpose and the clock-work plot.   This story of " Simple Susan " is not unlike a Kilner pastoral ; but the colours are fresher, the lines more definite.

" When the little girl parts with her lamb " said Scott, " and the little boy brings it back to her, there is nothing for it but just to put down the book and cry."

But perhaps his great love of children made him read more pathos into the story than is actually there.   Few

[1] The first tale of Rosamond :   " The Birth-day Present ". (P.A.   Vol. I.)

[2] See " The Mimic ".   (P. A.   Vol. II.)

[3] A remark of Scott's to Mrs. Davy, quoted in Lockhart's *Life.*

readers cry over these tales. They reflect the temper of the Edgeworth family.

Early Lessons[1] records the schooling of these children. Maria had scarcely discovered " the warmth and pleasure of invention " when her father recalled her to the School-room. She set about straightening her bright intricate patterns to make reading books for the little ones, much as Dr. Primrose's daughters cut up their trains into Sunday waistcoats for Dick and Bill.

To turn from the *Parent's Assistant* to *Early Lessons* is to agree with Byron that there ought to have been a Society for the Suppression of Mr. Edgeworth.

And yet there is something to be said for these chosen and deliberate little scenes. Acquaintance prospers where there is no plot-interest to engross attention. The " little boy whose name was Frank " steps as naturally into the story as he would into a familiar room. He is so obviously a real little boy that it is even possible to believe in his virtues :

"When his father or mother said to him, ' Frank, shut the door,' he ran directly and shut the door. When they said to him ' Frank, do not touch that knife,' he took his hands away from the knife, and did not touch it. He was an obedient little boy."

There is something arresting in this.

Frank's doings and his sayings are a model of simplicity ; but nobody could say of him what Charles Lamb said of Mrs. Barbauld's little boys. As surely as any critic is disposed to laugh at Frank, he finds himself watching with involuntary interest while Frank pulls the leg of the table, and finds out what would have happened to the tea-cups if he had not been such " an obedient little boy ". His adventures, moreover, are not all among the tea-cups.

[1] First edition (2 Vols.) 1801. A continuation in 2 volumes was published in 1815. See Appendix A. VIII.

He is interested in a carpenter and in kites, and he has a more than usually good eye for a horse. What really distresses the reader is that he is never allowed out of school ; his most casual experience contributes to his mental and moral advancement. Chestnuts, glow-worms, the flame of a candle and other enchanting things are impounded for object lessons. Frank's father and mother are his tutor and governess ; the only poetry they mete out to him comes from Dr. Darwin's *Botanic Garden*[1], and is " correlated " to Natural History ; and after that it has to be explained. For when Dr. Darwin sings of a moth's " trunk ", little Frank understands by that " a sort of box " ; when his mother repeats :

> "Alight, ye beetles, from your airy rings",

he asks (not without reason) " What does that mean, mamma ? " But the explanation would have come without asking. The Governess is giving a lesson, the tutor is at her elbow ; and because you should never laugh in lessons, it is all rather serious.

But here, as in every school, are the children ; the rest hardly counts. Here, for example, when a child has made friends with Frank, is Rosamond, who will make him forget all these lessons.

Readers of *The Parent's Assistant* had met her before, with a filigree basket. Here she is again, " about seven years old ", walking with her mother in the London streets, a very figure of childhood.

The mother disposes one by one of her bright interests : The toys (" *all* of them "), the roses in the milliner's window, the " pretty baubles " in the jeweller's shop. And then :

[1] *The Botanic Garden ; a Poem, in Two Parts.*   Part I containing The Economy of Vegetation.   Part II, The Loves of the Plants. With Philosophical Notes.   1789.
Quoted in Appendix A. VIII.

" ' Oh mother ! oh ! ' cried she, pulling her mother's hand ; ' Look, look ! blue, green, red, yellow and purple ! O mamma, what beautiful things ! Won't you buy some of these ? ' " (It was a chemist's shop, but Rosamond did not know that.)

Her mother answered, as before :

" What use would they be of to me, Rosamond ? " It is the purple jar that takes the child's fancy. Driven to invent a *use* for it, she thinks she could use it for a flower pot, but that was no part of her desire.

The story of Rosamond and the Purple Jar was meant to celebrate the usual triumph of the Perfect Parent ; but every child knows it is Rosamond who triumphs ; and this is the point where the Perfect Parent makes her first mistake. She does not warn Rosamond, she only *hints* :

" Perhaps, if you were to see it nearer, if you were to examine it, you might be disappointed ".

Now, Frank had his chance. They took away the tea-cups before he let down that table-leaf. But nobody helps Rosamond. The little reader follows, in close sympathy, as she goes on unwillingly, keeping her head turned " to look at the purple Vase till she could see it no longer ". And as she goes, it transpires that her shoes " are quite worn out ". That it should come to this, points to some pre-arrangement by the Perfect Parent. The occasion presents a unique opportunity for choice :

" Well, which would you rather have, that jar or a pair of shoes ? " The parental Economist cannot buy both ; she makes Rosamond understand that she will not have another pair of shoes that month.

Thus the purple jar repeats the theme of the filigree basket and the green and white uniform.

What Rosamond was never told, and what she could not reasonably have been expected to deduce, was that the beautiful purple colour was not in the glass. A child cannot forgive injustice ; all Rosamond's friends (and all children are her friends) cry out that it " wasn't fair ". They all say, " She wouldn't have chosen the jar if she had *known* " ; and they are right. But the story goes on relentless. Rosamond, sweet and unquestioning, survives the whole painful experience and hopes at the end of it that she will be " wiser another time " ; but the Perfect Parent has lost all the prestige she ever had with children. She lost it before her callous and unintelligent question, " Why should you cry, my dear ? " But that sealed her fate.

" I *love* Rosamond ", said a little twentieth-century girl, not long ago, " but, oh, how I *hate* that mother ! "

Miss Edgeworth drew none of her portraits from a single original ; but she often sat to herself for some part of them, and at least one likeness was recognised by the family. Writing in her sixtieth year to her aunt, of the " great progress " she is resolved to make, she adds : " ' *Rosamond at sixty*,' says Margaret."

Harry and Lucy, begun by Mr. Edgeworth and continued at intervals with Maria's help, was finished by her in 1825[1]. The four volumes, she says, complete the series of " Early Lessons ", in which Harry and Lucy had already figured ; but although her drawings of the two children add colour to the book, it is really an oblation, on Mr. Edgeworth's behalf, to the Giant Instruction.

At this stage, it is true, there is a laboratory as well as a museum in the giant's castle ; he can illustrate the marvels of steam and suggest experiments with electricity. Yet this is only a more practical Circle of the Sciences. The children's voices are trained to the question and answer

[1] Begun by Mr. Edgeworth and Mrs. Honora Edgeworth, to follow Mrs. Barbauld's *Lessons for Children*. The first part was printed for use in the family.

of a " Guide to Knowledge " ; their lives are marked off
in lesson-periods. Even when a dull journey offers the
means of escape, these little captives hug their chains.
They never travel without books, and when there is nothing
to observe from the carriage windows, they find education
in the forests of the Oroonoko, where the plague of flies
affords " an inexhaustible subject of conversation."

The " Grand Panjandrum " could never come better
than into this juvenile Cyclopædia.[1]

Mr. Foote's " droll nonsense " pleases Miss Edgeworth
chiefly because it was invented to test a man's memory ;
yet she can tolerate nonsense, at any rate when there is no
danger of its being confused with sense.

They are all there : "the Picninnies and the Joblillies
and the Garyulies, and the Grand Panjandrum himself
with the little round button at top." Lucy laughs and
enjoys it, Harry calls it " horrible nonsense " ; but their
father's opinion is final, and Miss Edgeworth agrees with
him :

" It is sweet to talk nonsense in season. Always sense
would make Jack a dull boy."

The didactic purpose, which hampers the story-teller
at every turn, becomes more irksome as an audience passes
from childhood into youth. Fixed patches of light and
shade appear unnatural ; the critical eyes of youth are
open to devices that passed unnoticed in the nursery.

Miss Edgeworth's *Moral Tales*, " for young people of a
more advanced age ",[2] followed Marmontel into his own
province ; but Marmontel drew his lessons from the world
as he found it ; Miss Edgeworth fits her world to her
father's theories.

[1] *Harry and Lucy*, Vol. II. " Young Travellers." A piece of
pure nonsense composed by Samuel Foote, comic actor and play-
wright. (*c.* 1720–1777). See Appendix A. VIII.

[2] First edition, 1801.

Here again she has admirable portraits : the Quixotic
Forester, a new and convincing likeness of Thomas Day ;
Angelina, that mirror of " romantic eccentricities " ;
Mademoiselle Panache, little changed since her first appear-
ance, but here balanced by a " good French Governess ".
The unconscious satire of Lady Catherine is twice barbed :

" I don't want to trouble you to alter his habits or to
teach him chemistry or *any of those things*."

Yet here, as in *Early Lessons*, the persons walk gingerly,
after the manner of Berquin's little boy who kept the
skirts of his coat under his arms, " for fear of doing any
damage to the flowers ". The paths of the Edgeworth
garden are purposely narrowed that their doings may
" neither dissipate the attention nor inflame the imagination."

Miss Edgeworth's books fitted into her busy life as a
natural occupation for long evenings. She wrote in the
common sitting-room with the family about her, not one of
them under any constraint, but talking freely, as if she had
been sewing instead of novel-writing. It was characteristic of her that she could turn to children's books in the
midst of the Defender troubles. An Irish rising claimed
no more attention than the play and laughter of the
children. She could refer to it in a letter, and pass on to
the next domestic detail without wasting a moment in
" useless reflection ". That is precisely the mood of her
stories. The *Moral Tales*, addressed to an emotional age,
do not merely ignore the common forms of " Sensibility " ;
they take no account whatever of the stronger affections
and more vigorous manifestations of life : a thing scarcely
tolerable to generous youth. In the nursery books, this
equanimity has its uses. It enables her to deal with one
thing at a time, to select from a mass of details the particular things that a child would waste time in choosing.
Nothing worries or puzzles her ; she sees the world in clear

and simple pictures, and reduces the inconsequent thoughts of children to a relentless order.

Her little figures stand out in firm outline and bright colour, and the background is interesting chiefly as it gives occupation or the means of life.

Madame de Staël was thinking of the *Tales of Fashionable Life*, when she said :

" *Vraiment Miss Edgeworth est digne de l'enthousiasm ; mais elle se perd dans votre triste utilité* "[1]. But it is not less true of the children's books.

Flowers in Miss Edgeworth's garden (she is a true lover of flowers) are beautiful symbols of human care and industry ; but they never encroach upon vegetables.

Rosamond was a rebel. " Mustard-seed, compared with pinks, carnations, sweet-peas or sweet-williams, did not quite suit Rosamond's fancy."[2]

Miss Edgeworth had chosen those flowers for Rosamond, but the Perfect Parent knew better. When the sweet thing planned a labyrinth of Crete " to go zig-zag—zig-zag " through one of her borders, she was reasoned out of it for the sake of some little green things that were going to be mignonette, and when she and Godfrey were thinking of digging a pond, a shocked voice cried :

" What ! in the midst of your fine bed of turnips ? "

Romance dies hard ; but the odds were against Rosamond :

" And now, Mamma, *lay out* my garden for me, as Godfrey says, exactly to your own taste ; and I will alter it all to-morrow to please you." This would be Emily and her mother over again, if it were not so like Maria and her father.

Dealing with a criticism by her cousin, Colonel Stuart,

[1] Madame de Staël made this criticism to M. Dumont.
[2] *Early Lessons*, Vol. II.

Miss Edgeworth wrote : " I *know* I feel how much *more is to be done, ought to be done*, by suggestion than by delineation, by creative fancy than by facsimile copying " ; but she wisely stuck to her own method. It is where she touches the magic circle that she is " spell-stopp'd." When Laura reads the fairy-tale to Rosamond (she is only allowed *one*), her passage into an unreasonable world is marked by a change of diction. The Edgeworth fairy is " inexpressibly elegant " ; her flowing robe is " tinctured with all the variety of colours that it is possible for nature or art to conceive ". But there is nothing supernatural about her. She is merely a new specimen for the Museum, to be " contemplated with attention ", like the others. The result, recorded in a scientific note, proves her a creature of flesh and blood :

" Small though she was, I could distinguish every fold in her garment, nay, even *every azure vein that wandered beneath her snowy skin.*"

Dr. Johnson and Miss Edgeworth took opposite sides on this question of the supernatural ; and since experience proves that both were right, both must have been wrong.

Mr. Edgeworth attacked the Doctor's belief that " babies do not want to hear about babies ", and Maria proved it a fallacy ; but neither disposed of his claim for " somewhat which can stretch and stimulate their little minds."

Mr. Edgeworth's questions are not arguments : " why should the mind be filled with fantastic visions, instead of useful knowledge ? Why should so much valuable time be lost ? Why should we vitiate their taste and spoil their appetite, by suffering them to feed upon sweetmeats ? " [1]

Dr. Johnson could have answered him, and perhaps Mr. Edgeworth knew it, for he adds :

" *It is to be hoped that the magic of Dr. Johnson's name will not have power to restore the reign of fairies.*"

[1] See Mr. Edgeworth's preface to *The Parent's Assistant.*

There was no great danger, so long as Miss Edgeworth upheld the republic of common sense ; but when at last she laid down her pen, all the spirits whose existence she had denied rose up and denounced her ineffectual successors.

Thus she brings the first century of children's books to a natural close. She gathers up the loose ends of the old stories and weaves them into a bright and symmetrical design. The pattern is not wholly original : it was set by Marmontel, followed by Berquin, attempted by Madame de Genlis and the English Rousseauists ; but Miss Edgeworth brought it to perfection, expressing traditional themes in terms of reason and benevolence.

The dramatic realism which marks her stories was the keynote of English ballads and folk-tales ; she found a substitute for romance in the wonders of science. Roger Bacon, that wizard of the chap-books, appears as a forerunner of the Royal Society. Harry and Lucy know him as the discoverer of gunpowder, the inventor of the camera obscura, the prophet of flying-machines.[1]

In Miss Edgeworth's tales, science has not merely succeeded to poetry ; it has changed the enchanter's instruments. The Balloon is the new Pegasus, or the Flying Horse of the Arabian Tales ; the Magician still cries " New lamps for old ; " but it is Davy's lamp that he carries.

Rosamond, when she cannot explore the India Cabinet, is encouraged to look for wonderful things in her own house ; which indeed was Miss Edgeworth's own practice. Her " Enchanted Castle " was the home of her aunt, Mrs. Ruxton,[2] and Aboulcasem's treasure was not more marvellous to her than a friend's " inexhaustible fund of kindness and generosity."

[1] *Harry and Lucy*, Vol. III (4th ed. 1846).
[2] Writing from Black Castle, Mrs. Ruxton's house, in 1803, Miss E. calls it " this enchanted castle ".

With the Lilliputians she had more in common than she would have acknowledged.

" When I was a child," wrote Mr. Edgeworth in the third volume of *Early Lessons*, " I had no resource but Mr. Newbery's little books and Mrs. Teachum."[1] He is too conscious of the superiority of the new children's books to do justice to Mistress Two-Shoes ; yet she, with her little scholars and her weather-glass, was Miss Edgeworth's Lilliputian prototype. Simple Susan could have compared notes with little Two-Shoes upon good and bad landlords, and in some of Miss Edgeworth's stories there are prudential maxims that recall *Giles Gingerbread* and *Primrose Prettyface*.

Some of Rosamond's features may be traced in the portraits by Miss Fielding, the Kilners and Mary Lamb. The quaint miniature of Goody Two-Shoes has the same grave intelligent look. If this little person, so wholly unconscious of her charm, can be regarded as an English type, then Emilie could not have been altogether French.

Like Madame d'Epinay, Miss Edgeworth let Rousseau's lifeless image of the parent or tutor stand between her and her readers. They listened to the talk of other children, but seldom heard her voice. " Little touches " in the *Letters*[2] would have made them better acquainted, for here she spoke freely, showing both tenderness and humour, making adventures of common incidents,—a journey or a visit to friends.

" I nearly disgraced myself ", she wrote, after a visit to Cambridge,[3] " as the company were admiring the front of

[1] See Mr. Edgeworth's " Address to Mothers ", *Early Lessons* (Vol. III). A list of books which he mentions is given in Appendix A. VIII.

[2] See *The Life and Letters of Maria Edgeworth*, edited by A. J. C. Hare.

[3] In a letter to C. Sneyd Edgeworth, May 1, 1813.

Emmanuel College, by looking at a tall man stooping to kiss a little child."

This betrays her attitude to art and life.

If she never understood the " fairy Way of Writing ", it was because she had built a school upon the fairy circles of her village green. Her children were so happy in and about the village that they never discovered an enchanted wood. They planted trees instead of climbing them ; they knew all the roads to Market, but nobody showed them the way to Fairyland.

When at last the " reign of fairies " was restored, children burst into an unknown world of adventure and poetry. Ever since that little boy of Shenstone's suffered for love of St. George, the fairies have fought shy of schools. It remains to be seen whether they will hold their own with modern pedagogues ; but they are still in league with the poets, and the understanding between them is this : that the child, once having tasted fairy bread, can spend but half his time upon solid earth. The rest he must have in the Land of Dreams.

CHAPTER IX

THE OLD-FASHIONED GARDEN OF VERSES

The Spectator on Gardens—" Cones, Globes, and Pyramids "—
Good counsels in rhyme—Verse in the Schoolroom—Didactic rhymes
—Dr. Watts's *Divine and Moral Songs*—*Puerilia ; or, Amusements
for the Young ; Gammer Gurton's Garland* and *Songs for the Nursery*
—The Sublime Truant—Rules and prescriptions—*Original Poems
for Infant Minds*—The old garden and the new—Jane Taylor's
verses—*Poetry for Children*, by Charles and Mary Lamb—*The
Butterfly's Ball* and other festivals—Miss Turner's cautionary
rhymes—" Edward, or Rambling Reasoned on "—The triumph
of nonsense and rhythm.

" I THINK there are as many Kinds of Gardening as
of Poetry ", wrote the Spectator. His own garden
ran into the " beautiful Wildness of Nature ";
he valued it more for being full of blackbirds than of
cherries, and very frankly gave them fruit for their songs.[1]

Nature, regarded as a landscape gardener of more than
ordinary skill, was even allowed to work under authority
in the domain of poetry ; but she neglected one corner of
it, and there the trees were still clipped after the old
fashion into " Cones, Globes, and Pyramids." This little
fenced-off portion was the eighteenth century Child's
Garden of Verses. The only way out of it was by a narrow
gate in the midst of a Yew hedge, and of this only
good nurses kept the key.

In the lane outside, the pedlar hawked his wares ; the
old ballads could still be heard, the seven lamps of enchantment burnt bright at nightfall.

But inside the garden there were curious knots, with
flowers of the older sort and fragrant herbs. As time went
on, some of the trees were allowed to grow as they would ;

[1] *Spectator*, No. 477. Sat. Sep. 6. 1712.

the open country could be seen through gaps in the hedge, and the children began to make friends with travellers upon the road.

Good counsels had run into rhyme from the beginning, that they might hang together among wandering thoughts. Thus might the *Whole Duty of a Child* be remembered.[1] It gave, in short couplets, without figure, all the matter of later exemplary and cautionary verse ; and since the lines were spoken in the person of the counsellor, there was a certain dramatic interest added ; for he that repeated the lines assumed the part of Monitor.

This is one of the secrets of a child's pleasure in didactic rhymes. School, dull enough in itself, becomes a live thing the moment it passes into the world of make-believe, and words of caution and authority are a delight when spoken in character.

Pedagogues and guardians of youth discovered in rhythm and rhyme a means of teaching facts otherwise unrelated. Emblem writers, feeling the weakness of their strained symbolism, clutched eagerly at an effectual prop. Emblems without verses had some measure of attraction, for if no natural correspondence seemed to exist between a hypocrite and a frog, or between an egg and a Christian,[2] the things had an interest of their own, and excited curiosity as to possible connections ; but without rhymes, it would have been impossible to pair them aright.

Verse, brought as an accessory into school, twinkled a small mirror of imagination. Figures lurked in the letters of the alphabet ; rhymed riddles were to be had for the piecing together of syllables. *A Little Book for Little Children* (1702)[3] had these elements of interest ; *The Child's*

[1] MS. Bodl. 832. There is a reprint in the *Babees' Book* (E.E.T.S.)

[2] See Bunyan's *Book for Boys and Girls ;* or, *Country Rhimes for Children*, 1686. See Appendix A. IX.

[3] See Appendix A. IX.

Week's Work[1] was further lightened by a wide uncurtained schoolroom window, set so low that very small persons could stand a-tiptoe, and get new lessons from the creatures of earth and air. The very moderation of the writer invites acceptance :

> " Come, take this Book
> Dear Child, and look
>   On it awhile and try
> What you can find
> To please your Mind ;
>   *The Rest you may pass by.*"

But most of it is too good to pass by ; the moral is lost in little phrases of real music, albeit the rhymer ties himself to words of one syllable :

> " Birds in the Spring
> Do chirp and sing
>   With clear, shrill and sweet Throats ;
> Some hop, some fly,
> Some soar on high,
>   Each of them knows its Notes.
>
> " Hear you a Lark ?
> Tell me what Clerk
>   Can match her ; he that beats
> The next Thorn-Bush
> May raise a Thrush
>   Would put down all our Wayts."

Other " clerks " were appointed henceforth to the business of instruction. Rhymed sermons grew up in the midst of hymns of praise ; these were marked by a forcible and rousing emphasis. If the voice of the Pharisee be heard no less distinctly than that of the Sluggard, in Dr. Watts's Divine and Moral Songs[2], it rises at times into something like a glow of patriotism :

> " I would not change my Native Land
> For rich Peru with all her Gold ;

[1] By William Ronksley, 1712. See Appendix A. IX.
[2] *Divine Songs for Children*, by the Rev. Isaac Watts, D.D., 1715. *Divine and Moral Songs for Children*, 10th ed., 1729.

> A nobler Prize lies in my Hand
> Than East or Western Indies hold."

Beneath the severity which his doctrine inspired, the learned Doctor had a genuine tenderness for children, a legacy not despised by the greatest and most revolutionary of his successors, William Blake. His Cradle Hymn, beginning :

> " Hush ! my dear, lie still and slumber ;
> Holy Angels guard thy bed ; "

is remembered the better for Blake's Cradle Song. In the old conventional but rhythmic fashion, he too could sing of lambs and children.

There is no answer to strictures on the more common errors of the nursery ; they are so obvious that admiration halts before the power of rhythm that could give them life. Here and there comes a thought fresh turned :

> " How proud we are, how fond to shew
> Our Clothes, and call them rich and new !
> When the poor Sheep and Silkworm wore
> That very Clothing long before."

The old indiscriminate approval that gave Dr. Watts a place of honour on the nursery shelf, started the echoes along two centuries. Critics could neither silence the triumphant march of the verse nor dispute a ring of sincerity that it has.

Few poets of the old-fashioned Child's Garden failed in loyalty to its first planter ; but editors made Lilliputian anthologies and filled " Poetical Flower Baskets " from other sources. Early in the new century, the author of *The Butterfly's Ball* fell by his frivolous choice from the company of the elect :

> " The Butterfly, an idle thing,
> Nor honey makes, nor yet can sing."[1]

[1] " The Butterfly ", by Adelaide O'Keefe. See below. *Original Poems* by the Taylors and A. O'K.

He encouraged a spirit of revolt, and talking beasts of divers kinds broke into the garden.

Of the old order, John Marchant was welcome, despite his lack of originality, for a trick of rhythm which he had learnt from Dr. Watts, and apart from this, as a champion of children's games.   He had " Songs for Little Misses ", " Songs for Little Masters ", and " Songs ", varying the martial beat of Dr. Watts, on " Divine, Moral and Other Subjects ".[1]

Children, he is persuaded, would be " delighted with the Humour of them because *adapted to their own Way of thinking and to the Occurrences that happen within their own little Sphere of Action.*"

Stevenson could not give a more detailed picture of these " occurrences " ; it is in the region of childish thought that his predecessor drifts into an uncharted sea. He knows nothing of the little mythologies of children ; there are no imaginary countries, no " Unseen Playmate ", no dreams.   It is the difference between the old garden and the new, which is of the child's own planting.

There was a truant in the *Babees' Book*[2] who sang :

> " I wolde my master were an hare
> & all his bokis houndis were
> & I myself a joly hontere."

In the years between this and *Puerilia*, no child was encouraged to put his own thoughts into rhyme ; but

[1] *Puerilia ; or, Amusements for the Young.* " Consisting of a Collection of Songs adapted to the Fancies and Capacities of those of tender Years, and taken from their usual Diversions and Employments : also on Subjects of a more elevated Nature.   Divided into three Parts, viz. : I. Songs for little Misses. II. Songs for little Masters. III. Songs on Divine, Moral and other Subjects, etc." By John Marchant, Gent.

London, Printed for P. Stevens and sold by the Booksellers in Town and Country. 1751.

[2] Preserved in a Balliol MS. Quoted by Mrs. E. M. Field in *The Child and His Book.*

Marchant's " Little Miss " is heard " Talking to her Doll ",
" Working at her Sampler ", " playing on her Spinet ",
even " learning to dance ". The " little Master " of 1751
whips his top, flies his kite and goes a-birds'-nesting in
verse, when he is released from Arithmetic and the Lan-
guages.

But the world of Make-believe is still unknown to grown-
up travellers : a mystery jealously hidden by the child
from unsympathetic eyes.

A doll, in the matter-of-fact view of Mr. Marchant, is
a " mere painted piece of wood " :

> " Legs thou hast, and tho' they're jointed,
>   Yet one Step thou canst not walk ;
> Head there is to thee appointed,
>   Yet thou canst not think or talk."

The rudest image could not be such a dead thing to a child.
The author is upon enchanted ground, and blind to all
its wonders.

He is safer following the needle in a child's hand, tracing
the " odd and various " crochets upon a sampler, or drawing a moral from the building of a " Pasty Pye ".

To music, whether of kit or spinet, he can keep time.
" Miss learning to dance ", in her saque and hooped petti-
coat, is a bewitching figure, and the musician, though his
skill is not great, contrives not to put her out :

> " How pretty 'tis to dance !
>   To curtsey and advance
> And wave about my Hands
>   To sound of Kit.
> My Steps true Measure keep,
>   Thus lightly do I trip,
> Along the Floor I sweep
>   With nimble Feet."

" Master ", watching a Puppet-show, plays Gulliver at the
Court of Lilliput, surveys the " pigmy Troop " and makes
appropriate reflections.

A boy's kite carries this quaint versifier for a moment into the upper air.   Even there his fancy cannot support itself ; he snatches a simile for the sake of the rhyme, then takes a header to earth and fastens on his moral :

> " He that soars a Pitch too high,
>   Riding on Ambition's Wings :
> Sudden in the Dirt may lie ;
>   Pride its Shadow ever brings."

But the Kite actually rises, waving a " knotty Tail," seeming now " a little Cloud," now " no bigger than a Spoon " ; the birds play round her or mistake her for a hawk, and the boy, were his string long enough, " *would send her to the Moon.*"

The rhymes of *Mother Goose's Melody* and *The Top Book of All* were wild flowers that sowed themselves in the midst of herbaceous borders.   Two garlands of folk-songs for children grew out of the same soil.   The date of *Gammer Gurton's Garland* is unknown.[1]   A Bodleian copy in flowered covers has some rhymes from *Mother Goose* ; but the most daring " Lulliputian " would not have chosen the fairy theme of impossible tasks :

> " Can you make me a cambrick shirt,
>   *Parsley, Sage, Rosemary and Thyme :*
> Without any seam or needle work ?
>   And you shall be a true lover of mine."

Here, also, is the singing-game of " London Bridge," and ' A very pretty little Christmas Carol : "

> " God bless the Master of this house
>   The Misteress also
>   And all the little Children
>   That round the table go
>   And all your kin and kinsmen
>   That dwell both far and near :

[1] *Gammer Gurton's Garland ; or, The Nursery Parnassus.*   " A choice Collection of pretty Songs and Verses for the Amusement of all little Children."
Stockton.   Christopher and Jennett, n.d.

> I wish them a merry Christmas
> And a happy New Year."

Ritson reprinted *Gammer Gurton*, with additions, in 1810 ; but in the meantime an unknown editor had collected new "Songs for the Nursery "[1] and adapted them " to favourite national Melodies ".

This is the biggest gap in the hedge. Here, at last, is the open country,—the cuckoo's song :

> The Cuckoo's a bonny bird ;
> She sings as she flies ;
> She brings us good tidings
> And tells us no lies :
> She sucks little birds' eggs
> To make her voice clear
> And never cries Cuckoo !
> Till Springtime of the year.",

the daffodil :

> " Daffy-Down-Dilly is new come to town
> With a yellow petticoat and a green gown.",

and the song of the North Wind :

> " The north Wind doth blow
> And we shall have snow
> And what will poor Robin do then ?
> Poor thing !
>
> " He'll sit in a barn
> And keep himself warm
> And hide his head under his wing,
> Poor thing."

It is even more surprising to find, in this trim garden, a nursery lyric that calls up the very spirit of child-thought :

> " How many miles is it to Babylon ?
> Three score miles and ten.
> Can I get there by candle-light ?
> Yes, and back again." [2]

[1] *Songs for the Nursery*, " collected from the Works of the most renowned Poets and adapted to favourite national Melodies." London, printed for Tabart & Co. at the Juvenile and School Library, 157, New Bond Street, 1805 (price sixpence).

[2] See Appendix A. IX for a reference by R. L. Stevenson.

There are no other songs like these. *The Poetical Flower Basket* [1] represents the Lilliputian tradition that prevailed between 1760 and 1789 : rhymed fables, epigrams and inscriptions from poets who never wrote for children, and the story of " Inkle and Yarico " in verse.

Of Blake [2], it is difficult to speak in such a company. He was a winged thing hovering over little formal beds of lavender, catching for a moment an echo of children's voices repeating the creed of " The Little Black Boy," dropping a tear for the Chimney-Sweeper, then flying off unseen and unheard to sing his own songs of joy and love, too much a child to suffer the interruptions of other children ; scarcely to be understood by those who were dreaming their own dreams under the noses of the pedagogues. A Pied Piper who never offered his services to the community ; a sublime truant from every school. Of the realistic faith that could map out a Geography of Heaven, he had no knowledge ; yet Laws and Moralities were the burden of some songs that had touched him. There is a magic in the simplest form of verse that may quicken the beat of a child's heart, and endow little forgotten rules and prescriptions of the nursery with unexpected significance. If Blake could have alighted in the starlight outside a window and heard Ann Taylor putting one of her children to bed, he might have come in and acknowledged the existence of naughtiness, just for the pleasure of being forgiven. Some voices can sweeten the longest homily, and the culprit waits patiently for the kiss that must come when the sermon begins :

" And has *my darling* told a lie ? " [3]

[1] *The Poetical Flower-Basket ;   or, The Lilliputian Flight to Parnassus.*   Price 4d., in Dutch flowered bds.   n.d. (*c.* 1780).

[2] Blake's *Songs of Innocence* appeared in 1789.

[3] " To a Little Girl That Has Told a Lie ", by Ann Taylor. (Original Poems, Vol. I.   See below.)

There is a triumphant contradiction in so tender a
severity ; a very rainbow of promise :

> " Do you think I can love you so naughty as this,[1]
> Or kiss you all wetted with tears ? "

" Idle Mary " can pass it all on to her doll.   Later on,
when she looks down from the height of the first speaker,
she understands how forgiveness and hope came with a
sudden rush at the end :

> " Oh, Mary, this will never do !
>   This work is sadly done, my dear,
> And then so little of it too !
>   You have not taken pains, I fear.

> " Oh no, your work has been forgotten,
>   Indeed you've hardly thought of that ;
> I saw you roll your ball of cotton
>   About the floor to please the cat.

>   .   .   .   .   .   .

> " The little girl who will not sew
>   Should neither be allowed to play ;
> *But then I hope, my love, that you*
>   *Will take more pains another day.*" [2]

The authors of the *Original Poems*[3] wore the laurels of
Dr. Watts " with a difference."   They remembered all his
tunes, they played variations on most of his themes, but
they added songs of their own.   In these, Walter Scott
caught a note of poetry, and wrote to thank " the Associate
Minstrels ".   Miss Edgeworth, who cared less for rhythm,
praised them for other excellences.   The songs were a
means of gentle intercourse between these writers and
" that interesting little race, the race of children " for
whom they had " so hearty an affection ".

[1] From the same : " For a Naughty Little Girl."

[2] " Idle Mary ". See *Rhymes for the Nursery*. By the authors
of *Original Poems*.   London, Darton & Harvey.   1806.

[3] *Original Poems for Infant Minds*. By Several Young Persons.
London, printed for Darton & Harvey.   1804.   (7th edition).
The authors were Ann and Jane Taylor and their friend Adelaide
O'Keefe.

The child of the new garden can join hands, " through the windows of this book ", with the child of the old. Ann and Jane and Adelaide were the great aunts-in-literature of Louis Stevenson. A hundred years before him they sang of stars and sun, of day and night and play in gardens. The contrast is the greater because not one or two, but all their poems turned upon " the whole Duty of Children ". Instead of following a child " up the mountain sides of dreams ", they were intent on pointing out to him a world of greater Reality.

The dream world lies all about Stevenson's " Garden ", there is no hedge to separate it from ordinary roads and rivers ; they all lead to Fairyland. Yet this most practical dreamer could speak in the very accents and call up the *silhouettes* of his gentle predecessors at any moment.

It is impossible to read of " The friendly cow all red and white ",[1] without thinking of Jane Taylor's

> " Thank you, pretty cow that made
> Pleasant milk to soak my bread." [2]

The child in her garden looked up and wondered at one star ; that other child in the hundred-years-distant garden, escaped at bedtime to watch " thousands and millions of stars ".

Who would recognise the theme of Stevenson's " Wind " symphony, under the old title of " The Child's Monitor " ?[3] Yet the first two lines proclaim it :

> " The wind blows down the largest tree
> *And yet the wind I cannot see—*"

The wind that brings mystery into the new Garden was an emblem of human thought in the old. Stevenson's myth is a real product of the child mind :

[1] " The Cow ", in *A Child's Garden of Verses*, by R. L. Stevenson. 1885.

[2] " The Cow ", by Jane Taylor : the first piece in *Rhymes for the Nursery*.

[3] By Adelaide O'Keefe. Compare " The Wind " by R. L. S.

> " O you that are so strong and cold,
>   O blower, are you young or old ?
>   Are you a beast of field and tree,
>   Or just a stronger child than me ? "

There could be no such heathen explanation for Adelaide
O'Keefe. The Wind took shape as an allegory in her day :
it changed into the Voice of Conscience, it became an
ever-watchful angel :

> " Thus, *something* very near must be,
>   Although invisible to me ;
>   Whate'er I do, it sees me still,
>   O then, Good Spirit, guide my will ! "

In another place the four elements are considered in a
modestly scientific light.[1] They balance a juvenile version
of *The Seasons*. Nature is regarded from the old didactic
point of view. Spring, when " the Creatures begin their
employ " invites to industry ; the Idle who in Summer
" love best in the shade to recline " are admonished by
the active joys of haymaking ; the innocent hare is
remembered in the hunting season, and in Winter, Charity
sits by a glowing hearth and comforts itself with the
sophistries of Dr. Watts for the unequal distribution of
faggots.

These are but echoes ; there are many touches that give
the personal records of keen and watchful eyes :

> " I saw a leaf come tilting down,
>   From a bare wither'd bough ;
>   The leaf was dead, the branch was brown,
>   No fruit was left it now :
>
> " But much the rattling tempest blew,
>   The naked boughs among :
>   And here and there came whistling through
>   A leaf that loosely hung.
>
> .   .   .   .   .
>
> " I saw an old man totter slow,
>   Wrinkled, and weak, and grey,

[1] Poems on " Fire ", " Air ", " Earth " and " Water ", by Ann
Taylor. *Original Poems.* Vol. II.

> He'd hardly strength enough to go
> Ever so short a way." [1]

The leaf and the old man had been seen and remembered, the one for the sake of the other.   There were times when Ann, in her gentle way, came very near the heart of things. The three could not have sung so well together if they had not practised different parts. Jane, comparing her own verses with the rest, modestly explained : " I allow my pieces to rank as the *leaves* which are, you know, always reckoned a necessary and even pleasing part of the bouquet."

The comparison is hardly just, or if so, they are bright leaves, more striking, though fewer than the flowers.

There is a crisp touch about her simplest work.   The verses are better turned than Adelaide's or Ann's.   She is content to take her subjects from the common stock of moral tales [2], to arrange her nursery pictures in twos and fours ; but in spite of convention, her " Morning " is a Reveillé :

> " O come, for the bee has flown out of his bed,
>   To begin his day's labours anew ;
> The spider is weaving her delicate thread,
>   Which brilliantly glitters with dew.

> .   .   .   .

> " Awake, little sleeper, and do not despise
>   Of insects instruction to ask,
> From your pillow with good resolution arise,
>   And cheerfully go to your task."

" Evening ", the companion picture, is no more original ; in due order all the properties of Morpheus move before tired eyes ; sheep, and the parting linnet and the owl, the setting sun, the friendly moon that peeps through the curtain.   Children know them all, and for that reason, the cradle-movement of the verse is the more soothing.   Conventional portraits, "The Shepherd Boy " and "The Gleaner"

---

[1] " The Yellow Leaf ", by Ann Taylor.

[2] See Appendix A. IX.

stand out in clear simplicity, one on each side of the nursery mantel-piece, as "Evening" and "Morning" go over the bed. But when all the pictures are arranged, some of the figures walk out of them and begin to dance upon the floor.

"The Creatures" are never mere moral messengers. Jane has the same eye for character in beasts as in flowers or children. "The Toad's Journal" in *Q. Q.* is a better example of this than any of her nursery pieces. This "venerable reptile", supposed to have been found alive in the ruins of an Egyptian temple, records the events of his *first thousand years* :

> "Crawled forth from some rubbish and wink'd with one eye ;
> Half opened the other, but could not tell why ;
> Stretched out my left leg, as it felt rather queer,
> Then drew all together and slept for a year.
> Awaken'd, felt chilly—crept under a stone ;
> Was vastly contented with living alone.
> One toe became wedged in the stone like a peg,
> Could not get it away—had the cramp in my leg :
> Began half to wish for a neighbour at hand
> To loosen the stone which was fast in the sand ;
> Pull'd harder—then dozed as I found it no use ;—
> Awoke the next summer, and lo ! it was loose."

The next sleep ("for a century or more ") gives time to dream ; the dreamer, awakened,

> "Grew pensive—discovered that life is a load ;
> *Began to be weary of being a toad :* "

It is a daring moralist who laughs at her own moral :

> "To find a moral *when there's none*
> Is hard indeed—*yet must be done :* "

The moral, just because "*there's none,*" presses the unspoken analogy :

> "Age after age afforded him
> To wink an eye or move a limb,
> To doze and dream ;—and then to think
> Of noting this with pen and ink ;]

> Or hieroglyphic shapes to draw,
> More likely with his hideous claw ;
> Such length of days might be bestowed
> On something better than a toad !
> Had his existence been eternal,
> What better could have filled his journal ? "

To go back to the Nursery (the Original Poets were scarcely more than children when they wrote), Jane's talking beasts quickened the old stuff of fables by a new sense of likeness and incongruity. The spider and his wife (Jane loved spiders) are as real to a child as any married couple of his acquaintance. He follows their fortunes with personal concern ; he would forego a feast to dine with them :

> " One day when their cupboard was empty and dry
>   His wife, (Mrs. Hairy-leg Spinner,)
> Said to him, ' Dear, go to the cobweb, and try
> If you can't find the leg or the wing of a fly,
>   As a bit of a relish for dinner ' ".

The Cow and the Ass, meeting where the child may see them on any summer day, reconcile nonsense and natural history. The small actor can take both parts, and laughs the more at his own drollery.

> " ' Take a seat,' cried the cow, gently waving her hand.
> ' By no means, dear Madam,' said he, ' while you stand.'
> Then stooping to drink, with a complaisant bow,
> ' Ma'am, your health,' said the ass :—' Thank you,
>   Sir,' said the cow."

Thus laughter crept into the garden under the eye of Caution and Example, and, for his coaxing ways, was allowed to stay as a probationer.

Charles and Mary Lamb wrote their *Poetry for Children*[1] as a task. It was probably suggested by Mrs. Godwin,

[1] *Poetry for Children*, " Entirely Original. By the Author of Mrs. Leicester's School. In 2 Vols. 18 mo., ornamented with two beautiful Frontispieces. Price 1s. 6d. each, half-bound and lettered." Published by Mrs. Godwin in 1809.
See Appendix A. IX.

anxious to rival the publishers of *Original Poems*. In a letter to Coleridge (June, 1809), Lamb says : " Our little poems are but humble, but they have no name. You must read them, remembering they were task-work ; and perhaps you will admire the number of subjects, all of children, picked out by an old Batchelor and an old Maid. Many parents would not have found so many."

The Lambs could do nothing together without enjoying it ; they could not speak in a child's voice, and had almost forgotten the way to Babylon, but there are fewer subtleties of child-thought here than in *Mrs. Leicester's School*. The verses are full of practical interests. The humour of the writers brought tenderness and delight to the " task ", and children, who are quick to catch the note of sympathy, would feel this without understanding it.

Lamb had already tried his hand at children's rhymes. In 1805 he had written *The King and Queen of Hearts*[1], a careless and farcical impromptu which he sent by carrier to " Mr. Johnny Wordsworth ", begging his " acceptance and opinion ".

It is not easy to decide his exact share in *Poetry for Children*. The pieces reprinted in 1818[2] are not children's poems. One of them, " To a River in which a Child was drowned ", was suggested by the translation of a Spanish ballad in Percy's *Reliques*. " Love, Death and Reputation " was recognised by Swinburne as a translation from Webster's *Duchess of Malfi*.

Lamb seems to have amused himself now and then by casting fragments of mature flavour into this jar of nursery simples.

Of children, but assuredly not for them is the beautiful " Parental Recollections " which suggests understanding as well as love :

[1] Printed for Thomas Hodgkins. London, 1805.
[2] See Appendix A. IX.

14

" A child's a plaything for an hour ;
    Its pretty tricks we try
For that or for a longer space ;
    Then tire and lay it by.

" But I knew one that to itself
    All Seasons could controul,
That would have mock'd the sense of pain
    Out of a grieved soul.

" Thou, straggler into loving arms
    Young climber up of knees,
When I forget thy thousand ways
    Then life and all shall cease."

Charles Lamb knew the Child that Wordsworth rever-
enced : the child of imagination

        " . . . . *that to itself*
            All seasons could controul ".

The verses he would have repeated in that child's company
were nonsense rhymes or metrical " wild tales " ; not
without a song or two from Shakespeare (after the wise
example of Mother Goose) ; for he never could keep the
things he loved best out of talk or writing.

Poetry for Children was written to fit parental ideals,
just as stories were sometimes invented to accompany
stock illustrations ; yet Lamb's gay humour played pranks
here and there, as in the gratulatory ode, " Going into
Breeches " :

" Joy to Philip, he this day
Has his long coats cast away
And (the childish season gone)
Puts the manly breeches on.
Officer on gay parade,
Red-coat in his first cockade,
Bridegroom in his wedding trim,
Birthday beau surpassing him,
Never did with conscious gait
Strut about in half the state,
Or the pride (yet free from sin)
Of my little Manikin :

> Never was there pride or bliss,
> Half so rational as his.
> Sashes, frocks, to those that need 'em—
> Philip's limbs have got their freedom—
> He can run, or he can ride,
> And do twenty things beside,
> Which his petticoats forbade :
> Is he not a happy lad ? "

And is not this a mischievous poet, that dares sympathise thus openly with nursery vanities ? A dangerous man, with a tendency to romantic, unlawful sentiment. He places the revolutionary effusion between two tender and wholly innocent little poems of Mary's.[1] It should have been pilloried instead in a column facing " George and the Chimney Sweeper ", by Adelaide O'Keefe :[2]

> " His petticoats now George cast off,
> For he was four years old ;
> His trousers were nankeen so fine,
> His buttons bright as gold,—
> ' May I,' said little George, ' go out
> My pretty clothes to show ?
> May I, papa ? May I, mamma ? '
> *The answer was—' No, no ! '* "

Here, retribution is foreshadowed in the first stanza, if a second glance be given at the title.

In another mood, Lamb could sit patient under his reverend predecessor, or give new life to an old text :

> " In your garb and outward clothing
> A reserved plainness use ;
> By their neatness more distinguish'd
> Than the brightness of their hues.

> " All the colours in the rainbow
> Serve to spread the peacock's train ;
> Half the lustre of their feathers
> Would turn twenty coxcombs vain.

> " Yet the swan that swims in rivers,
> Pleases the judicious sight ;

[1] " The Lame Brother " and " Nursing ".
[2] *Original Poems,* Vol. I

> Who, of brighter colours heedless,
> Trusts alone to simple white.

> " Yet all other hues, compared
>   With his whiteness, show amiss ;
> And the peacock's coat of colours
>   Like a fool's coat looks by his."

Lamb's instincts were all against the timid doctrine of cautionary tales. A sermon is a thing that may be borne, even enjoyed, at the appointed hour ; but there is no escape from regulations which cramp and restrict every natural movement. Philip is not encouraged to eschew games and concentrate on " little books " ; he is not warned on promotion that all the things he wants to do are dangerous ; he may play Baste the Bear, Leap-frog, Foot-ball and Cricket, he may run in the snow, he may even

> " *Climb a tree, or scale a wall,*
>   *Without any fear to fall.*"

If a branch will not bear his weight,

> " If he get a hurt or bruise,
>   To complain he must refuse,
> Though the anguish and the smart
>   Go unto his little heart."

It was at this point that some of the trees in the Child's Garden put forth new shoots and began to grow into their natural shapes.

But there was no revolt against wholesome discipline ; traditional virtues were still honoured in verse, cleanliness as well as courage :

> " Come, my little Robert near—
> Fie ! what filthy hands are here—
> Who that ere could understand
> The rare structure of a hand,
> With its branching fingers fine,
> Work itself of hands divine,

> " Who this hand would choose to cover
> With a crust of dirt all over,

> Till it look'd in hue and shape
> Like the fore-foot of an Ape ? "

The romance of antiquity induces reverence for Age :

> " My father's grandfather lives still,
> His age is fourscore years and ten ;
> He looks a monument of time,
> The agedest of aged men."

These were town-bred poets ; Nature figures only in side-glances. " The Ride " gives the town child's delight in fields, but two children are the real subject of the picture. The Rainbow, regarded from a honeysuckle bower, is sweet after a tempest, but it is a messenger of earth : each precious tint is dear to Mary Lamb, " which flowers, which fields, which *ladies wear*." The robe of Iris is unwoven to find the colours of gardens, of living things, and of the human face. The magic bridge is dissolved with " half of its perfect arch " yet visible.

" The Boy and the Skylark " is the most revolutionary of these pieces. Bees and lambs, ants and silkworms, had been noted for the docility with which they entered into the business of human improvement. This sky-lark asserts the independence of his race. He scorns the limitations of human imagination which conceives of " the feathered race " as serving the little ends of man. Richard, hearing the lark's song, confesses his sin, under the impression that the " little bird " will betray him, as indeed Dr. Watts and all Lilliput would have had him believe.

This, says the bird, is folly " fit to move a sky-lark's mirth."

> " Dull fool ! to think we sons of air
> On man's low actions waste a care,
>   His virtues, or his vices ;
> Or soaring on the summer gales,
> That we should stoop to carry tales
>   Of him or his devices !
>
> " Our songs are all of the delights
> We find in our wild airy flights,

> And heavenly exaltation ;
> The earth you mortals have at heart
> Is all too gross to have a part
> In sky-lark's conversation."

Mrs. Trimmer would have been inexpressibly shocked at
this bird's attitude ; Ann Taylor would have been grieved
that he was not more friendly; Jane might have seen his
point of view. But this lark is a literal poet ; there is no
attempt here to interpret a real ecstasy of song. The poem
is but an argument that hits a popular fallacy. This is
still the voice of the town and of common sense. The
Spectator might have said as much for the birds that
sang in his cherry trees.

There is only one fairy in *Poetry for Children* ; fairies,
like dreams, were outside the pale of the Garden. This
one is a spirit of the age, but springs from the brain of a
child. Little Ann was a friend of Mary Lamb's, and knew
what the poet " prettily " wrote about Titania ; but
because she had not been admitted to fairy Society, it was
entirely natural that she should project into fairyland the
most diminutive creature of her acquaintance (an Edge-
worthian method of setting imagination to work upon
experience) and describe the " fabulous being " to her friend :

> " ' You'll confess, I believe, I've not done it amiss.'
> ' Pardon me,' said Matilda, ' I find in all this
> Fine description you've only your young sister Mary
> Been taking a copy of here for a fairy.' "

There is a thrill of adventure in the true tale of a child
that took an adder for a " *fine grey bird* ", and shared with
it, in perfect fearlessness, his breakfast of bread and milk ;
children laugh over the odd choice of the little Creole who
saw a crowd of dancing chimney sweepers on a May
morning, thought they were his fellow countrymen, and
became ambitious for a sooty coat. These stories could
have been told as well in prose ; but the charming fancy
called " The Desert " is a feast of the nursery muse :

" With the apples and the plums
Little Carolina comes,
At the time of the dessert she
Comes and drops her last new curt'sy ;
Graceful curt'sy, practis'd o'er
In the nursery before.
What shall we compare her to ?
The dessert itself will do.
Like preserves she's kept with care,
Like blanch'd almonds she is fair,
Soft as down on peach her hair,
And so soft, so smooth is each
Pretty cheek as that same peach,

.　　.　　.　　.　　.　　.　　.

Whiter drapery she does wear
Than the frost on cake ; and sweeter
Than the cake itself, and neater,
Though bedeck'd with emblems fine,
Is our little Caroline."

Studies of children, in the warm and tender colouring of
personal reminiscence, are the chief matter of the book ;
children do not appreciate the love and insight that makes
it poetry ; they will not stand still to trace, in these
portraits of brothers and sisters, a likeness to the gentle
authors. Grown-up persons, acquainted with the family
history, understand the little girl's patience over her
broken doll and her studied kindness to " dear little craving
selfish John ".

There is a bending-down in many of the poems that
only grown-up persons understand ; the writers stoop to
conquer childish reserve, not at all in the disconcerting
manner of Wordsworth, though they sometimes adopt his
way of recording the result :

" Lately an Equipage I overtook,
And help'd to lift it o'er a narrow brook.
No horse it had except one boy, who drew
His sister out in it the fields to view.
O happy town-bred girl, in fine chaise going
For the first time to see the green grass growing.
This was the end and purport of the ride

> I learn'd, as walking slowly by their side
> I heard their conversation . . . "

The " task " is forgotten in the pleasure or pathos of such incidents :

> " In a stage coach, where late I chanc'd to be,
>   A little quiet girl my notice caught ;
> I saw she look'd at nothing by the way,
>   Her mind seem'd busy on some childish thought.
>
> " I with an old man's courtesy address'd
>   The child, and call'd her pretty dark-eyed maid
> And bid her turn those pretty eyes and see
>   The wide-extended prospect. ' Sir,' she said,
>
> " ' I cannot see the prospect, I am blind.'
>   Never did tongue of child utter a sound
> So mournful, as her words fell on my ear.
>
> .   .   .   ."

Mary Lamb's poem " The Two Boys ", quoted by Lamb in " Detached Thoughts on Books and Reading ", records an incident of Martin Burney's youth :[1]

> " I saw a boy with eager eye
> Open a book upon a stall,
> And read, as he'd devour it all,
> Which, when the stall-man did espy,
> Soon to the boy I heard him call
> ' You, sir, you never buy a book,
> Therefore in one you shall not look.'
> The boy pass'd slowly on, and with a sigh
> He wish'd he never had been taught to read,
> Then of the old churl's books he should have had no need."

This is an unexpected link with Stevenson ; the proprietor of the shop " which was dark and smelt of Bibles " (that quaint store-house of romance)[2] is a reincarnation of this bookstall man ; he repeats the old growl in prose:

" I do not believe, child, that you are an intending purchaser at all ! "

[1] See Appendix A. IX.

[2] " A Penny Plain and Twopence Coloured," by R. L. S. *Memories and Portraits.* Paper XIII.

To compare these verses with Stevenson's is to discover an essential difference. The Lambs had the same delight in memories, but they looked back with tenderness to a childhood which they had been forced to leave behind. Stevenson was a boy to the end. The Child in his Garden is heard singing his own deeds. These gentle Olympians looked down at

" Horatio, of ideal courage vain,"

saw him now as Achilles, brandishing his sword, now Hector in a field of slaughtered Greeks, or the Black Prince, driving the enemy before him ; but lest vain imagination should grow bold upon encouragement, he must strike his milk-white hand against a nail, and seal the moral with his blood :

" Achilles weeps, Great Hector hangs his head,
And the Black Prince goes whimpering to bed."

The " Mimic Harlequin " who transforms a whole drawing-room full of furniture into matter of imagination is brought back to reality by his practical mother :

" You've put the cat among my work, and torn
A fine lac'd cap that I but once have worn."

Yet in another rhyme, the monitress relents, and indulging the idle fancies of Robert, allows him, though late for breakfast,

" To sit and watch the vent'rous fly
Where the sugar's piled high,
Clambering o'er the lumps so white,
Rocky cliffs of sweet delight ".

There is not enough of this to make a book of children's poetry. Romance knocked timidly at the gate and tendered a moral as the price of admission ; but it would be a dull child that could not find him somewhere in this corner of the garden.

The two small volumes had a short life ; some of the pieces were reprinted in collections, but the book failed to hold its own against Mr. Roscoe's bright fancy, *The Butterfly's Ball* [1], written for the birthday of his little boy Robert, and set to music by order of their Majesties for Princess Mary.

Children responded with one accord to the invitation of the first couplet :

> " Come take up your Hats, and away let us haste
> To the Butterfly's Ball and the Grasshopper's Feast."

Here was an entertainment which made no demands on attention or understanding, which had no " moral " ; it was all pure enjoyment. The rhymes were as simple as any in *Mother Goose's Melody ;* the pictures, early efforts of Mulready's [2], presented the various creatures in glorious independence, no more constrained by laws of proportion than the inhabitants of a willow-pattern landscape. They come, a gay and irresponsible procession, with a hint of fairy-land for all their reality :

> " A Mushroom their table, and on it was laid
> A Water-Dock leaf, which a Table-Cloth made."

There is " the sly little Dormouse " and " his blind Brother the Mole " ; the Frog (found still in the same attitude by Alice in Wonderland) and the Squirrel, who watches the feast from a tree. The rest are mostly winged :

> " : . . . . the Gnat and the Dragon-fly-too,
> With all their Relations, Green, Orange, and Blue."

[1] *The Butterfly's Ball and the Grasshopper's Feast*, by Mr. Roscoe. Illustrated with Elegant Engravings. London, Printed for J. Harris, Successor to E. Newbery, at the Original Juvenile Library, the Corner of St. Paul's Churchyard, 1807. Facsimile reprint, with introduction by Charles Welsh, Griffith and Farran, successors to Harris, 1883.

[2] Mulready, whose history was told in *The Looking-Glass* (See below, Appendix A. VIII), was supposed to have drawn these illustrations in his childhood.

The Harlequin Spider performs feats on the tight line, a giant Bee hovers over an absurdly inadequate hive, a snail bigger than either offers to dance a Minuet; and at nightfall the Watchman Glow-worm is ready with his light.

The feast is soon done, but for a third reading it can be got by heart.

" A Sequel ", *The Peacock " At Home "*,[1] appeared in the same year, with a frank and humorous acknowledgment of its predecessor's success. A pleasing mystery about its authorship was solved some years later in the preface of " *The Peacock and Parrot on their Tour to discover the Author of ' The Peacock At Home '.*"

> " A path strewed with flowers they early pursued,
> And in fancy, their long-sought Incognita viewed.
> Till, all their cares over, in *Dorset* they found her,
> And, plucking a wreath of green bay-leaves, they crowned her."

Mrs. Dorset, thus discovered, was a sister of Charlotte Smith, the writer of *Minor Morals* and *Rural Walks*.

All the birds left out of the Butterfly's Ball, including foreigners, such as the Taylor Bird and Flamingo, were guests of the Peacock. They offered a variety of absurd analogies.

The Lion's Masquerade, rhymed in the same quaint humour, was a sort of Æsop in Ranelagh :

> " The guests now came thronging in numbers untold,
> The furious, the gentle, the young and the old,
> In dominos some, but in characters most,
> And now a brave warrior, and then a fair toast.
> *The Baboon* as a *Counsellor* : Alderman Glutton :
> A Lamb, Miss *in her teens*, with her aunt, an old mutton.
> It was easy to see, as this couple past by,
> The Wolf, very cunningly, cast a sheep's eye."

A guest of unusual interest is the " *Great Hog in Armour* " who stalks, in Mulready's illustration, like the ghost in

[1] For this and other sequels to *The Butterfly's Ball*, see Appendix A. IX.

Hamlet, under a full moon ; and there is a Bear in the " character " of Caliban,

> " . . . . loaded with wood,
> His bones full of aches, from Prospero's rod."

Those were great naval days ; the English sailor is repre-sented by a Mastiff :

> " Britannia receiv'd him with mark'd condescension
> And paid him all night, most distinguish'd attention."

Bewick's beasts and birds forsook their natural haunts and danced in the most carefully preserved parterres. They came in their thousands, of all sizes and nationalities. " W. B." followed Mrs. Dorset with *The Elephant's Ball*, and the Season was extended till all " the Children of Earth and the Tenants of Air " were exhausted. Children ran out of the Lambs' quiet parlour into a garden of per-petual Feasts. What could come better after the Butterfly's Ball than a Wedding Among the Flowers ?

But there was still an old-fashioned lady, one Miss Elizabeth Turner, who held aloof, wielding the rod of Dr. Watts. With the perversity of their race, the Lilli-putians fell into step as they approached her, and listened to her warnings with a fearful joy. She told them, in simple numbers, how Miss Sophia would not wait for the garden gate to be opened, and demonstrated by her fall, that " little girls should never climb " ; she expected them to believe that every little boy with a craving for adventure must share the fate of one who

> " Once was pretty Jack
> And had a kind Papa ;
> But, silly child ! he ran to play
> Too far from home, a long, long way,
> And did not ask Mama.
> So he was lost, and now must creep
> Up chimneys, crying, Sweep ! Sweep ! Sweep ! "

Poor Jane and little Tom excited a thrill as " cautionary "
Babes in the Wood. They succumbed to the fatal fascination of scarlet berries :

> " Alas ! had Tommy understood
> That fruit in lanes is seldom good,
> He might have walked with little Jane
> Again along the shady lane."

Small listeners decided privately that Peter was an
indifferent sportsman to turn the red-hot poker against
himself ; they would prove at the first opportunity that
he bungled the thing. But when other children cried, it
amused them to agree with Miss Turner that

> " A rod is the very best thing to apply
> When children are crying and cannot tell why ! "

The names of her two little books [1] have no obvious
connection with the verses. She explains *The Daisy* in a
Cowslip rhyme :

> " Like the flow'ret it spreads, unambitious of fame,
> Nor intrudes upon critical gaze."

But names are pictures to a child : daisies and cowslips
should have a place in his garden. In open defiance of
the calendar, these were succeeded by *The Snowdrop* and
The Crocus. Mary Elliott suffered herself to be turned
by the Muse from Precept and Example ; she added *The
Rose* [2] to this serial garland. Little feet went willingly
after her, for she led the way through a village, and visited
many friends. At the window of the village shop they
loitered together, forgetting all the penalties of pleasure-

---

[1] *The Daisy ; or, Cautionary Stories in Verse*, 1807.
The Cowslip ; or, More Cautionary Stories in Verse, 1811.
For additions, reprints and imitations, see Appendix A. IX.
[2] *The Rose*, Containing Original Poems for Young People. By
their friend Mary Elliott.

seeking in a glory of gingerbread, candy, little gilt books and many sorts of toys :

> " How many bright eyes have I seen
> Examine each article o'er,
> Still looking, while pausing between
> The window and latch of the door.
>
> " For well the young customers know
> The Dame does not like to be teased,
> And when indecision they show,
> Cries ' children can never be pleased ! '
>
> " Such grumbling, however, is borne
> While thus she displays such nice fare,
> And her threshold, uneven and worn
> Proves how many footsteps go there ! "

The Giant Instruction sent a few spies into the garden, disguised as poets. Wise children saw through the deception at once ; others, lured into encyclopædic mazes, yawned while the guide recited " Edward, or Rambling reasoned on ",[1] and described the delights of town for the benefit of those who hankered after foreign travel :

> " The pictures in the Louvre
> Display their bright perfections,
> But we should first manœuvre
> To see some home collections.
>
> .   .   .   .
>
> " The Royal Institution
> Gives knowledge, taste and skill,
> And change without confusion
> Attends its lectures still.
>
> " Some folks have wished to be
> Whole years in the Museum :
> So much there is to see,
> No fear it should *ennui 'em*."

The unconscious humorist rambles thus through a dozen stanzas. But the last lines are drowned by the voice of

[1] From *Mamma's Verses ; or, Lines for Little Londoners*, said to have been suggested by *Original Poems*. Brentford, P. Norbury, n.d.

the Pedlar at the door. He is singing new rhymes to old tunes : *Whimsical Incidents, Cinderella in Verse, Mother Hubbard, Dame Trot* and *Goody Flitch*.[1] The Lady of Ninety who wrote *Dame Wiggins of Lee* [2] must have heard him singing in her youth.

Nonsense rhymers, whipped out of the Court of Stupidity, found a refuge in the purlieus of the child's garden ; nobody recognised them as descendants of the citizens of Cockayne, or suspected that they would one day be honoured as predecessors of Edward Lear. Yet who shall gauge their influence on the character of Englishmen, or decide how far the eccentricities of certain theorists depended on the exclusion of nonsense from the nursery ?

The History of the *Sixteen Wonderful Old Women*[3] came too late for Mr. Day :

> " There was an Old Woman from France
> Who taught grown-up Children to dance,
> But they were so stiff,
> She sent them home in a miff,
> This sprightly Old Woman from France."

While Mr. Edgeworth was " explaining " poetry to children, and later, when Young Reviewers were being taught to " dissect poems ",[4] the Pedlar was still singing for truant minds. If he knew nothing of poetry, at least he knew enough to let it alone ; and his songs were good to dance to, which every child knows is an excellent thing in songs.

[1], [2], [3], [4]. See Appendix A. IX.

APPENDIX A.

I.

p. 14. 1. *List of chap-book romances and tales in order of reference.*

(1) Bevis of Southampton.—First English edition, Wynkyn de Worde (a fragment, n.d.)
Chap-book: *Sir Bevis of Southampton*, London, n.d.

(2) Guy of Warwick.—First English edition, W. Copland (1548–68).
Chap-book: *Guy, Earl of Warwick*, n.d. (*c.* 1750).

(3) The Seven Champions of Christendom.—By Richard Johnson (1596).
Chap-book: London, n.d. (*c.* 1750).

(4) Don Bellianis of Greece.—Earliest edition, 1598. Black Letter.
Chap-book: The History of Don Bellianis of Greece, London, n.d. (*c.* 1780).

(5) The Famous History of Montelyon. By Emanuel Forde (1633).
Chap-book: The History of Montellion, London, n.d.

(6) Parismus, the Renowned Prince of Bohemia. —1598. Black Letter.
Chap-book: London, n.d. (*c.* 1760).

(7) The History of Fortunatus.—Stationers' Register (1615).
Chap-book: London, n.d. (eighteenth century).

(8) Valentine and Orson.—French edition, 1489. Two editions by W. Copland.

(9) Friar Bacon.—Greene's play, mentioned in Henslowe's Diary under the years 1591–2 was based on an earlier tract. Eighteenth century chap-book: London, n.d.

(10) The Historyes of Troye.—Caxton, 1477.
Folio Black Letter.
Chap-book : *Hector, Prince of Troy*, London,
n.d.

(11) Patient Grissel.—Chap-book : The History
of the Marquis of Salus and Patient Grissel,
London, n.d. (*c.* 1750).

(12) The King and the Cobbler.—Chap-book :
London, n.d. (King Henry VIII).

(13) The Valiant London Prentice.—" Written
for the Encouragement of Youth " by John
Shurley. For J. Back, B.L.
Chap-book : " Printed for the Hon. Company of Walking Stationers ", London,
n.d. (after 1780).

(14) *Tom Long the Carrier* (with woodcut of
Tudor pedlar), London, n.d.

(15) " The Seven Sleepers of Ephesus ", a
mediæval tale in Caxton's *Golden Legende*.

(16) *The History of Laurence Lazy*, London, n.d.
(eighteenth century).

(17) *Joseph and his Brethren.*—Chap-book :
London, n.d.

(18) The Glastonbury Thorn (Joseph of Arima-
thea).—Wynkyn de Worde, n.d.
Chap-book : The History of Joseph of
Arimathea, n.d. (*c.* 1740).

(19) *The Wandering Jew*, etc.
Chap-book (dialogue), London, n.d.

p. 20.   1.   Another chap-book of this sort is The History
of Dr. John Faustus (Aldermary Churchyard,
n.d.).
" A Ballad of the Life and Death of Doctor
Faustus, the Great Congerer ", was entered in
the Stationers' Register in 1588 ; and Marlowe
produced his play in 1589.

p. 22.   1.   The humour of " topsy-turveydom " dates
back to the fourteenth century *Land of Cockayne,* and survives to-day in nursery-rhymes
and " drolls ". " The Wise Men of Gotham "
was still popular in the eighteenth century.
This famous nonsense-book was written by

Andrew Boorde, and a Bodleian copy is dated 1630.

p. 22. 2. (a) *Memoirs of the late John Kippen*, "to which is added an Elegy on Peter Duthie, who was for upwards of eighty years a Flying Stationer".

(b) Mr. R. H. Cunningham, in a note prefixed to his *Amusing Prose Chap-books* (1889) gives an account of a book-pedlar, Dougal Graham, who hawked books among Prince Charlie's soldiers in the '45, and afterwards became an author and printer of chapbooks.

p. 25. 1. *The Adventures of Philip Quarll*, by Edward Dorrington (1727) was probably inspired by *Robinson Crusoe*. It was afterwards used to illustrate revolutionary theory. See Chapter V.

p. 26. 1. (a) "Chevy Chase", praised by Sir Philip Sidney for its "trumpet note", was included in Dryden's Miscellanies, 1702, in the Collection of 1723 and in Percy's Reliques, 1765.

(b) The ballad of "The Two Children in the Wood" was printed in 1597 as "The Norfolk Gentleman, his Will and Testament", etc. There is a prose chap-book of 1700, "to which is annex'd the Old Song upon the same".

The ballad is included in the collection of 1723.

p. 27. 1. "The Noble Acts of King Arthur and the Knights of the Round Table; with the Valiant Atchievements of Sir Launcelot du Lake. To the Tune of, *Flying Fame*".

The first stanza (of which Falstaff quotes the first line in Henry IV, Part 2) runs thus:

"When Arthur first in Court began,
And was approved King,
By Force of Arms great Victories won,
And conquest home did bring".

The episode is from Malory.

Other ballads based on romances in the Collection of 1723 are : " St. George and the Dragon ", The Seven Champions of Christendom ", " The London Prentice " and " Patient Grissel ".

The Percy Folio includes " King Arthur and the King of Cornwall ", " Sir Lancelott of Dulake ", " The Marriage of Sir Gawaine ", " Merline ", and " King Arthur's Death ".

p. 30.   1. (a) Legendary ballads in the Collection of 1723 include : " Fair Rosamond ", " King Henry (II) and the Miller of Mansfield ", " Sir Andrew Barton's Death ", " King Leir and his Three Daughters ", " Coventry made free by Godiva ", " The Murther of the Two Princes in the Tower ", " King John and the Abbot of Canterbury ".

Many others deal with historical themes, such as " The Banishment of the Dukes of Hereford and Norfolk ", or with famous battles. " King Henry Fifth's Conquest of France " probably belongs to the reign of George I.

(b) " The Blind Beggar's Daughter " was adapted from a favourite Elizabethan ballad, " Young Monford Riding to the Wars ".

There is a prose chap-book, printed by T. Norris, London, 1715.

p. 31.   1.   Other sea-ballads in Child's collection are :—
" The Sweet Trinity " (or, " The Golden Vanity ").—Pepys, 1682-5 ; " Captain Ward and the Rainbow ",—Roxburghe and Aldermary copies ; " The Mermaid " (or, " The Seamen's Distress ").—Garland of 1765, etc. ; " Sir Patrick Spens ".—Percy's *Reliques*, 1765, Herd's *Scottish Songs*, 1769, and Scott's *Minstrelsy*, 1803.

II.

p. 40.   1.   There is a list of great men given in *The Tatler* (No. 67), Sept. 13, 1709; and in No. 78, one Lemuel Ledger writes to put Mr. Bickerstaff in mind of " Alderman Whittington, who began the World with a Cat and died with three hundred and fifty thousand Pounds sterling ".

The Spectator (No. 5) March 6, 1711, says that " there was once a Design of casting into an Opera the Story of Whittington and his Cat, but that Mr. Rich abandoned the Idea for Fear of being overrun by Mice which the Cat could not kill."

Suspicion seems to have been cast on the cat in the second half of the century, and it is interesting to find Goldsmith (" On Education", 1759) advocating instead of romances " the old story of Whittington, *were his cat left out* " as " more serviceable to the tender mind than either Tom Jones, Joseph Andrews, or a hundred others, where frugality is the only good quality the hero is not possessed of ".

Mr. Wheatley in his *Chap-books and Folk-lore Tracts*, notes that in 1771 the Rev. Samuel Pegge brought the subject of Whittington and his Cat before the Society of Antiquaries, " but he could make nothing at all of the Cat ".

p. 48.   1.   Other early editions of the Arabian Tales: 1712 and 1724.

The translation of the *Arabian Nights* was followed by English versions of Pétis de la Croix.

The Persian Tales, or the Thousand and One Days appeared in 1714, and was followed in the same year by *The Persian and Turkish Tales Compleat*.

The pseudo-translations of Gueullette were translated into English in 1725, as *The Chinese Tales, or the Wonderful Adventures of the Mandarin Fum-Hoam*.

p. 56. 1. Moralised ballad-stories :—

    (a) Robin Hood, J. Harris, London, n.d. (*c.* 1807).

    (b) *The Tragical History of the Children in the Wood*, " containing a true Account of their unhappy Fate, with the History of their Parents and their unnatural Uncle. Interspersed with Morals for the Instruction of Children. To which is added the favourite Song of the Babes in the Wood. Embellished with Cuts." London, n.d.

    (c) *The Children in the Wood (Restored by Honestus)*. J. G. Rusher, Banbury, ½d. (*c.* 1810).

III.

p. 60. 3. " According to Act of Parliament (neatly bound and gilt) a little Pretty Pocket Book, intended for the Instruction and Amusement of little Master Tommy and pretty Miss Polly, with an agreeable Letter to read from Jack the Giant-Killer, and also a Ball and Pincushion, the Use of which will infallibly make Tommy a good Boy and Polly a good Girl ", etc.

p. 62. 1. *The Philosophy of Tops and Balls* is explained as " The Newtonian System of Philosophy adapted to the Capacities of Young Gentlemen and Ladies, and made entertaining by Objects with which they are intimately acquainted ".

p. 62. 3. *The Lilliputian Magazine; or, the Young Gentleman and Lady's Golden Library.*

From the preface :—" the Authors concerned in this little Book have planned out a Method of Education very different from what has hitherto been offered to the Public : and more agreeable and better adapted to the tender Capacities of Children ".

p. 64. 1. In Mr. John Newbery's list for 1762, *A Pretty*

Book of Pictures for little Masters and Misses has the alternative title of " Tommy Trip's History of Beasts and Birds, with a familiar Description of each in Verse and Prose ".

To this was added " The History of little Tom Trip himself, his Dog Jowler, and of Woglog the Great Giant ".

This was the earliest edition known to Mr. Welsh; but an edition of 1752 was afterwards discovered and noted in *The Times Literary Supplement*, Dec. 18, 1919, under " Notes on Sales ". This seems to be the first edition of *Tommy Trip's History*; but an earlier account of him is given in *The Lilliputian Magazine*, first advertised in 1751. Goldsmith came to London after his travels on the Continent, in 1756, so that he could not have written *Tommy Trip*, although the rhyme of " Three Children ", as Mr. Welsh observed, is remarkably like the " Elegy on a Mad Dog ".

p. 64. 2. *Note on Novels and Plays abridged or adapted for children :—*

Among these were *Pamela ; or, Virtue Rewarded*, with a prefatory address " To the Parents, Guardians and Governesses of Great Britain and Ireland ". (E. Newbury's list, 1789) ; and *Tom Jones, the Foundling* (the story of his childhood only), published about 1814 by Pitts of Seven Dials, with a foreword to the " little Friends " for whom it was designed.

Plays were also fashioned into children's books. Garrick's Masque from Dryden's *King Arthur* (1770) produced a " Lilliputian " romance closely modelled on Dryden : *The Eventful History of King Arthur ; or, the British Worthy*. London, printed for H. Roberts & W. Nicholl. Price 6d., in Dutch paper boards. (A.S. Kensington copy is dated 1782.)

Early in the 19th century, the story of *Cymbeline* was published as *The Entertaining History of Palidore and Fidele*, in flowered covers, for the " amusement and instruction of youth ".

p. 65.   1.   (a) *Tommy Thumb's Pretty Song Book.* Vol. II. " Sold by M. Cooper, according to Act of Parliament ".

The frontispiece shows a boy playing a flute and two girls seated with a book of songs. At the foot of each page is a musical direction : " Recitatio ", " Toccato ", " Vere Subito ", etc. At the end are two cuts, one a portrait of the writer " Nurse Lovechild ", the other advertising *The Child's Plaything*, with the date 1744, and the following rhyme :—

> " The Child's Plaything
> I recommend for cheating
> Children into Learning
> Without any Beating."

(b) The author of *The Little Master's Miscellany* (1743) condemns the popular song-books, and instead of these, provides children with moral dialogues, " On Lying ", " On Fishing ", " On Death ", " On Detraction ", " On the Tulip ", etc.

(c) John Marchant in his *Puerilia ; or, Amusements for the Young* (1753) offers a better substitute for the " Ribaldry " which he complains that children are " instructed to con and get by Heart " as soon as they can read,—" to trill it with their little Voices in every Company where they are introduced ".

See above.—Chapter IX.

p. 65.   2.   *Mother Goose's Melody ; or, Sonnets for the Cradle*, in Two Parts. Part I.—The most celebrated Songs and Lullabies of the old British Nurses, calculated to amuse the Children and excite them to sleep ; Part II.—Those of that sweet Songster and Muse of Art and Humours, Master William Shakespeare. Adorned with Cuts and illustrated with Notes and Maxims, historical, philosophical and critical ".

The addition, in Part II, of Shakespeare's songs makes a fitting sequel for older children.

A facsimile of the New England edition of 1785 was printed in 1892, with the following description :—

" The original Mother Goose's Melody, as issued by John Newbery of London, *circa* 1760 ; Isaiah Thomas of Worcester, Mass., *circa* 1785, and Munro and Francis of Boston, *circa* 1825. Reproduced in facsimile from the first Worcester edition, with introduction and notes by William H. Whitmore. To which are added the Fairy Tales of Mother Goose, first collected by Perrault in 1696, reprinted from the original translation into English by R. Samber in 1729. Boston and London,—Griffith, Farran & Co., 1892.

p. 65.   2. (b) Another early book of rhymes is *The Top Book of all for little Masters and Misses*, " Containing the choicest Stories, prettiest Poems and most diverting Riddles, all wrote by Nurse Lovechild, Mother Goose, Jacky Nory, Tommy Thumb and other eminent Authors . . . also enriched with curious and lovely Pictures, done by the top Hands, and is sold only at R. Baldwin's and S. Crowder's, Booksellers in Pater Noster Row, London, and at Benjamin Collins's in Salisbury for 2d. (Date, on woodcut of a shilling, 1760)."

(c) A later Miscellany, *Mirth without Mischief c.* 1790, has similar rhymes.

p. 67.   1.   A third edition of *Goody Two-Shoes* appeared in 1766, in Dutch flowered boards, " printed for J. Newbery at the Bible and Sun in St. Paul's Churchyard.   Price 6d."   This was reproduced in facsimile with an introduction by Charles Welsh, by Griffith and Farran, successors to Newbery and Harris, in 1881.

Later editions : 1770.—T. Carnan & F. Newbery, Jun.; 1783.—T. Carnan ; 1786— Isaiah Thomas, Worcester, Mass. (First Wor-

cester ed.) ; 1793.—Darton & Harvey, Grace-
church St. ; 1796 (with MS. note by Mr. J.
Winter Jones), 32 mo.

Penny chap-book edition (*c*. 1815).—J.
Pitts, Seven Dials : " The Toy and Marble
Warehouse ". Many " modernised " editions
were printed during the 19th century ; the last
recorded, in 1884 ; and G.T.S. was included in
Charlotte Yonge's *Storehouse of Stories* (1870).

p. 68. 1. (a) From Carnan's list, 1787.—" The Valentine's Gift ; or, the whole History of Valentine's Day, containing the Way to preserve
Truth, Honour and Integrity unshaken. Very
necessary in a trading Nation. Price sixpence,
bound.

A later edition (Kendrew, Glasgow, *c*. 1814)
in the S. Kensington collection, has significant
additions :—

" The Valentine Gift ; or, a Plan to enable
children *of all Denominations* to behave with
Honour, Integrity and Humanity. To which
is added some Account of old Zigzag, and of
the Horn which he used to understand the
Language of Birds, Beasts, Fishes and Insects.
The Lord who made thee made the Creatures
also ; thou shalt be merciful and kind unto
them, for they are thy fellow Tenants of the
Globe.—Zoroaster."

(b) *The Twelfth Day Gift* (advertised April 18,
1767). The title-page of the 1783 edition is
as follows :—

" The Twelfth Day Gift ; or, the Grand Exhibition, containing a curious Collection of
Pieces in Prose and Verse (many of them
Originals) which were delivered to a numerous
and polite Audience on the important Subjects
of Religion, Morality, History, Philosophy,
Polity, Prudence and Economy, at the most
noble the Marquis of Setstar's by a Society of
young Gentlemen and Ladies, and registered
at their request by their old Friend Mr. Newbery. With which are intermixed some occa-

sional Reflections and a Narrative containing the Characters and Behaviour of the several Persons concerned.

> Example draws where Precept fails
> And Sermons are less read than Tales.

London : Printed for T. Carnan, Successor to Mr. J. Newbery in St. Paul's Church Yard. Price one shilling."

In an enveloping cautionary story, there is some account of a gigantic Twelfth Day Cake ; but the book consists chiefly of " Pieces ", which include the story of " Inkle and Yarico ", taken by Addison from Ligon's *Account of Barbados* (*Spectator*, No. 11), " versified by a Lady ", Addison's hymns ; Pope's Universal Prayer ; " The Progress of Life ", an Eastern story from the *Rambler* ; Parnell's " Hermit " ; the character of Antiope from Fénélon's *Telemachus*, translated in 1742, and the King's speech to Westmoreland (Henry V. iv. 3), a sign of the revived interest in Shakespeare.

This is almost a perfect specimen of the Lilliputian Miscellany.

p. 76. 1. From Nichols's *Literary Anecdotes* (1812–16) :—" It is not perhaps generally known that to Mr. Griffith Jones, and a brother of his, Mr. Giles Jones, in conjunction with Mr. John Newbery, the public are indebted for the origin of those numerous and popular little books for the amusement and instruction of children which have been ever since received with universal approbation. The Lilliputian histories of Goody Two-Shoes, Giles Ginger-bread, Tommy Trip, etc., etc., are remarkable proofs of the benevolent minds of the projectors of this plan of instruction, and respectable instances of the accommodation of superior talents to the feeble intellects of infantine felicity."

2. Examples of grammatical faults in *Goody Two-Shoes* :—

Ch. vi.—" She was in Hopes he *would have went* to the Clerk."

Ch. viii.—" Therefore she laid very still."

Part II. Ch. iii.—" Does not the Horse and the Ass carry you and your Burthens ; don't the Ox plough your Ground ?"

John Newbery's private memoranda show mistakes of the same kind.

p. 76. 3. (a) John Newbery died in 1767, when the business was divided into two branches, one under his son Francis, in partnership with T. Carnan, the other under Francis Newbery the nephew, whose widow Elizabeth succeeded him in 1780. T. Carnan afterwards set up on his own account.

(b) In the curious " appendix " to *Goody Two-Shoes*, there is " an Anecdote respecting Tom Two-Shoes, communicated by a Gentleman who is now writing the History of his Life ". This is the chief incident in *Tommy Two-Shoes*, published at the close of the century by Wilson and Spence of York.

Imitations only mark the distinction of the Newbery books. Many were published by John Marshall (*c.* 1780). These include *The Orphan ; or, the Entertaining History of Little Goody Goosecap ;* and *The Renowned History of Primrose Prettyface,* " who, by her Sweetness of Temper and Love of Learning, was raised from being the Daughter of a poor Cottager, to great Riches and the Dignity of Lady of the Manor. . . . London, printed in the Year when all little Boys and Girls should be good ", etc.

One copy is inscribed " Thos. Preston, March 22nd, 1788 ". If this be the date of purchase, the book may be earlier ; but it may be the date of the child's birth.

p. 76. 4. " The Lilliputian Masquerade : recommended to the Perusal of those Sons and Daughters of Folly, the Frequenters of the Pantheon, Almack's and Cornelly's. Embellished with Cuts, for the Instruction and Amusement of the rising Generation. Price of a Subscription Ticket, not Two Guineas, but Two Pence ".— Carnan's List for 1787.

The Masquerade was "occasioned by the Conclusion of Peace between those potent Nations the Lilliputians and Tommy-thumbians ", after a quarrel "concerning an Affair of no less Importance than whether, when a Cat wagged her Tail, it was a Sign of fair or foul Weather " ; and the Peace had been made by "an old Lady *whose Name was Reason* ".

A later edition in Dutch paper covers (probably after 1800) published by P. Norbury at Brentford, has no reference to the Pantheon, etc., but is recommended by the couplet :

> " Behind a Mask you'll something find
> To please and to improve the mind."

p. 78. 2. First Worcester edition : *The Juvenile Biographer,* " containing the Lives of little Masters and Misses. Including a Variety of Good and Bad Characters. By a little Biographer. . . . Worcester, Mass. Printed by Isaiah Thomas and sold at his Book Store. Sold also by E. Battelle, Boston, 1787."

p. 81. 1. *Juvenile Correspondence ;* " or, Letters designed as Examples of Epistolary Style, for Children of both Sexes ". By Lucy Aikin. 2nd Edition. London, for Baldwin, Cradock & Joy, Paternoster Row, and R. Hunter, St. Paul's Churchyard, 1816.

Miss Aikin's aim was to supply children with " juvenile equivalents of Gray, Cowper and Lady Mary Wortley Montague " ; but the influence of Mrs. Barbauld adds natural touches not found in " Lilliputian " books.

p. 82. 1. *A Father's Memoirs of his Child,* by Benjamin Heath Malkin (1806), contains letters written by a child from his third to his seventh year (1798–1802).

The little boy, Thomas Williams Malkin, born

in October, 1795, died when he was seven. His father, beginning the *Memoirs*, says : " It is not intended to run a parallel of his infancy with that of Addison in his assumed character of Spectator, who ' threw away his rattle before he was two months old, and would not make use of his coral until they had taken away the bells from it ' " ; but the disclaimer proves that he was conscious of the parallel.

On his own showing, he had made the child into a " little Philosopher " who never had so much as a rattle to throw away, whose first toy was a box of letters. The boy's letters show a pathetic struggle between natural simplicity and the artificial system on which he was being trained. Some are more precocious and pedantic than any in *Juvenile Correspondence*.

The tendency of parents to encourage stilted " epistolary patterns " was shown earlier in the childish letters of Mrs. Trimmer (See *The Life and Writings of Mrs. T.*)

p. 83. 2. Canning deals with the Newbery books much as Addison does with the ballads, though Canning's classical parallels are not serious. He begins by recommending to novel-readers, instead of " the studies which usually engross their attention ", the " instructive and entertaining Histories of Mr. Thomas Thumb, Mr. John Hickathrift and sundry other celebrated Worthies ;   a true and faithful account of whose adventures and atchievements may be had by the Curious and the Public in general, price two-pence gilt, at Mr. Newbery's, St. Paul's Churchyard, and at some other Gentleman's whose name I do not now recollect, the *Bouncing B., Shoe-Lane* ". (This refers to John Marshall's sign of the " Great A and Bouncing B ".)

He identifies " Tom Thumb " with Perrault's " Little Thumb ", and draws a parallel between that hero and Ulysses ; and between the Ogre and Polyphemus, comparing the incidents in a mock-heroic vein. There is no trace of the " Lilliputian " Hickathrift which he mentions.

p. 84. 1. " Jemmy " Catnach, and " Johnny " Pitts of the " Toy and Marble Warehouse ", were rival printers of ballads and chap-books in Seven Dials.

Catnach's nursery books include rhymed versions of Perrault's Tales, *The Butterfly's Ball*, *The Tragical Death of an Apple Pie* (a very old alphabet rhyme) and various " gifts ". (See Charles Hindley's *History* of *the Catnach Press*, 1886.)

Pitts printed a penny edition of *Goody Two-Shoes* (*c.* 1815). His farthing books include *Simple Simon* and other nursery rhymes.

John Evans, another Seven Dials printer, also published a farthing series including *Dick Whittington*, *Cock Robin* and *Mother Hubbard*. (See Edwin Pearson's *Banbury Chap-books*, etc., 1890.)

IV

p. 91. 1. Armand Berquin was born in France in 1749. He refused an appointment as tutor to the son of Louis XVI. Towards the end of his life he was denounced as a Girondist, and driven into exile. He died in 1791.

Mr. Charles Welsh gives a most interesting account of him in his introduction to the reprint of *The Looking-Glass for the Mind*, published by Griffith, Farran, Okeden and Welsh, 1885.

p. 100. 1. Mrs. Pilkington, writing " on the Plan of that celebrated work *Les Veillées du Château*, by Madame de Genlis ", produced *Tales of the Cottage ; or Stories Novel and Amusing for Young Persons*, printed for Vernor & Hood in the Poultry, and sold by E. Newbery, 1799.

She was the wife of a naval doctor, and became governess to a family of orphans, for whom she wrote. Other books published for her by E. Newbery include *Biography for Boys*, 1808 ; *Biography for Girls*, 1809 ; *Marvellous Adventures ; or the Vicissitudes of a Cat*, and a translation (abridged) of Marmontel's *Contes Moraux*.

p. 102. 1.   *Le Théâtre d'Education* was followed, in England, by Hannah More's *Sacred Dramas* (1782).

Moral plays by the German Rousseauists, Engel and Weisse, were translated in *The Juvenile Dramatist* (1801), and *Dramas for Children*, imitated from the French of L. F. Jauffret, by the Editor of Tabart's *Popular Stories*, was printed for M. J. Godwin, at the Juvenile Library, Skinner Street, in 1809. The table of contents includes " The Curious Girl ; " " The Dangers of Gossipping " ; " The Fib Found Out " ; " The Little Coxcomb ".

These educational dramas are no more dramatic than the average moral tale. They may be regarded as a result of Rousseau's realism, an effort on the part of educators to use the dramatic instincts of children to impress the lesson.

V

p. 106. 1.   Thomas Day (1748–1789) was educated at the Charter House and Corpus Christi College, Oxford. He was an intimate friend of Richard Lovell Edgeworth, although he had paid his addresses in turn to Honora and Elizabeth Sneyd, afterwards the second and third Mrs. Edgeworth.

Day was a member of Dr. Darwin's literary circle at Lichfield, and was the author of verses and political pamphlets. The third edition of his poem " The Dying Negro " was dedicated to Jean Jacques Rousseau.

p. 113. 2.   *The History of Prince Lee Boo* (1789) is an early example of this interest in coloured races. Children's books of the early nineteenth century include many stories of the Slave Trade and adventures of Negroes. Some of the most popular were *The Adventures of Congo* (1823) ; Mary Ann Hedge's *Samboe ; or, the African Boy* (1823) ; *Radama ; or, the Enlightened African* (1824).

p. 114. 1.   Third edition, 1759 ; new version in *The Children's Miscellany*, 1787 ; Children's chapbook in Dutch flowered boards, *c.* 1789 : *The English Hermit ; or, The Adventures of Philip Quarll*, "who was lately discovered by Mr. Dorrington, a Bristol Merchant, upon an uninhabited Island, where he has lived above fifty years, without any human assistance, still continues to reside and will not come away. Adorned with cuts and a Map of the Island ". London, John Marshall. Price Six Pence bound and gilt. (Inscribed " Margaret H. Haskoll, (Au. 14th, 1789)." Other editions : 1795, 1807, 1816.

The 1807 edition, repeated in Newcastle, York and Banbury chap-books, has cuts attributed to Bewick.

VI

p. 124. 1.   *The Life and Adventures of a Fly*, "supposed to have been written by himself ". Price Sixpence. (E. Newbery's list, 1789.)

Another edition, with cuts by John Bewick, was printed in 1790 (*Bewick Collector*).

p. 125. 2.   *The Young Misses' Magazine* was reviewed in the *Critical Review*, Aug., 1757. It consists of " Dialogues of a wise Governess with her Pupils ", and was almost certainly inspired by Miss Fielding's *Governess*. The studies of Madame de Beaumont's pupils, under the names of *Ladi Sensée, Ladi Spirituelle, Ladi Tempête*, etc., although they represent types, are made from life.

Madame de Beaumont also wrote " *Moral Tales* ", designed to counteract supposed dangers in Richardson's novels. " The whole," she says, " is drawn from the pure source of Nature, which never fails to move the heart."

p. 127. 1.   Other books by " M. P." include :
Anedcotes of a Boarding School, *Anecdotes of a Little Family*, and *Letters from a Mother to her Children*.
See below :—" Adventures " of things, by " S. S."

p. 131. 1.   Other stories by Elizabeth Sandham are :
The Happy Family at Eason House, 1822 ; *The History of Elizabeth Woodville*, 1822 ; *The Orphan*, n.d. and *The Twin Sisters*, n.d.

p. 133. 2.   Other books by Arabella Argus :
The Adventures of a Donkey (1815) ; *Further Adventures of a Donkey* (1821) ; *Ostentation and Liberality* (1821).

p. 136. 1.   (a) On the occasion of a literary dispute at Reynolds's house, Mrs. Trimmer, then Miss Kirby, fifteen years old, produced from her pocket a copy of *Paradise Lost*.   Johnson marked his appreciation of the incident as recorded above.
(b) From 1802 to 1804, Mrs. Trimmer edited *The Guardian of Education* (published monthly) which exercised a kind of censorship over children's books.   A reference by Mrs. T. to Perrault's *Tales*, which she had read as a child, called forth the criticism of a correspondent who denounced " Cinderella " in particular as encouraging envy, jealousy, vanity and other evil passions in children.   Mrs. Trimmer's principles forced her to agree with this stern moralist.

p. 140. 2.   Bird stories by Mr. Kendall include :
The Crested Wren.   E. Newbery, 1799 ; *The Swallow*. E. Newbery, 1800 ; *The Sparrow* and *The Canary Bird* are also mentioned in *The Stories of Senex ; or, Little Histories of Little People*, by the same author.

p. 141. 2.   Elizabeth Sandham also wrote :
The Adventures of a Bullfinch.   J. Harris, 1809.

and *The Perambulations of a Bee and a Butterfly*,
1812.

p. 144. 2.   Other " adventures " of things :
The Adventures of a Silver Penny.   Price 6d.
E. Newbery. (Advertised in the London
Chronicle, Dec. 21–29, 1787, " just published ";
The Adventures of a Doll, by Mary Mister, 1816 ;
Memoirs of a Peg Top, by S. S.   Author of
The Adventures of a Pincushion.   Marshall's
list, *c*. 1788.

VII

p. 155. 1.   In the preface to *The Adventures of Ulysses*,
Lamb says :   " This work is designed as a
supplement to the Adventures of Telemachus ";
and in a letter to Manning (1808) he says it is
" intended as an introduction to the reading of
Telemachus ".

Fénélon's *Télémaque* (1699) which, like his
Fables and *Dialogues des Morts*, was written
for his pupil, the grandson of Louis XIV, was
translated into English in 1742.   It is a kind
of sequel to the fourth book of the *Odyssey*,
describing the further adventures of Telemachus in search of his father.   Fénélon
turned his " adventures " into a moral tale,
and Lamb, in his preface, also lays stress on the
moral of his book.

p. 156. 1.   At the back of the third edition of *Mrs.
Leicester's School* is a list of " new books for
children ", published by M. J. Godwin, at the
Juvenile Library, Skinner Street.   Many of
these are school texts, some by Godwin, writing
under his pseudonym of " Edward Baldwin ".
Others include the *Tales from Shakespear* ; the
*Adventures of Ulysses ; Poetry for Children ;
Stories of Old Daniel ; Dramas for Children*, from
the French of L. F. Jauffret ;   Mrs. Fenwick's
Lessons for Children (a sequel to Mrs. Bar-
bauld's) ; and Lamb's *Prince Dorus*.

Stories of Old Daniel, which has been attributed to Lamb, has the alternative title "*or Tales of Wonder and Delight*". It contains "Narratives of Foreign Countries and Manners", and was "designed as an Introduction to the study of Voyages, Travels and History in General ": a sufficient proof that Lamb had nothing to do with it.

p. 161. 2.   The passage in " Susan Yates " runs thus :

"Sometimes indeed, on a fine dry Sunday, my father would rise early, and take a walk to the village, just to see how *goodness thrived*, as he used to say, but he would generally return tired, and the worse for his walk."

Mr. Lucas points out that Charles Lamb's father came from Lincolnshire, and that the saying was probably his.

p. 161. 3.   Isaac Taylor, the father, was the author of several moral and instructive tales for youth.

Jefferys Taylor, the brother of Jane and Ann, wrote *Æsop in Rhyme* (1820) ; *Harry's Holiday* (1822) ; and other books for children.

p. 170. 1.   (a) Some of Mrs. Sherwood's most popular books were : *Little Henry and his Bearer* (her first book) *c.* 1815 ; *The History of Henry Milner* (4 parts) 1822–1836 ; *The Little Woodman and his Dog Cæsar* (1819).

Many of the chap-books were written for stock illustrations.

(b) Mrs. Cameron, Mrs. Sherwood's sister, was also a prolific writer of children's chap-books; but these are undistinguished in style and matter. (See B. M. collections under title : "Cameron's Tales ".)

p. 171. 1.   The introduction to Mrs. Sherwood's version of *The Governess* states that " the little volume was published before the middle of the last century, and is said to have been written by a sister of the celebrated Fielding ".

p. 172. 1.   Mary Elliott (afterwards Mrs. Belson, a Quaker, wrote many other tales for children. Among these are : *Precept and Example* (*c.* 1812) ; *The Modern Goody Two Shoes* (*c.* 1818) ;

The Adventures of Thomas Two Shoes : " being a sequel to the Modern G. T. S." (*c.* 1818) ; *The Rambles of a Butterfly* (1819) ; *Confidential Memoirs, or the Adventures of a Parrot, a Greyhound, a Cat and a Monkey* (1821).

Priscilla Wakefield, another Quaker, was the author of *Mental Improvement, The Juvenile Travellers* and other instructive books.

VIII

p. 176. 2.   The Stories in *The Parent's Assistant* (1845) are :—

Vol. I.   Lazy Laurence ;   Tarlton ;   The False Key ; The Birth-day Present ; Simple Susan.

Vol. II.   The Bracelets ;   The Little Merchants ;   Old   Poz ;   The Mimic ; Mademoiselle Panache.

Vol. III.   The Basket Woman ;   The White Pigeon ; The Orphans ; Waste Not, Want Not ;   Forgive and Forget ; The Barring Out ; or, Party Spirit ; Eton Montem.

A modern edition, with an introduction by Anne Thackeray Ritchie, was published by Macmillan in 1903 ;   and a selection, *Tales from Maria Edgeworth*, with an introduction by Mr. Austin Dobson (Wells, Gardner, Darton & Co.), appeared in the same year.

p. 180. 1.   *Little Plays* (1827) contains " The Grinding Organ " (written May, 1808) ; " Dumb Andy " (written in 1814) and " The Dame School Holiday ".

" Old Poz " and " Eton Montem " in *The Parent's Assistant*, are also in dialogue form.

2.   From the letter to Mrs. Ruxton (March 19, 1803), describing a visit to Madame de Genlis in Paris :

(*a*) " . . . . She looked like the full-length picture of my great-great-grandmother Edgeworth you may have seen in the garret, very thin and

melancholy, but her face not so handsome as
my great-grandmother's ; dark eyes, long
sallow cheeks, compressed thin lips, two or
three black ringlets on a high forehead, a cap
that Mrs. Grier might wear,—altogether an
appearance of fallen fortunes, worn-out health,
and excessive, but guarded irritability."

(b) From the same letter :

". . . Forgive me, my dear Aunt Mary,
you begged me to see her with favourable eyes,
and I went to see her after seeing her ' Rosière
de Salency' " (a play in the *Théâtre d'Education*) " with the most favourable disposition,
but I could not like her."

At this time it would seem that the old
countess was soured by neglect and disappointment.

p. 180. 3.   The school stories in the *P. A.* are : "The
Bracelets " (an early story of a girls' school) ;
" The Barring Out " and " Eton Montem ",
both theoretic studies of schoolboys.

p. 183. 1.   The four volumes of *E. L.* contain the
following stories :

Vol. I.   The Little Dog Trusty ; The Cherry
Orchard ; Frank.

Vol II.   Rosamond ; Harry and Lucy.

Vol. III.   The Continuation of Frank and part
of the Continuation of Rosamond.

Vol. IV.   The Continuation of Rosamond and
of Harry and Lucy.

These were followed by *Rosamond : a Sequel
to Rosamond in " Early Lessons ".* 2 vols.,
1821 ; and *Frank : a Sequel to Frank in
" Early Lessons ".* 3 vols, 1822.

p. 184. 1.   Dr. Darwin attempted to deal poetically
with matter of Science ; but his couplets show
all the worst features of eighteenth century
verse. The passage quoted in *Frank* (E. L.,
Vol. I.) runs thus :—

" Stay thy soft murmuring waters, gentle rill ;
Hush, whispering winds ; ye rustling leaves, be
still ;

> Rest, silver butterflies, your quivering wings ;
> Alight, ye beetles, from your airy rings ;
> Ye painted moths, your gold-eyed plumage furl,
> Bow your wide horns, your spiral trunks uncurl ;
> Glitter, ye glow-worms, on your mossy beds ;
> Descend, ye spiders, on your lengthen'd threads ;
> Slide here, ye horned snails with varnish'd shells ;
> Ye bee nymphs, listen in your waxen cells."

p. 187. 1.   The lines, repeated to test Harry's power of attention, are these :—

> " So she went into the garden to cut a cabbage leaf, to make an apple-pie ; and at the same time a great she-bear coming up the street, pops its head into the shop. ' What! No soap ? ' So he died, and she very imprudently married the barber ; and there were present the Picninnies, and the Joblillies, and the Garyulies, and the grand Panjandrum himself, with the little round button at top ; and they all fell to playing the game of catch as catch can, till the gunpowder ran out at the heels of their boots."

" The Great Panjandrum Himself " was later " pictured " as a schoolmaster in cap and gown, by Randolph Caldecott.

p. 192. 1.   Children's books recommended by Mr. Edgeworth in his " Address to Mothers " (E. L. Vol. III) :—

" Fabulous Histories " ; " Evenings at Home "; Berquin's " Children's Friend " ; " Sandford and Merton " ; " Little Jack " ; " The Children's Miscellany " ; " Bob the Terrier " ; " Dick the Pony " ; " The Book of Trades " ; " The Looking-glass, or History of a Young Artist"; " Robinson Crusoe " ; " The Travels of Rolando " ; " Mrs. Wakefield on Instinct " ; *parts* of White's Natural History of Selborne ; and *parts* of Smellie's Philosophy of Natural History.

The Dog of Knowledge ; or Memoirs of Bob the Spotted Terrier (1801) and *Dick the Pony* were by the same author.

The Book of Trades is a modern equivalent of *Dives Pragmaticus* (see above—Introd :)

The Looking-glass, etc., by " Theo Marcliffe ", is the story of the early life of Mulready the painter, written by Godwin under this pseudonym.

IX

p. 195. 2.   A revised and abridged edition of Bunyan's " Rhimes " appeared in 1701, under the title : *A Book for Boys and Girls ; or, Temporal Things Spiritualised.*

A ninth edition was published in 1724 under the new title *Divine Emblems ; or, Temporal Things Spiritualised.*

3.   *A Little Book for Little Children,* " wherein are set down in a plain and pleasant Way, Directions for Spelling and other remarkable Matters. Adorned with Cuts. By T. W." (Thomas White).

London, printed for G. C. and sold at the King in Little Britain.

p. 196. 1.   *The Child's Week's Work ;* " or, A Little Book so nicely suited to the Genius and Capacity of a little Child, both for Matter and Method, that it will infallibly allure and lead him into a Way of Reading, with all the Ease and Expedition that can be desired." By William Ronksley. London, printed for G. Conyers and J. Richardson in Little Britain, 1712.

p. 201. 2.   R. L. Stevenson quotes this rhyme in the lines " To Minnie " (*A Child's Garden of Verses,* pp. 130–1) :

      " Our phantom voices haunt the air
      As we were still at play ;
      And I can hear them call and say :
      ' How far is it to Babylon ? '

      " Ah far enough, my dear,
      Far, far enough from here—
      Yet you have farther gone !
      ' Can I get there by candlelight ? '

      " So goes the old refrain.
      I do not know—perchance you might—
      But only children hear it right,
      Ah, never to return again !

> " The eternal dawn, beyond a doubt,
> Shall break on hill and plain,
> And put all stars and candles out,
> Ere we be young again."

p. 206. 2.   Few of the themes are original. Two by
Adelaide O'Keefe, " The Boys and the Apple
Tree " and " The Vine ", are verse readings
of stories in *The Looking Glass for the Mind*.
So also is " The Two Gardens " by Ann Taylor.

p. 208. 1.   *Poetry for Children* was praised in the *Monthly
Review* for Jan., 1811, but soon went out of
print. The original edition was lost sight of
until 1877, when it was sent from Australia
" a courteous and most welcome gift from the
Hon. William Sandover " to Mr. R. H. Shepherd. (See the Introduction to Mr. Shepherd's
reprint.—Chatto & Windus, 1878.)

In the meantime, twenty-two of the pieces
had been preserved in a *First Book of Poetry*
printed by W. F. Mylius, a master at Christ's
Hospital, " For the Use of Schools. Intended
as Reading Lessons for the Younger Classes."
This was mentioned in the *Monthly Review*
for April, 1811.

p. 209. 2.   The following poems were reprinted in the
1818 edition of Lamb's Works :—
" To a River in which a Child was Drowned " ;
" The Three Friends " ;   " Queen Oriana's
Dream ".

p. 216. 1.   Lamb says that Martin Burney read *Clarissa*
in snatches at a book-stall, until discouraged
by the stall-keeper. He adds : " A quaint
poetess of our day has moralised upon this
subject in two very touching but homely
stanzas ".

p. 219. 1.   (a) *The Peacock " At Home."* " A Sequel to the
Butterfly's Ball. Written by a Lady and
illustrated with elegant engravings ". Harris,
successor to E. Newbery, 1807.
(b) *The Lion's Masquerade.* " A Sequel to the
Peacock ' At Home '. Written by a Lady."
London, J. Harris, etc., 1807.

(c) *The Elephant's Ball and Grand Fête-Champêtre :* Intended as a Companion to those much admired Pieces, The Butterfly's Ball, and The Peacock " At Home ". By W. B. London, J. Harris, etc., 1807.

Facsimile reprints by Charles Welsh, 1883.

p. 221. 1. (a) *The Daisy*, " Adapted to the Ideas of Children from four to eight years old "—was illustrated with 30 copperplate engravings.

(b) *The Cowslip* was announced as " By the Author of that much admired little work entitled The Daisy ". Both were published by Harris, and reprinted with introductions by Charles Welsh in 1885.

(c) Imitations were :—

The Snowdrop ; or, Poetry for Henry and Emily's Library. By a Lady. Harris, 1823 (3rd edition) ; and *The Crocus ; or, Useful Hints for Children,* " being Original Poems on Popular and Familiar Subjects ". London, R. Harrild, 1816.

p. 223. 1. *The Journey of Goody Flitch and her Cow,* a variant of *Old Mother Hubbard,* 1817.

2. *Dame Wiggins of Lee and Her Seven Wonderful Cats,* " A Humorous Tale. Written Principally by a Lady of Ninety. Embellished with sixteen coloured Engravings. Price one shilling ". London, Dean & Munday, 1823.

The rhyme was reprinted by Ruskin, who admired its strong rhythm.

3. *The History of Sixteen Wonderful Old Women,* " Illustrated by as many Engravings, exhibiting their principal Eccentricities and Amusements ". London, Harris & Son, 1821.

4. *Readings on Poetry.* By Richard Lovell Edgeworth and Maria Edgeworth (London, 1816), followed the plan used with the Edgeworth children. No word or phrase is allowed to pass without explanation.

This may have inspired the author of *The Young Reviewers ; or, the Poems Dissected.* London, William Darton, 1821.

APPENDIX B

Chronological List
of
Children's Books from 1700 *to* 1825

The List shows only books studied in the foregoing chapters. It includes no undated chap-books.

A.D.

1700.   Anon.   The History of the Two Children in the Wood.

1701.   Bunyan, John.   A Book for Boys and Girls; or, Temporal Things Spiritualised.

1702.   White, Thomas.   A Little Book for Little Children (12th edn.).

1708.   Chap-books mentioned in *The Weekly Comedy* (Jan. 22): Jack and the Gyants, Tom Thumb, etc.

1709.   Romances given in Steele's paper (Tatler, Nov. 15-17): Don Bellianis of Greece, Guy of Warwick, The Seven Champions, etc.

1712.   Anon.   The Child's Week's Work.

1715.   Watts, Isaac.   Divine Songs for Children.

1727.   Anon.   The Hermit; or, Philip Quarll.

1738.   Wright, J.   Spiritual Songs for Children. (2nd edn.)

1743.   Anon.   The Little Master's Miscellany.

1744.   Anon.   A Little Pretty Pocket Book.
        Anon.   Tommy Thumb's Pretty Song Book. 2 vols.

1745–66.   Anon.   The Circle of the Sciences.

1746.   Anon.   The Travels of Tom Thumb.

1749.   Fielding, Sarah.   The Governess; or, The Little Female Academy (2nd edn.).

1751.   Anon.   The Lilliputian Magazine.
        Marchant, John.   Puerilia; or, Amusements for the Young.

1752.   Anon. A Pretty Book of Pictures for Little Masters and Misses ; or, Tommy Trip's History of Beasts and Birds.

1760.   Anon. The Top Book of All for Little Masters and Misses.

1760–65. Anon. Mother Goose's Melody ; or, Sonnets for the Cradle.

1761.   The Philosophy of Tops and Balls. (Adv. Apr. 9.)

1765.   Anon. The Renowned History of Giles Gingerbread : a Little Boy who lived upon Learning.

         Anon. The History of Little Goody Two-Shoes.

1767.   Anon. The Twelfth Day Gift : or, the Grand Exhibition.

1768.   Anon. Tom Thumb's Folio.

1770.   Anon. The Letters between Master Tommy and Miss Nancy Goodwill.

         Anon. Robin Goodfellow ; " A Fairy Tale written by A Fairy ".

1777.   Anon. The History of the Enchanted Castle ; or, The Prettiest Book for Children.

c. 1777. Anon. Juvenile Correspondence ; or, Letters suited to Children from four to above ten years of age.

1780.   Anon. The Poetical Flower Basket.

         Anon. The Governess ; or, Evening Amusements at a Boarding School.

         Barbauld, Anna Laetitia. Easy Lessons. Hymns in Prose for Children.

c. 1780. Cooper, W. D. The Oriental Moralist.

1781.   Anon. Juvenile Trials.

1782.   Anon. The History of King Arthur (from Dryden).

         Anon. Oriental Tales : The Ruby Heart and The Enchanted Mirror.

         More, Hannah. Sacred Dramas.

1783.   Day, Thomas. The History of Sandford and Merton, Vol. I.

c. 1783. Fenn, Eleanor (Lady Fenn). The Juvenile Tatler.

1786.   Day, Thomas. Sandford and Merton, Vol. II.

           Trimmer, Sarah. Fabulous Histories.

1787.   Anon. The Adventures of a Silver Penny.

           Anon. The Juvenile Biographer (New England edn.).

           Anon. The Lilliputian Masquerade.

           Day, Thomas. The Children's Miscellany.

c. 1787.   Anon. The Adventures of a Silver Three-pence.

1788.   Kilner, Dorothy ("M. P.") The Life and Perambulation of a Mouse.

           The Village School.

           Kilner, Mary Jane ("S. S."). The Adventures of a Pincushion.

           Jemima Placid ; or, The Advantage of Good-Nature.

           Memoirs of a Peg Top.

c. 1788.   Anon. The Renowned History of Primrose Prettyface.

1789.   Anon. The Adventures of Philip Quarll (adapted).

           Anon. The History of Prince Lee Boo.

           Anon. The Life and Adventures of a Fly.

           Cooper, W. D. Blossoms of Morality.

           Day, Thomas. Sandford and Merton. Vol. III.

           Fenn, Eleanor (Lady F.). The Fairy Spectator.

c. 1789.   Tom Thumb's Exhibition.

1790.   Anon. Mirth without Mischief.

           Kilner, Dorothy (?). Anecdotes of a Boarding School.

1791.   Wollstonecraft, Mary. Original Stories from Real Life.

1792–96.   Aikin, A. L. and J. (Mrs. Barbauld and Dr. Aikin). Evenings at Home. 6 vols.

1794–5.   Wakefield, Priscilla. Mental Improvement. 2 vols.

1796–   Edgeworth, Maria. The Parents' Assistant ;
1800.   or, Stories for Children.

1798.	Kendall, Edward Augustus. Keeper's Travels in Search of his Master.
1799.	Kendall, E. A. The Crested Wren.
	Pilkington, Mrs. M. S. Biography for Girls.
	Tales of the Cottage.
1800.	Kendall, E. A. The Stories of Senex; or, Little Histories of Little People.
	The Swallow.
	Pilkington, M. S. The Asiatic Princess.
	Porter, Jane. The Two Princes of Persia.
	Sandham, Elizabeth. The Boys' School.
1801.	Anon. The Dog of Knowledge; or, Memoirs of Bob, the Spotted Terrier.
	Edgeworth, Maria. Early Lessons. 2 vols.
	Moral Tales.
	Wakefield, Priscilla. The Juvenile Travellers.
1802.	Pilkington, M. S. Marvellous Adventures; or, the Vicissitudes of a Cat.
1804.	Taylor, Ann and Jane; and O'Keefe, Adelaide. Original Poems for Infant Minds.
1805.	Anon. Songs for the Nursery.
	Lamb, Charles. The King and Queen of Hearts.
1806.	Taylor, A. & J.; and O'Keefe, A. Rhymes for the Nursery.
1807.	Anon. The Children in the Wood (moralised).
	Anon. Robin Hood (moralised).
	B., W. The Elephant's Ball.
	Dorset, Mrs. C. A. The Lion's Masquerade.
	The Peacock " At Home ".
	Lamb, Charles and Mary. Tales from Shakespear.
	Roscoe, William. The Butterfly's Ball and the Grasshopper's Feast.
	Turner, Elizabeth. The Daisy; or, Cautionary Stories in Verse.
1808.	Anon. The Academy; or, a Picture of Youth.
	Anon. Stories of Old Daniel.
	Lamb, Charles. The Adventures of Ulysses.
	Pilkington, M. S. Biography for Boys.
	Taylor, Ann. The Wedding among the Flowers.

1809.   Lamb, Charles and Mary. Mrs. Leicester's School. Poetry for Children.

Pilkington, M. S. Biography for Girls.

Sandham, Elizabeth. The Adventures of a Bullfinch.

The Adventures of Poor Puss.

1810.   Argus, Arabella. The Juvenile Spectator.

Ritson (ed.). Gammer Gurton's Garland.

1811.   Anon. Felissa ; or, The Life and Opinions of a Kitten of Sentiment.

Lamb, Charles. Prince Dorus.

Turner, Elizabeth. The Cowslip ; or, More Cautionary Stories in Verse.

1812.   Elliott, Mary (formerly Belson). Precept and Example.

Sandham, Elizabeth. The Perambulations of a Bee and a Butterfly.

1815.   Argus, Arabella. The Adventures of a Donkey.

Edgeworth, Maria. Early Lessons. Vols. III and IV.

c. 1815.   Sherwood, M. M. Little Henry and his Bearer.

1816.   Aikin, Lucy. Juvenile Correspondence.

Anon. The Peacock and Parrot on their Tour to discover the Author of The Peacock " At Home ".

Edgeworth, Richard Lovell and Maria. Readings on Poetry.

Elliott, Mary. The Orphan Boy ; or, A Journey to Bath.

Mister, Mary. The Adventures of a Doll.

1818.   Elliott, Mary. The Modern Goody Two Shoes.

The Adventures of Thomas Two Shoes.

Sandham, Elizabeth. The School-fellows.

Sherwood, Martha Mary. The History of the Fairchild Family.

Taylor, Jefferys. Harry's Holiday.

1819.   Elliott, Mary. The Rambles of a Butterfly.

Sherwood, M. M. The Little Woodman and His Dog Cæsar.

1820.   Sherwood, M. M. (ed.). The Governess.

1820.   Taylor, Jefferys. Æsop in Rhyme.
1821.   Anon.   The Sixteen Wonderful Old Women.
        Anon.   The Young Reviewers ; or, The Poems
            Dissected.
        Argus, Arabella.   Further Adventures of a
            Donkey.
        Ostentation and Liberality.
        Edgeworth, Maria.   Rosamond, A Sequel
            to Rosamond in Early Lessons.
        Elliott, Mary.   Confidential Memoirs ; or,
            the Adventures of a Parrot, a Greyhound, a
            Cat and a Monkey.
        Hack, Maria.   Harry Beaufoy ; or, The Pupil
            of Nature.
        Sherwood, M. M.   The Infant's Progress.
1822.   Edgeworth, Maria.   Frank.   A sequel to
            Frank, in Early Lessons.
        Sandham, Elizabeth.   The Happy Family at
            Eason House.   The History of Elizabeth
            Woodville.
1823.   Anon.   The Adventures of Congo.
        Anon.   The Court of Oberon ; or, The Temple
            of the Fairies.
        Hedge, Mary Ann.   Samboe ; or, the African
            Boy.
        Lady of Ninety, A.   Dame Wiggins of Lee
            and her Seven Wonderful Cats.
1824.   Hedge, Mary Ann.   Radama ; or, the
            Enlightened African.
        Taylor, Jane.   The Contributions of Q. Q.
            2 vols.
        Taylor, Jefferys.   The Little Historians.
1825.   Edgeworth, Maria.   Harry and Lucy " con-
            cluded ; being the last part of Early
            Lessons ".   4 vols.

Foreign Books and Translations

1707.   D'Aulnoy, Madame la Comtesse.   Collected
            Works.
1708.   The Arabian Nights' Entertainments ; Trans-
            lated from the French of M. Galland.

1708. Perrault, Charles. Histoires ou Contes du Temps passé, avec des Moralités. " Par le fils de Monsieur Perrault de l'Academie François ". 1st edn. 1697.

1722. Æsop. Fables. Croxall's edition.

1729. Perrault, Charles. First English translation by R. Samber.

1742. Fénélon, François de Salignac de la Mothe. Adventures of Telemachus. 2 vols. 1st French edn. 1699.

1757. Beaumont, Jeanne Marie Le Prince de. Le Magazin des Enfans. 2nd edn. 2 vols. Translated as the Young Misses' Magazine. (Adv. Critical Review, Aug.)

1763. Marmontel, Jean François. Moral Tales. Translated by Miss R. Roberts.

1775. Beaumont, J. M. Le P. de. Moral Tales. Trans. Anon. 2 vols.

1779. Genlis, Madame la Comtesse de. Le Théâtre d'Education.

1782. Genlis, Madame de. Adèle et Théodore.
1782-3. Berquin, Armand. L'Ami des Enfans.
1783. Berquin, Armand. The Children's Friend. Translated by M. A. Meilan. 24 vols.
Epinay, Madame d'. Les Conversations d'Emilie.
Genlis, Madame de. Adelaide and Théodore. Trans. Anon. 3 vols.

1784. Genlis, Madame de. Les Veillées du Château.
1786. Marmontel, J. F. Contes Moraux collected.
1787. Berquin, Armand. The Looking-Glass for the Mind. (Selections from L'Ami des Enfans. ed. Cooper.)
Epinay, Madame d'. Conversations of Emily. Trans. Anon.

1788. Campe, J. H. Robinson der Jüngere. Trans. as The New Robinson Crusoe.

1791. Berquin, Armand. The History of Little Grandison. Trans. Anon.

1792. Salzmann, C. G. Elements of Morality. Trans. from the German.

1801. Engel, J. and Weisse, F. The Juvenile

Dramatist. (Educational plays, trans. Anon.)

Genlis, Madame de. Le Petit La Bruyère translated as La Bruyère the Less.

1809. Jauffret, L. F. Dramas for Children. " Imitated from the French of L. F. J. By the Editor of Tabart's Popular Stories ".

1823. Grimm, J. L. C. and W. C. Popular Stories.

Other children's books of the 18th and 19th centuries are given in Mr. F. J. Harvey Darton's bibliography : Cambs. Hist. of Eng. Lit. Vol. XI, Chap. XVI.

There is also a useful list of Essays, Magazine Articles, etc.